GIVE THE WINDS
A MIGHTY VOICE

Charles Fuller and thirty years of radio sermons.

The Story of
CHARLES E. FULLER

GIVE THE WINDS
A MIGHTY VOICE

by Daniel P. Fuller

WORD BOOKS, Publisher
Waco, Texas

Give the Winds a Mighty Voice

Library of Congress catalog card number: 72-83342
Printed in the United States of America

Contents

Foreword

During the last months of my father's life, another member of the Board of Trustees of the Gospel Broadcasting Association remarked that perhaps a final biography of Charles E. Fuller should now be written. Two biographies had already been published: Dr. J. Elwin Wright's *The Old Fashioned Revival Hour and the Broadcasters* (1940) and Dr. Wilbur M. Smith's *A Voice for God* (1949), and my initial reaction was that there was not enough additional material to justify a third one.

But after my father passed on and I was spending days sorting through his papers, I began to see how much knowledge about his life and deep intentions could be gleaned from these and other sources. As a scholar I have reflected particularly on the historical foundations of the biblical faith, and this has involved considering the kinds of data and the methodology a historian uses to learn what happened in the past. Knowledge of the past is available only from the "tracks" that people have left. Here were all these "tracks" left by my father, and no doubt there were many others that research could uncover. But if someone did not work them over, much knowledge of his life would be lost.

Therefore the historian in me simply could not allow these sources of knowledge about Charles Fuller to be stacked away in some filing cabinet. But I still recoiled from writing the biography myself. Surely someone besides his sole survivor would be a more objective biographer! A Christian writer expressed an interest in taking on the task, so I turned all these papers over to him. He spent many hours interviewing people who had known my father and began to write the story of his life. But it became apparent after awhile that the final biography of Charles Fuller could be written only by someone who, because he was salaried, had the indefinite amount of time required to work over these papers, comb through old newspapers on microfilm or in musty stacks in public library basements, and then trace out the chronology.

As a faculty member and administrator at Fuller Seminary, I was

7

in a position to do this. So for the past three years there have been blocks of time during summers, a four-month sabbatical, and weekends when this research and writing could be done. Then too, because I was so involved in my father's life and remembered events pretty well from 1930 onwards, I had the feel for how and where things fitted in.

Now that the task is behind me, I am so glad that the Lord gave me no choice but to see it through. As I carried on this research, new funds of information about my father came to light. Miss Pauline Hagen of the R. H. Alber Radio Advertising Company casually remarked one day that in her office there were some scrapbooks of clippings regarding the broadcast from 1938 onwards. These were of immense value. I am very grateful to the Placentia Presbyterian Church, and to Mr. George Key in particular, for letting me read through the session minutes during the years when my father was a member and an elder there. I also want to thank Miss Ruth Brown, secretary of the Calvary Church, Placentia, for helping me get information about the church's early days; Mr. Gerald L. Gooden, the librarian at Biola College, La Mirada, for loaning out some volumes of *The King's Business* for the years when my father was president of the board of trustees there; Dr. Arnold Ehlert of Biola College for procuring the file on my father during his student days from 1919 to 1921; and Dr. James O. Henry, professor of history at Biola, who helped answer certain inquiries. The librarians at Fullerton State University and at the city libraries of Placentia, Fullerton, Santa Ana, and Los Angeles graciously showed me how to get at their newspaper holdings.

Although two biographies about my father have already been written and widely read, there is justification for this third one. For one thing, it covers the last twenty years of his life. How one runs and finishes the last laps of the race is the perspective which best shows the significance of the earlier laps.

Then, too, in writing a biography of a person who has died, one works more energetically to glean information from written documents than he would if the subject were still alive. He is not vulnerable to the overpowering temptation to regard the subject's memory and reconstruction of the past as having an absolute authority. It seems almost absurd to go through documents and microfilms that might cast light on a person's past when he himself is at hand for interrogation. But memory is not a perfect source for knowledge. It seems that my father forgot that he had not commenced continuous radio broadcasting until early in 1930. He had also said that the turning point in his life came when he heard Paul Rader in July, 1917. Church ads of the *Los Angeles Times* show that he must have heard him in July, 1916. While research has raised many questions about which I wish I could have asked my father, I believe I have learned more about him from written sources than I ever could by simply interrogating him.

Here then is this biography of Charles E. Fuller, completed almost four years after his homegoing. In writing this I have had to retrace as much of his life as can be known and to try to understand something of his contribution to the history of the Church. I believe his life is important because, more than anyone else, he used radio to get the Gospel out to the world in that era before television became the primary mass communication medium. His life is also significant because in his zeal to get the Gospel out, he never forgot how necessary is the time-consuming, expensive, and difficult task of training young people to be preachers of the Gospel themselves.

In closing I want to say how much I appreciate the devoted time my wife, Ruth, has given to criticizing and typing the manuscript.

DANIEL P. FULLER

Henry Fuller (1846-1926), father of Charles Fuller.

1. Boyhood

CHARLES FULLER'S EARLIEST impressions were of the booming town of Los Angeles where he was born on April 25, 1887. His father, Henry Fuller, owned and managed a furniture store at the corner of Third and Main Streets, and his home was just off the nearby Plaza which from the earlier Spanish days had been the hub of Los Angeles. The fire station around the corner was a source of great excitement as its horse-drawn wagons, bells clanging, answered alarms. Young Charles spent much of his time there and became so well liked by the firemen that they would let him ride in the wagon with them to fires.

His mother, Helen Day Fuller, became worried about this. One morning as she left to go shopping, she warned, "Now, Charles, while I'm away, I don't want you going off to fires." Dutifully he promised to stay home until she returned. But when the bells began to ring, he completely forgot about his promise. Running to the fire station, he climbed onto the wagon and was off on another glorious adventure. As the wagon was returning to the station, however, with Charles sitting beside the driver, who should spy him but his mother. Sternly she ordered him off the wagon and at the corner of Second and Spring Streets gave him a sound thrashing.

In 1874, at the age of twenty-eight, Henry Fuller had come from Vergennes, Vermont, to Southern California on the railroad that had reached Los Angeles just a few years previously. The journey took thirty days because he had brought a carload of sheep with him in hope of selling them for a profit. He settled on new land near present-day Covina and then sent for his wife to come and join him. Though he had planned to raise turkeys and wheat, a drought caused him to lose his investment, and he had to move into downtown Los Angeles. In Vermont Henry Fuller had made a living managing a store and an excelsior factory which he had started. This earlier experience now proved valuable as he opened up a small furniture store in Los Angeles with an initial inventory of only two dozen rockers and ten dozen chairs. His store prospered, however, through the boom Los Angeles was experiencing in those years as well as through the manufacture and sale of a line of very successful bed springs. Thus Henry Fuller was well able to provide for his family which now included four sons, Charles being the youngest.

But a year or so after Charles was born, his mother began to suffer increasingly severe asthma attacks. She could find relief from them only when she went inland to the drier climate of the Redlands area, seventy miles to the east. Henry Fuller realized that he would have to relocate. The orange industry was thriving, so he began to look for suitable land around Redlands where he might start a new orange grove. While driving through the Barton Flats area (near present-day Loma Linda) one frosty February morning, he noticed that the sunflowers and vegetation were untouched by frost. Orange groves in this spot, he reasoned, would be less vulnerable to the killing frosts which could wipe out a whole year's crop. So in 1889 with the savings he had accumulated from the furniture business, he purchased seventy acres in this location.

Commuting between Redlands and Los Angeles, Henry Fuller supervised the building of a red barn and a three-story, heavily ornamented house with vaulted roof and bay windows, front and back parlors, and all the other appointments of a fine family residence of the Victorian period. He also managed the clearing of the land and the planting of orange trees, thirty acres for navels and forty for Valencias. After making a large profit in his furniture business by selling a shipment of surplus furniture from the Chicago World's Fair in 1893, he sold the store and completed the task of moving to Redlands.

The life the Fuller family lived on an orange ranch was in sharp contrast to the life they had known in the city. Now they were out in the country, four miles from the center of the sleepy town of Redlands. Instead of being surrounded by people on every side, there were perhaps no more than a dozen people within the radius of a mile. Gone were the fire bells and the shouting of the teamsters. Now there was the majestic stillness of the sparsely settled San Bernardino valley and the awe-inspiring view of the mountains to the north and the eleven-thousand-foot snow-capped peaks just fifteen miles to the east. Nestled on the edge of this valley, the new orange grove and its ornate ranch house were at the beginning of rolling foothills, scarcely touched as yet by the hand of man, that extended for several miles to the south.

With no fire station nearby, it was to this foothill wilderness that the young Charles Fuller was constantly drawn. Here he could satisfy that longing for the wide open spaces that he felt all during his life. He whiled away many a sunshine-filled day exploring these hills and drinking in the beauty of God's handiwork. There were still some California Indians who lived in the hills in the way their ancestors had for centuries past.

Now that Henry Fuller was no longer a merchant but a farmer, hard physical labor characterized his life style, and he saw to it that his four sons did their share to make this new orange grove a financial success. Nursing the young orange trees until they were hardy enough to bear high-quality fruit often required eighteen-hour workdays. But all this physical exertion, in combination with sunshine, fresh air, and eating oranges grown in virgin soil, equipped Charles Fuller with a stamina and physique which enabled him in later years to bear up under heavier tasks than many men could have endured.

In line with his Yankee heritage, Henry Fuller trained his sons to be thrifty as well as to be hard workers. The Fuller boys would occasionally chuckle at the lengths to which their father would go in the name of thrift. One day Charles saw his father trudging through the groves with his trousers flapping oddly at each step. "Dad, what in the world have you got on?" he asked. But then he noticed that his father, having worn out the knees of his trousers, had simply put them on backwards to get more wear out of them.

Charles Fuller's particular responsibility was to set traps to keep gophers from coming into the seventy acres and destroying the roots of the young orange trees. Setting traps each morning, he would then return from school in the afternoon to see how many gophers had been caught. For every gopher tail he could lay out before his father, he would get a dime. By catching hundreds of gophers he was finally able to buy a watch and then an L. C. hammerless shotgun. He loved to go on hunting excursions with his dog in the hills to the south and bring home quail and rabbits. One day, however, as he was out hunting he noticed a covey of quail across the canyon. In his haste to get within range he stumbled and

Above: *The ranch house surrounded by young orange trees, 1892, with two Fuller boys in foreground.* **Below:** *During a broadcast, Charles Fuller plays an old-fashioned organ similar to that used by his parents in family devotions.*

the gun fired, shooting off the right side of his hat brim. For five minutes he sat dazed, wondering whether he was dead or alive and afraid to touch his head for fear that half of it was blown off.

Henry Fuller made it clear that his son must tithe part of his gopher money to support the Methodist Church of Redlands to which the entire family belonged. Charles Fuller also remembered how, after hearing a particularly stirring sermon one morning, he pledged twenty-five dollars to help build the new sanctuary that was completed in 1901. Fifty years later it was destroyed by fire; and when he heard about it, he phoned a former high-school friend and commented, "Hundreds of my gopher tails went up in smoke last night!"

Charles Fuller's parents were dedicated Christians. Family devotions were held each morning. His father would read a portion of Scripture and then the family would gather around his mother and sing hymns as she accompanied them on the pump organ. But though he sat through these daily devotions at home as well as two church services each Sunday, Charles Fuller had no great interest in spiritual things during these days. Nevertheless his parents' faithfulness in exposing him to the Christian faith did leave an indelible impression upon him. In later years he would mention in his broadcasts, often with tears in his voice, those times when the family would gather around the organ to sing hymns. Although the seed sown did not seem to accomplish much at that time, Henry Fuller lived long enough to rejoice in the way God was beginning to use his youngest son to preach the Gospel.

In those earlier years Henry Fuller felt that Charles showed the least promise of any of his sons. He was shy, and sometimes he was found sleeping under an orange tree when the rest were working, or he would be off hunting in the hills with his dog. Then, too, he was something of a prankster. There was an elderly Chinese man who lived in a little house behind the ranch. One day Charles slipped a rock into his slingshot and landed a rock on the old man's roof. The man came running out screaming and flailing his arms, while Charles ran to hide.

Henry Fuller was not planning anything more ambitious than for Charles to spend his life in helping manage the ranch. But one older son, Percy, prepared to be a lawyer, and another son, Leslie, was particularly impressive for he wanted to be a minister and seemed to have the qualifications.

Therefore when Henry Fuller went around the world in 1902, it was Leslie who went with him. He took this trip partly because he had become so interested in foreign missions through the ministry of Dr. A. B. Simpson, the founder of the Christian and Missionary Alliance. The orange grove had now reached maturity, and "Fuller's Fancy Oranges" were bringing in good profits. Henry Fuller wanted to visit missionaries and get a better idea of how to further the cause of foreign missions. He wanted Leslie also to get a vision for foreign missions as he toured the world with him.

They visited Japan, China, India, Ceylon, Egypt, and Palestine. Henry Fuller wrote letters describing this trip and sent them back to the Redlands newspaper. After his return he had them all published in a 341-page book entitled *A Californian Circling the Globe*. From India, where he was appalled at the misery and degradation of the people, he wrote:

The real cause and want of greater success in missions is in so-called Christian lands. The man or woman in England or America that gives a few dimes to missions and one hundred dollars to build and adorn some costly home church that never prays for a foreign mission, that breathes a sigh of relief when the missionary collection is raised, knows of and cares but little for missionary work. With the scanty funds with which missionaries are provided, I think they are accomplishing real miracles.

In 1905 he took another trip around the world, and by then the grove had prospered sufficiently for him to undertake the full support of three missionaries, one in Japan and two in India. Toward the end of his life he was supporting, in full or in part, fifty-five missionaries and Christian workers around the world.

But for some time the only way Charles Fuller figured in his father's vision for spreading the Gospel was that he should help manage the ranch so it would continue to make a profit. Charles, however, became captivated by an interest which had no bearing on managing an orange ranch. Through the dimes earned by gopher tails he ordered a telegraph set from a mail-order catalog. When it arrived, he busied himself in learning Morse code and in stringing wire through the ranch house so that he could transmit messages between several points. Then, too, on his way home from high school he would sometimes stop at the Southern Pacific railway station nearby and persuade the old station manager, Jim Rimpaw, to let him practice sending and receiving real messages on the railroad circuits. He became so good at it that before long Mr. Rimpaw was even allowing him to send instructions to the main dispatcher in Los Angeles.

Charles Fuller also installed a buzzer down at the ranch gate so the postman could signal the family that he had left mail in the box. In addition he set up a telephone connection between his house and the neighbors' who lived a few hundred yards away. Later as a senior in high school, Charles also had the first amateur wireless telegraph receiver in the Redlands area. One hot July day he bounded down the stairs from his room waving a slip of paper. "Listen to this," he cried excitedly. "I just took a message from the wireless station on Catalina Island. Some congressman has just hooked a tremendous bass weighing three-hundred pounds!"

"Oh, pshaw!" his father muttered. "You're just joking." He went back to his paper. But the next day in the *Los Angeles Times* the same story appeared which Charles had reported the day before. "Look here, Dad—just as I told you!" he exclaimed. His father's only words were, "Well, I'll be jiggered."

Here was evidence that the Heavenly Father had different plans for Charles Fuller than the earthly father. In Henry Fuller's eyes, Charles's task was simply to help manage the ranch. But in God's plan, Charles Fuller was a chosen vessel to use radio to give the winds a mighty voice for spreading the Gospel to multitudes all over the world.

2. Joining with His Life Partner

DURING HIGH SCHOOL Charles Fuller was big for his age. At fifteen he was six feet tall and wore a size twelve, double E shoe. He was shy and did not enter much into the school's social activities. But because of his size and strength he distinguished himself as a football player and was even the captain of the team.

In his same class at high school was a young lady named Grace Leone Payton. Her first recollection of Charles Fuller was when she and her mother were attending a high-school program. Charles was seated directly across the aisle from them, and as Grace glanced across the aisle, she noticed with amusement this boy wearing very large shoes.

Charles Fuller knew about Grace Payton. She was well known because her father had become one of Redlands' chief physicians. As a young boy in 1849, John Payton had come across the plains to Oregon with his parents in a covered wagon. Like his father, he became a doctor and practiced in rural Oregon for several years. But his poor health had forced him to move to the warm, dry climate of Redlands. Charles Fuller felt that he had no chance with a girl of such prominence because, unlike his brothers who had traveled and studied abroad or were going into business, he was destined simply to finish high school and then be a foreman on the orange grove.

But one day after a football scrimmage, a friend said, "Come over here. I want you to meet a real nice girl." Charles was all covered with mud and perspiration, but he quickly borrowed someone's cap so he could tip it when he was introduced to Grace Payton. He was bashful, but Grace remembered that she thought he was very nice.

Some months passed after that first meeting during which each simply knew who the other was because they were in the same class. Then came the day when Henry Fuller, after returning from his round-the-world tour, invited the leading citizens of Redlands to come the four miles out to his ranch house to view the pictures he had taken and the souvenirs he had collected in various parts of the

18

world. Tables holding the displays almost filled two parlors, and Grace and her parents—she was an only child—were among those who came. When it was time to leave, Grace could not find her hand-carved ivory fan which she had brought along to give relief from the oppressive heat.

But after the guests had all left that Sunday afternoon, the fan did turn up, and Charles gladly volunteered to return it. He phoned Grace to tell her he would bring the fan right over. Shyly he stood at the front door of her house, holding the fan, but she reassured him by inviting him to come in and stay for a few minutes. The few minutes stretched into hours, and it was decided that instead of returning home before the evening church service, he should simply stay on and go with Grace to the young people's meeting at the Baptist church which she attended.

This became the pattern that was followed Sunday after Sunday until they graduated from high school in 1906. Charles and Grace were indeed high-school sweethearts, and while still in high school Charles wanted to become engaged. But by the time he had made the marriage proposal, Grace had learned about the inner urgings of his heart to give his life in service as a missionary. Sometime in 1903 Charles Fuller had heard a sermon at the Methodist church, and this, coupled with his father's great interest in foreign missions, had made him feel he must give his life in service to others.

Grace Payton was not sure she wanted to be a missionary's wife, and she asked a close friend whether she would marry a man who wanted to be a missionary. Her friend replied, "I would marry him if I loved him." But Grace said, "Well, I'm not so sure *I* would."

Thus for the time being Grace's reply to Charles was, "We are both much too young. I want to get a college education. Let's not mention engagement again for awhile. Later on, if we find we are suited for each other, you might ask me again." But even though there was no formal engagement during high-school years, Charles nevertheless presented Grace with a beautiful cedar hope chest, and she reciprocated with a gift of several shirts and a sweater, all of which had to be exchanged for larger sizes.

After graduation from high school in the spring of 1906, Grace went with her parents to spend the summer in the East. But the two wrote each other faithfully twice a week. In the fall Grace entered the Cumnock School of Expression in Los Angeles, where she studied

Shakespearean dramatics, English, diction, public speaking, and French.

Charles entered Pomona College, located about halfway between Los Angeles and Redlands. Henry Fuller had not planned to send Charles to college, but his wife had finally convinced Henry that this youngest son should have the advantage of a college education. Charles himself had some misgivings. He had not been thinking in terms of college, but now that he was there, could he measure up to Percy, and especially to Leslie's academic achievements?

However, he soon found that he could do quite well in his studies, and he excelled in athletics, especially football. As left-tackle he had an uncanny ability to anticipate and break up the opposing team's plays. Charles quickly became a great favorite among his classmates. In his senior year at Pomona he was elected both president of his class and captain of the team, which wound up in first place in the league championship.

Grace sometimes came to watch Charles play football. On one particular afternoon she watched with pride as Pomona defeated its rival, and afterward the team carried Charles around the field on their shoulders. But at a banquet that evening, as she looked admiringly at him, all dressed up in his tuxedo, she noticed that some of the mud of the ball field had eluded his clean-up and remained behind one ear.

Charles Fuller was featured in the evening edition of the *Herald Express* as Pomona's star left-tackle. In addition to winning his letter and gold football fob, he also earned a letter in the hammer-throw and shotput division of track. In his studies he had some difficulty in language and English but did quite well in mathematics and science. He majored in chemistry and was chosen to teach the freshman chemistry class. In 1910 he graduated cum laude from Pomona College.

Charles had majored in chemistry so that as an orange grower he could analyze the soil and prescribe the proper fertilizer to use. But it is also interesting to note that while his wife-to-be was learning to be a good speaker at the Cumnock School, he had joined the Lyceum Debating Society. It would seem that God was training both Charles and Grace to improve their ability at public speaking, since He would be using them as a team to spread the Gospel by radio.

As Grace Fuller read the letters over the radio in later years, many

20

Charles Fuller (right) and the Pomona College football line.

Boat in which Charles Fuller almost drowned in the American River in 1910.

Charles (right) and a brother during a workday in the grove.

were impressed with her unaffected yet beautiful, flowing diction. She often thanked God for helping her to prepare for her life work during the year she spent studying elocution. Charles also felt that what he learned in debating was vital to his future life work. "You have to organize your materials for debating," he told me in later years. "You have to be able to anticipate your opponent's arguments, and you have to build up your case to a climax and bring it to a good conclusion. Debating certainly helped me in organizing my sermons."

Charles took up debating because his budding ambition moved him to take on a number of challenges. But he did not succeed in debating as he had in athletics. There was one particular failure in debating which Charles Fuller never forgot. He was trying to bring a speech to a climax by denouncing "anarchy in Cuba," but instead of saying "anarchy" he used the word "Arnica," a brand name for a medicinal salve common in that day. "Down," he shouted, "with Arnica!" The audience roared with laughter, and when they finally quieted down, the professor looked over his glasses and with pretended solemnity said, "We are going to have to put some salve on the case Charles Fuller has made . . ." It was such an experience which caused Charles Fuller in later years to remark that God, in calling him to be a preacher, surely loved to take the weak and foolish things of the world to confound the wise.

The very load that Charles Fuller carried in college—studies, football, debating, presidency of the senior class, being an assistant teacher—helped to prepare him for the many loads that he would carry in the years ahead. Under his picture in the college annual the following words were inscribed: "Mastodon, largest specimen on the coast." Then under his name in a group picture were the words, "Physically the biggest man in school, mentally a fine student, morally every inch a man."

But spiritual development did not keep pace with physical and cultural development. While studying in the zoology and biology departments of the school, Charles began to find that the views of his professors clashed with the beliefs his parents had taught him. These beliefs now seemed old-fashioned in contrast to the evolutionary theory of Darwin. Nevertheless he still attended church regularly and entertained some thoughts about using his life to help his fellow-man.

Neither did Grace Payton's spiritual development keep pace with her cultural achievements. After a year in the Cumnock School, she enrolled at Western College for Women in Oxford, Ohio. Indeed, there was a healthy spiritual atmosphere here with a daily chapel service required for everyone as well as a twenty-minute "quiet time" every evening which was to be spent in Bible study and prayer. But when, in the following year, she enrolled at the University of Chicago, she started attending a Unitarian church because the minister's diction was so fine and he quoted from Emerson and Shakespeare. By the end of that year Grace had been virtually won over to the Unitarian faith.

But just before the school year ended at Chicago, her father died, and she left school without completing the year in order to be with her mother. Later that summer Grace Payton told several people that she felt that Unitarianism was the most reasonable faith that one could accept. What could be more simple than to worship God as one and to see Christ as the great example for daily living but not as the One who is the Son of God?

One of her mother's close friends was Mrs. Leonora Barnhill. This woman had had a very hard life. She had come from the East to the dry climate of Redlands to overcome tuberculosis. While taking special courses to qualify her to teach in California, she had to support herself by working in a novelty shop six days a week, eleven hours a day for five dollars a week. But despite all these difficulties, she was a radiant Christian, and she became a close friend of the Paytons.

One evening Grace and Mrs. Barnhill were seated in front of the fireplace, and Grace was saying to her, "You know, Barney dear, I worship only God. Christ was merely our example." Mrs. Barnhill replied, "Oh, Grace, Christ said, 'No man cometh unto the Father but by Me,' and my dear, you have no way of approach to a holy God unless you come through Christ, His Son, as your Savior." Grace said later, "The Scripture she quoted was the sword of the Spirit, and at that moment Unitarianism was killed forever in my heart. I believed that moment, though I said nothing, and believing God's Word, I instantly became a new creature in Christ."

She did not resume her college studies in the fall since it seemed best that she stay with her bereaved mother. She and Charles had become engaged the previous summer, and Charles was now beginning his last year at Pomona. It is interesting that as graduation drew near, he again felt, as he had in high-school days, a strong urge to "be of some help to humanity." This time, however, he was not thinking of foreign missions but of being a YMCA secretary. By graduation he had definitely decided to go to Boston to enroll in the YMCA Secretarial Training School.

But again Henry Fuller had other plans for his son. He had invested a large sum of money in a gold dredging operation on the American River in northern California. This venture, however, was not paying off as he had hoped, and so he commissioned Charles to become one of the employees on the gold dredger to see if he could not discover why so little gold was being recovered. Obediently he carried out his father's wishes and spent the next year living the rough life of a miner among the coarsest sort of men. As he threaded pipe, his hands, unaccustomed to such manual labor, soon were covered with blisters.

By orders of Henry Fuller, the workmen had to stop all dredging on Sundays. With nothing else to do, they walked over to the town of Forest Hill which had a population of only five hundred people but twenty-five saloons. Charles saw two shootouts in the town during those months, and once he had to duck behind a tree to protect himself from flying bullets.

While working on the dredge one day, Charles Fuller came close to losing his life. Word had come that there had been a cloudburst back in the mountains and that the river was expected to go on a rampage soon. The foreman told Charles to cross the river in a boat and tighten the cable that was holding the dredge in place. But when he was halfway across, the great mass of water hit and swept the boat out from under him. As he desperately clung to the cable, the torrents whipped him around, and he felt that at any moment he would lose his grip and be dashed against the rocks. Somehow he became conscious of his whole life in just a fleeting moment, and he had a profound sense of being afraid to die and to meet God. He cried out, "Oh, God, save me, and I'll serve you always!" And God did enable him to hang on and to pull himself back to the shore.

On the graveyard shift one night, Charles began talking with the winchman as they kept dredging the bottom for gold. This man was an experienced gold miner who had worked a dredge during the

24

Klondike gold strike at the turn of the century. Charles asked, "What do you think? Will we ever dredge deep enough to reach the gray mud which has the highest gold concentration?" The veteran miner replied, "I don't think your father will ever make any money here. There are so many jagged rocks on the bottom that the dredge can't get down to the gray mud." Charles thanked him, and the next day he telegraphed his father that he thought the operation should be discontinued. His father agreed, and Charles returned to Redlands in the summer of 1911.

By that time he seemed to have forgotten his plan of training to become a YMCA secretary. He wanted to marry Grace Payton and get settled in his own home. To earn enough to do this he accepted his father's offer to become a workman on the ranch. Charles spent monotonous days doing the arduous work of stacking boxes of "Fuller's Fancy Oranges" in freight cars, sometimes having to lift them high above his head. For a young man who, fifteen months before, held the aspirations and challenges of college life, this was more of the sheer drudgery that he had known when working on the gold dredge. But now he could visit Grace often, and they made plans for their wedding in the fall.

On October 21, 1911, they were married in the living room of Mrs. Payton's large house on Eureka Street in Redlands. Grace had washed her hair the previous day and this had brought on a terrible head cold. During the wedding ceremony she could scarcely speak above a whisper. And then after the reception, their Redlands friends mischievously put them into an open truck and sped through the streets of the dark and chilly city. Charles gave them a fight, knocking down one man who got in his way in the process. The new Mr. and Mrs. Fuller didn't get started on their honeymoon trip until well past midnight, and by the time they arrived at the Riverside Inn some fifteen miles to the south, Grace had no voice left at all.

The Fullers set up housekeeping in a house owned by Grace's mother on property adjoining the Fuller ranch. In addition to his work on the ranch Charles took on a job as salesman for a fertilizer company. He would travel from ranch to ranch on a motorcycle, and using his training in chemistry he tested ranchers' soils and recommended the kind of fertilizer they should use.

25

Grace worked hard to cook the dishes she knew her husband liked best, nervously competing, as brides often do, with the reputation of her mother-in-law. Grace chose Charles' favorite hash for their first meal in the new house and proceeded to cook it in a new iron skillet which had been a wedding present. She forgot, however, to fill it first with ashes and grease and boil the iron out of it. When the hash was served and Charles took the first bite, he thought to himself, "My conscience! What in the world is this?" But when Grace asked proudly, "Well, did you enjoy it?" he was able for love's sake to stretch a point and reply, "Sure! I liked it!"

The thought of her mother-in-law living in the ranch house so close at hand no doubt spurred Grace Fuller on to become the neat housekeeper that she was always known to be. Once when she was a student at Western College in Ohio, Charles' mother had unexpectedly dropped by for a visit, and rather than let her see the chaotic condition of her room, Grace let her future mother-in-law wait for thirty minutes in the lobby while she and her roommate tidied everything up in a frenzy. Grace felt very close to Charles' mother, but she had no desire to let the Ohio experience happen again.

During their second year of marriage Charles had prospered enough to make the down payment on a ten-acre orange grove of his own. The Fullers were getting along well financially and moved with ease in their social set. They attended church quite regularly, but ever since that conversation with Mrs. Barnhill, Grace Fuller had been more interested in spiritual things than her husband.

A few months after the purchase of the ten-acre orange grove, a freeze came which destroyed almost the entire crop for the year. Charles Fuller then tried to protect his investment against the repetition of such a calamity by equipping his grove with smudge pots. In January, 1913, however, there came a very severe freeze. A chill wind blew from the north. As night fell the thermometer dropped alarmingly. During a freeze an orange grower tries to keep the smudge pots burning well enough so that the temperature will not go below twenty-six degrees for more than two hours. Anything beyond that limit means the loss of one's crop for the year. Grace Fuller, dressed in her husband's work clothes, joined him in the battle all that evening. She helped fill smudge pots and took tempera-

Courting days.

ture readings, but despite all their efforts the thermometer plummeted right past the 26-degree mark. By midnight they knew they would have no crop again that year.

By morning the thermometer had dropped to thirteen degrees—very, very cold by Southern California standards! Bone weary, discouraged, and blackened by smudge, Charles and Grace dragged themselves home. The cold had been so intense that it had split the bark of their trees and killed them. Their grove, as well as their crop, was gone; but as they looked into each other's smudgy faces, they could laugh because they still had each other and could make a fresh start.

Later that morning Charles drove over to see his father. The groves were brown. Icicles hung from the branches. Ruptured water pipes lay gnarled and twisted on the ground as if ravaged by a terrible fire.

"I guess everything is gone," Charles said sadly.

"It's the worst I've ever seen," Henry Fuller replied. "But we have a little saved. We'll make it all right."

Grace Fuller urged her husband to search for a better line of work. When they heard that a packing house in Orange County was looking for a manager, she encouraged Charles, despite his youth, to apply for it. The job would pay one hundred dollars a month.

He did apply and was hired for the job. They then moved to Placentia for what they thought would just be a new phase of work in the orange industry. Little did they realize, however, that in Placentia the urge Charles had felt to be a missionary near the close of high-school days and to be a YMCA secretary as he graduated from college would be experienced again. But this time he would fully yield to God's leading and give his life to preaching the Gospel.

3. Called to Preach

A BEAUTIFUL VISTA unfolded before the Fullers as they drove into Placentia in April of 1913. The city had been given this name because in Spanish it meant "pleasant place." The sign denoting entrance into the city today reads, "Smile, you are entering Placentia, a pleasant place." Situated in a twenty-five-mile-square valley bounded by hills on three sides and by the Santa Ana River to the south, the area had been nothing but a continuous sweep of orange groves until 1910. Then the Santa Fe railroad came through, linking Fullerton and Los Angeles to the west with Riverside and other points to the east. The orange growers knew their savings would be considerable if their oranges, lemons, and grapefruit could be packed and shipped from the railroad now crossing the center of this valley instead of being hauled four miles to Fullerton or Anaheim.

In 1910 Mr. John C. Tuffree, one of the leading orange producers in the area, organized a cooperative association of orange growers, with a board of directors, to establish the Pacific Mutual Orange Association packing house. Two or three other associations and packing houses were established to take advantage of the new railroad, and this required the building of a town where the employees of these packing houses could live. Oil had also been discovered under the surrounding foothills, and the influx of oil workers added to the town's population.

Placentia was situated in the midst of one of the richest and most highly developed orange districts in California. It was one of the few places where oranges could be picked and shipped every month of the year. From December to April there was the harvest of the Washington navels; from April to June the pickers gathered the Saint Michaels and the Mediterranean sweets; but the area's most famous product, the sweet Valencias, were packed and shipped from April to November.

In this spring of 1913 as the Fullers drove into Placentia, the small town of about two hundred people which had grown up had

29

certainly not spoiled the beauty of the place. In an article appearing in the *Santa Ana Register* in August, 1913, is a description of Placentia which helps us recapture the beauty of this spot which has now been somewhat blighted by smog, a freeway interchange, electronics factories, and urban sprawl.

If one were lifted in a captive balloon, he would look down on an immense field of rich dark green, in the center of which would be grouped bits of squared brown and white roofs. To the north would be lighter green rolling foothills, covered with barley with high wooden frameworks [oil derricks] protruding skywards. All that would be Placentia. But this is no way to see Placentia. Drive forth by automobile or team and pass through scores of acres of orange groves loaded down with fruit famous the world over. See dozens of handsome homes. . . . Turn to the north. There you come to vast grain fields on low hills where huge derricks mark the presence of an oil well or a place where men are sending down a drill in search of oil. Down to the very edge of the orchards, and even into them, have come the oil wells. Here one finds a highly developed land. . . . Placentia orchards are irrigated under the Anaheim Union Water Company. With its bounteous supply coming both from gravity and pump, the orchards need not want for moisture. Practically all the orchards are supplied through the cement pipelines and standpipes for the regulation of the water into the furrows. . . . With at least one automobile upon every ranch, telephones and good roads, Placentians are not far from any point in Southern California. They have all the delights of outdoor life with glorious sunshine and delightful climate, and at the same time they are not far separated from the cities. With its splendid orchards and beautiful homes, Placentia has become a veritable park. . . . Placentia is altogether fair and lovely. It is one of the most remarkable districts of the county that has many remarkable districts, but only one Placentia.

The town already had a bank and a schoolhouse erected at the cost of fifty thousand dollars. In 1912 the Placentia Presbyterian Church had been organized and met in the schoolhouse until its own edifice was finished and dedicated on June 1, 1913. The hub of the town's social life was the Placentia Round Table. This was a women's club, limited to fifty members, which met in a club house at the corner of Bradford and Chapman Streets, the main intersection of the town.

Because of their heavy losses in Redlands, the Fullers could afford only a very small house just to the south of the women's club. Their new home had twenty-four by twenty-four feet of floor space. Neighbors jokingly remarked that the biggest man in town lived in the smallest house. Charles Fuller joked with them and said, "To enter I have to take my shoes off outside and back in."

He immediately threw himself wholeheartedly into managing the operations of the Mutual Packing Association. The directors had some misgivings about hiring a man only twenty-seven years old for such a responsible position. But good recommendations from associates in Redlands, the fact that he was a college graduate, and his rather extensive experience in various phases of the orange business had finally prevailed. What remaining doubts they may have had vanished after a few days. As they saw his efficiency and diligence, his salary was raised from one hundred to one hundred fifty dollars a month. In partnership with another man, he also launched a trucking company. Fuller's big White trucks helped haul the fruit from the groves around Placentia to the packing house. Whites were the best trucks that money could buy, and he added to his fleet until there were four or five trucks in operation.

A SPIRITUAL TURNABOUT

There is evidence that Charles Fuller also gave a good deal of time and energy to the church. In the record book of the Placentia Presbyterian Church for September 13, 1913, we read, "The following persons appeared desiring to unite with the church. Mr. Charles E. Fuller from the Redlands Methodist Episcopal Church and Mrs. Grace Payton Fuller, his wife, from the Redlands Baptist Church." Nine months later, in April, 1914, he was ordained as a ruling elder in this church of eighty members. From April to October, 1915, he was Sunday school superintendent. A note for April 6, 1916, reports his giving a talk to the session on his work as leader of the young men's club. The records also show that he was clerk of the session from June, 1916, onwards.

Charles Fuller said virtually the same things about himself when he made application to the Bible Institute of Los Angeles in the summer of 1919. The Biola application form asked, "What Christian work have you done and what are you now doing?" and he

31

replied, "Leader of YMCA club at Placentia for three years. Teacher of Adult Bible Class for four years. Have charge of the Christian Endeavour work of the church at Placentia. Clerk of the session. Sunday school superintendent for one year."

Furthermore, during these years and even in 1919 when he made application to Biola, he regarded himself as having been a Christian for some time. In answer to the question, When did you accept Christ as your Savior and Master? he replied, "1903." His interpretation of his Christian experience in 1919 is thus somewhat different from that which he gave after he had graduated from Biola. In later years he regarded himself as having been only a nominal Christian when he moved to Placentia. Although he was conscious of no hypocrisy in those early days, he later felt that he joined the church, accepted the responsibility of being a ruling elder, and superintended the Sunday school partly because this was how he could acquire the image of civic-minded responsibility needed by a new packing house manager who was only twenty-seven years old.

Despite all this activity in the church, however, Charles Fuller did not share his wife's interest in spiritual things. While she wanted to attend church regularly, he sometimes preferred to stay home Sundays to polish the car and read the Sunday paper. Then, too, Grace Fuller had become very interested in attending a large Bible class in Anaheim taught on Thursday evenings by Dr. H. A. Johnston, one of Orange County's leading physicians. Charles Fuller would drive his wife the four miles to this class, but he would leave her there to go to the theater to enjoy such silent films as *Tillie's Punctured Romance.* He also loved to spend evenings with the Placentia card club, but his wife would not join him in this.

Mrs. Barnhill often visited the Fullers in their little house in Placentia, and Grace Fuller found great spiritual help in conversing with this woman who had led her to Christ. During one of these visits Mrs. Barnhill brought a book on biblical prophecy by a Plymouth Brethren writer, F. W. Grant, entitled *The Mysteries of the Kingdom.* Following the dispensational system of biblical interpretation originated by John Darby and popularized by the *Scofield Reference Bible,* this book talked of how God would restore the kingdom to Israel, of the apostasy of the professing church, of the rapture of the true believers before the Great Tribulation, and of Christ's return to set up His millennial kingdom. Grace Fuller read this book with great interest; and when she got her husband to read it, he also found it fascinating. When in 1965 someone asked Charles Fuller to write up his conversion for a book, he said, "My first interest in spiritual matters was awakened by the book *The Mysteries of the Kingdom.*"

However, the interest aroused by this book soon died away. A baby was on the way, but toxemia plagued Mrs. Fuller's pregnancy and the baby had to be taken stillborn. In the aftermath of this ordeal, tuberculosis set in, and she was an invalid for the next three and a half years. During this time she had to lie in a special reclining bed on the screened-in front porch of their little home, and in the hot summers she would spend much time with her mother at Big Bear Lake in the San Bernardino Mountains. The fever that she developed almost every day reminded her of the virulence of her infection and made her realize that the only way she could hope to be restored to health was to discipline herself to remain completely inactive and rest. The fever also showed how easy it would be to transmit this infection to someone else. For two years her husband could not even kiss her.

Mrs. Fuller's outlook on life was changed profoundly through the loss of the baby and the ensuing tuberculosis. How hard it was for her who had been so vivacious, so surrounded by friends, and so well received by everyone now to have to spend most of her time in bed, not even being able to read but having to concentrate on relaxing as much as possible! It deeply grieved her to have become such a burden to her husband, but her admiration and love for him increased as she saw the uncomplaining love and tenderness with which he cared for her during this extended convalescence.

During July, 1916, Grace Fuller was in the mountains with her mother. Her husband had to remain in Placentia to manage the packing house. This work occupied his time Monday through Saturday, but on Sundays he was very lonesome. Saturday, July 29, he read in the paper that Paul Rader, former wrestler and boxer, would be preaching at the Church of the Open Door in Los Angeles that Sunday. This man was now the thirty-eight-year-old pastor of the Moody Memorial Church in Chicago. He had just completed an eight-month evangelistic campaign in which he had preached nightly to large crowds. Charles Fuller was interested in this former athlete who was now being called the "new Elijah," and with nothing else to do, he decided to drive in to Los Angeles and hear what he had to say.

Arriving at the Church of the Open Door, he slipped in and sat behind one of the pillars upholding the balcony. Peering around, he took a good look at Paul Rader. He was powerfully built, and for a moment or two Charles Fuller visualized how he must have looked in the ring with his gloves on. But as Paul Rader began to preach, his attention shifted from the speaker's physical prowess to his message. His theme was "Out of the Cave," and his text was: "Having the eyes of your hearts enlightened, that you may know what is the hope to which he has called you, what are the riches of his glorious inheritance in the saints" (Eph. 1:18, rsv). Paul Rader explained how, apart from the Holy Spirit's illumination, people were in a cave, as it were, blinded and unaware of the glorious and marvelous things God had in store for them. They needed to "come out of the cave" and realize the blessings God had promised to impart. As Charles Fuller listened to this message, the Holy Spirit convicted him that he was not living as one who looked forward to such blessings. Leaning his head on the seat in front of him, he trembled under deep conviction, not quite understanding what had come over him. At the close of the service he did not respond to the invitation but left and drove to Franklin Park in nearby Hollywood. He stopped in the shade of a eucalyptus tree and knelt on the floor of the back seat of his car, yielding his life to God to live as one who looked forward to such a great inheritance. There he remained in prayer until it was time to return to the afternoon meeting.

With his heart fairly bursting with joy, Charles Fuller went back to hear Paul Rader preach again. He felt freed from all desire to get ahead in the business world and to make money. The great concern of his life now was for God to use him to win souls. Returning to Placentia, he penned a letter to his wife:

There has come a complete change into my life. Sunday I went up to Los Angeles and heard Paul Rader preach. I never heard such a sermon in all my life. Ephesians 1:18. Now my whole life aims and ambitions are changed. I feel now that I want to serve God if He can use me instead of making the goal of my life the making of money. I may have a call to go to the mission field in Africa. ◡

Mrs. Fuller received the news with mingled delight and apprehension, wondering whether she could be a missionary. "I'll go with him anywhere in the world," she thought, "but oh, my goodness, I hope it isn't to a hot climate!"

When she returned from the mountains and saw her husband again, it was clear that he had had a radical spiritual turnabout. The first Sunday they were together, he remarked that he needed to get his bearings in understanding the Bible. "So," he said, "the first thing I'd better do is memorize the books of the Bible." Leaning back in his chair and putting his feet on a table, he went to work. As the days went by, Grace Fuller also noticed that instead of spending his spare time poring over the *Saturday Evening Post* he now read his Bible for long periods. He also found great delight in talking over spiritual things with Mrs. Barnhill during her visits. She loved to discuss the wonderful truths of the Second Coming of Christ, and he began to study this subject. Through Mrs. Barnhill's encouragement, he read William E. Blackstone's *Jesus Is Coming* and A. C. Gaebelein's books on Daniel and Revelation.

He became so excited by the things he was learning that he felt he must share them with others. Not wanting to be in conflict with any other classes or teachers, he announced that he would begin teaching a class at 8:00 on Sunday morning and that all who were interested were welcome to come. About five of the church's Sunday school teachers joined with him for these sessions which someone aptly named "The Unearthly Hour Bible Class." Charles Fuller began by taking them through the Book of Daniel.

The fall of 1916 he worked as clerk of the church's session and leader of the Placentia YMCA club. In addition to being an elder, he became a trustee of the church in April, 1918. In February, 1919, he took charge of the church's Christian Endeavour program.

But some Sundays after the Unearthly Hour Bible Class was over, the Fullers would drive into Los Angeles to hear Dr. Reuben Torrey preach at the Church of the Open Door. They were embarrassed to have the people of Placentia know that they were leaving to go elsewhere to worship, and so they tried to go as unobtrusively as possible. But their collie, Gillie, excited at the prospect of an automobile ride, would start to bark and thus announce to the town that the Fullers were leaving.

On some Sunday afternoons, between the morning and evening services at the Church of the Open Door, the Fullers would go to a little mission on Main Street called Victoria Hall. Charles Fuller was seeking deeper spiritual truths and a closer walk with God, and he received much help from the Bible readings and discussions at this mission. On other Sunday afternoons they would go to the Bethel Temple where a Dr. Eldredge was pastor. A number of people spoke in tongues there, and Charles Fuller thought that he should seek this gift. But he never spoke in tongues. Some years later he had Dr. Eldredge come out to his church in Placentia to preach. Taking him back to the train station after the services were over, Charles Fuller was still concerned that he had not received the gift of tongues and he talked to Dr. Eldredge about it. The older man put his hand on his shoulder and said, "Charlie, what you need to seek is the Giver, not the gifts." God settled the whole matter for him right then and there. He saw in a flash that Christ dispensed His gifts sovereignly to His people, and that he had received not the gift of tongues but of expository evangelistic teaching. Thereafter he was content simply to exercise this gift.

Preparing to Preach

In the spring of 1919 Charles Fuller became restless and increasingly convinced that God wanted him to resign his position as manager of the packing house and go to the Bible Institute of Los Angeles to train to become a preacher. He liked the orange business and the challenge to buy and sell so that the growers would get the very best prices. His desire now to go into Christian work was not motivated by his having done poorly as a packing house manager, for one of those who wrote a recommendation for his acceptance at Biola in the fall of 1919, a Mr. R. C. Harris who was an orange grower and a member of the Placentia Presbyterian Church, said, "He has sure made a success as manager of the Placentia Mutual Association's packing house."

But God was working to make him want to preach the Gospel.

36

He now began to view his work in the packing house (as he put it) "as just a continuous whirlygig and year-round race to get a cent a box more for the growers' fruit, and when it was all said and done, not much was accomplished for eternity. It was just a matter of getting the best prices."

One morning in April, 1919, as Charles Fuller sat in his office in the packing house, the conviction that he should go into full-time service became so powerful that he had to leave his desk and find some place where he could be alone to pray. He went downstairs, through the packing house where men and women were working, and back to a storage room where the makings of orange boxes were stored. He knelt behind a stack of these.

There was the strong urge to give his life fully to preaching the Gospel, but he remembered from his debating experience in college that he didn't have the fluency and style in public speaking that preachers are supposed to have. Satan tried to tell him that he would be a complete failure if he tried to preach. Then, too, he wondered how he would support himself if he left his position as manager of the packing house. It wasn't simply a problem of how to get enough money to live on each month; it was also the question of how to continue payments on the twenty-acre orange grove he had just bought with a five-thousand-dollar down payment.

At first these obstacles seemed too great, and he rose to go back to his desk, but God's hand was so heavy upon him that he sank to his knees again and said, "Oh, Lord, I will walk in your path. I will even try to preach. I will resign my position and trust you to supply our needs as I prepare for the ministry." Peace came to his soul, and he soon notified the board members of the packing house that by the fall of that year (1919) he would be resigning so he could study at Biola. They took this news sadly, one even going so far as to say, "Charlie, you're too good a man for the ministry. You should stay here. Why, a minister only has to work one day a week—on Sundays when he preaches. Furthermore, I don't think you're qualified for the ministry. You might well starve." But for Charles Fuller there was no turning back. From that day on he felt like Paul who said, "Woe is me if I preach not the Gospel."

The crop that year from his twenty acres of oranges didn't give him much encouragement either. It brought in less than was needed to make the yearly payment. But he and his wife were praying and looking to God to supply their needs, and God answered their prayer in a way more abundant than they could have asked or thought. An oil well had just come in to the northeast of town, and suddenly oil companies and their geologists were scrutinizing the whole Placentia area to detect where more oil might lie. One oil company contacted Charles Fuller and immediately offered him ten thousand dollars for the right to drill somewhere on his twenty acres. He accepted it, greatly amazed at how God had supplied his needs after he had resigned from his position in order to train for the ministry. He was so astounded that he made a special trip back to Redlands to show the check to his father. True to form, the taciturn and thrifty Yankee simply said, "Charlie, that's an awful lot of money." For some reason the oil company never did drill, but the money was his and with it the way was open to spend the next two years studying for the ministry.

We have seen how Charles Fuller, in his application to Biola in 1919, thought he was converted in 1903, and thus did not view his experience in July, 1916, as anything more than a radical spiritual turnabout. In later years, however, that 1916 experience became to him the time of conversion. Possibly this resulted from the profound influences that began to mold him as he commenced studies at Biola in the fall of 1919. By becoming a student there, he exposed himself fully to the mood characterizing all that was best in the Bible institute and Fundamentalist movement. To understand Charles Fuller and his ministry, it is necessary to understand a little of the Bible institute movement as it expressed itself in the lives of the three founders of Biola—Lyman Stewart, Thomas Horton, and Reuben Torrey.

Lyman Stewart was born in western Pennsylvania in 1840. In 1859 oil was first discovered near his home, and as a young man he made a fortune in it. Though he had been raised as a Christian, in the mad scramble to make money in oil, he had failed to give anything to Christian work. When he tried to duplicate the fortune he had made in oil by investing in a machinery company, he lost everything and felt that God had chastised him for not tithing. Lyman Stewart then moved to California where through various partnerships and after many discouragements he opened up several new oil fields and was able, in 1890, to establish the Union Oil

The smallest house for the biggest man in town!

Fuller (right) with railroad car on which he traveled into the mountains to preach to the lumberjacks in early 1920s.

As manager of packing house at Placentia about 1918.

As member of student body at the Bible Institute of Los Angeles in 1921.

Company. Now that God had prospered him again, he diverted great sums of money for the rest of his life to various Christian enterprises.

In 1894 he had attended one of the famous Niagara-on-the-Lake Bible conferences which stressed biblical teaching about the Lord's return and living the victorious Christian life. The speakers at these conferences were prominent ministers, evangelists, and professors in theological seminaries who were interested in biblical prophecy. Some of these had been influenced by John Darby, the founder of the Plymouth Brethren, and his system of dispensationalism that was later made so popular by the footnotes in the *Scofield Reference Bible.*

One of the emphases in dispensationalism is that God has been testing man down through the ages through a sequence of several dispensations in order to make it evident that men are sinners and unable to obey God no matter what set of terms (dispensations) God sets before them. Despite the offer of free grace in Christ during the dispensation of this present Church age, the great majority of professing Christendom is nevertheless apostate. There is only a small remnant who are true members of the body of Christ.

Lyman Stewart picked up this strand of teaching at the Niagara conference of 1894, and thereafter he often expressed a great concern about the apostasy of the Church. Through a committee organized by A. C. Dixon, the pastor of Moody Memorial Church, he provided the money necessary for publishing the twelve volumes of *The Fundamentals,* a series of pamphlets that were published between 1910 and 1915. Some 300,000 of each of these volumes were printed and distributed free to English-speaking Protestant leaders throughout the world. Comprising ninety articles written by sixty-four men, these pamphlets defended the basic Christian doctrines. Lyman Stewart also contributed a thousand dollars to the publication of the *Scofield Reference Bible.*[1]

In 1906 Thomas C. Horton came on the staff as an assistant minister at the Immanuel Presbyterian Church in Los Angeles where Lyman Stewart was a member. After being a YMCA secretary for some years in Minneapolis, Thomas Horton became convinced

---

[1] Letter from Lyman Stewart to C. I. Scofield, dated July 21, 1908, preserved at Biola College Library, La Mirada, California.

that the YMCA had turned liberal. So he resigned and founded the Gospel Tabernacle in Minneapolis. He served as pastor of that church for seven years, and then was pastor for seven years at the Scofield Memorial Church in Dallas—the church founded by the editor of the *Scofield Reference Bible*—before coming to Los Angeles.

Soon after coming to Los Angeles, he heard a sermon which struck him as epitomizing the Liberalism which was gaining control of so many seminaries, denominations, and churches. Liberalism denied that man was so sinful that his only hope for being restored to fellowship with God was through Christ's substitutionary death on the cross and through the regenerating work of the Holy Spirit. Instead Liberalism regarded man as essentially in harmony with God and looked to Darwin's theory of evolution as supporting the idea that men already had powers inherent within them which would eventually enable them to live in peace and harmony. Such a view of man fitted in with a postmillennialism which denied that only Christ, by a special intervention at His Second Coming, could bring in the peace and brotherhood of the millennium. Dispensationalism, which affirmed that Jesus must come to establish the millennium, seemed to many to offer an excellent antidote to Liberalism.[2]

Like Stewart, Horton wanted to help stem the tide of Liberalism. He felt the best way to do this was to found a school which would teach the Bible to laymen and train them to be effective soul winners. He persuaded Lyman Stewart to provide money for such a school. Early in 1908 the great evangelist Reuben Torrey was coming to Los Angeles for a campaign, and with Stewart's help Thomas Horton established a school to train enough personal workers for that campaign.

Horton wanted to draw people from all denominations into this

---

[2]Thus in many circles of Fundamentalism, not to be premillennial and dispensational in one's understanding of Scripture implied that one was a Liberal. In oversimplifying things in this way, Fundamentalists forgot that it was possible to be postmillennial and yet orthodox. Jonathan Edwards, the great American theologian and revivalist of the eighteenth century, was postmillennial, without being at all Liberal. They also forgot that many noted theologians and Bible expositors have been premillennial without being dispensationalists. Nathaniel West, one of the chief speakers at the Niagara conferences, is an example of a nondispensational premillennialist.

41

school, so he sought for the Church Federation of Los Angeles to endorse both it and the campaign which Reuben Torrey was to conduct. He did not, however, want this school to be under the control of the Church Federation, because, as he said, "There is opportunity for criticism concerning their kind of teaching. The need is so definite along dispensational lines that I want to give it out and yet there are no doubt many federation men who would no doubt object [to dispensational teaching]."[3]

The school commenced with six hundred students enrolled. At the last minute, Torrey's campaign was canceled. But the training program had already been running for some weeks with Lyman Stewart as president, Thomas Horton as superintendent, and William E. Blackstone, who wrote the dispensational treatise *Jesus Is Coming,* as dean. It had had such a successful beginning that these men felt it should continue permanently, campaign or not. By 1911 Lyman Stewart made it financially possible for this school, now called the Bible Institute of Los Angeles, to locate at Sixth and Hope Streets. Reuben Torrey had agreed to come as dean of the new Bible institute on the condition that it would have, among other things, a three-thousand-seat auditorium where he could preach on Sundays.

He was well qualified for this new task. Twenty years before, D. L. Moody had appointed him to start the Moody Bible Institute of Chicago, and he had been its dean for ten years. During that time he was also the pastor of the Moody Memorial Church. Then for three years he went on a world-wide evangelistic tour during which there were 115,000 decisions for Christ. After this tour he continued as an evangelist and Bible conference speaker.

Reuben Torrey was also a dispensationalist. The text that he wrote for his classes in Bible doctrine, entitled *What the Bible Teaches,* sounds the dispensational note when it declares that the Church will be raptured out of the earth before the Great Tribulation. The large auditorium which he wanted was completed in 1913, and at its dedication a *Scofield Reference Bible* was placed in its cornerstone.

The Biola which had been shaped by these three men and which

---

[3] Quoted by James O. Henry, "Black Oil and Souls to Win," *The King's Business* (February, 1958), p. 22.

Charles Fuller entered in 1919 had certain strong emphases. First and foremost there was the emphasis on the study of the English Bible. Reuben Torrey had attended a theological seminary, but he felt that the approach he had developed in founding the Moody Bible Institute trained Christian workers more effectively. According to the 1920 catalog, Biola was for

. . . graduates of colleges and theological seminaries who desire to supplement the knowledge gained in college and seminary by a more thorough study of the English Bible, practical methods of aggressive Christian work, and the most effective methods of teaching the Bible [and also for] men already in the ministry, who feel the need of a more thorough, accurate and practical knowledge of the Bible.

There was also a heavy emphasis on evangelism, soul winning, foreign missions, and all forms of Christian service. From the preceding quotation we see how the study of the English Bible was regarded as all of a piece with "aggressive Christian work." As the outgrowth of their study of the Bible in the classroom, students were required to give many hours each week in a number of forms of practical Christian outreach. Week by week Charles Fuller had to turn in a report not only of the number of hours he had spent in Bible study (he averaged about twelve hours a week) in addition to classes but also the kinds of Christian work he had engaged in each week. The registrar kept elaborate records of the various ways each student was spending his time. Thus, for example, during the month of May, 1920, Charles Fuller reported that he had distributed twelve tracts; talked with eight people about their souls (the previous month he had talked with eleven, one of whom had been converted); conducted one youth meeting; and had taught four adult Bible classes. The records also indicate that by the fall of 1920 he had become assistant to the pastor at the Placentia Presbyterian Church. A recent writer on the history of Fundamentalism has observed that one of the chief innovations of the Bible institute movement was "learning by doing."[4]

This heavy stress on practical work naturally required a high

---

[4] Louis Gasper, *The Fundamentalist Movement* (The Hague: Mouton & Co., 1963), p. 95.

degree of dedication from students. The first quality that was to characterize a Biola student was "genuine and thorough consecration." The catalog then devoted a whole section to describing the kind of devotional life which the students were to develop. Definite times each day were to be set aside for private and corporate prayer and devotional Bible reading. There was also the emphasis that each student was to seek "enduement with power by the filling of the Holy Spirit."

From the vantage point of later years, Charles Fuller felt that the teachers who influenced him the most at Biola were Reuben Torrey, William Evans, and Mrs. Anna Dennis. Reuben Torrey took his students through a summary of Bible doctrine in his book *What the Bible Teaches*. Here was where Charles Fuller received his basic grounding in Bible doctrine. In this book Reuben Torrey would state a proposition and then back it up by quoting several verses of Scripture. In examining Charles Fuller's own copy of this text with the many notes written in and around its propositions and verses, we begin to understand the influence its author had on Charles Fuller's preaching which was so characterized by the quotation of Scripture used to drive home the message of God to the hearts of men.

Reuben Torrey was impressed with Charles Fuller as a student. After hearing him give a practice Bible lesson on Cain and Abel, he sat for awhile without saying a word, and then said, "Young man, God has a great work ahead for you." It was Reuben Torrey who taught Charles Fuller never to preach a sermon on any subject without bringing in the cross of Christ and also to repeat often what the Bible has to say about heaven.

Mrs. Anna Dennis showed him how to give concrete illustrations of the truths of God's Word from the Bible itself. She taught him to understand how incidents in the history of Israel and details regarding the construction of the Tabernacle in the wilderness were types of Christ and His work of redemption.

The earliest sermon of Charles Fuller that still exists is the one he gave as speaker for the graduating class of 1921. His topic was the pillar of cloud which guided the children of Israel in the wilderness. He pointed out how insubstantial a cloud appeared to be, and yet it was through this cloud that Israel enjoyed the presence of

God, the power of God, and the protection of God. That such an apparently insubstantial thing as a cloud could give Israel such marvelous blessings was emblematic of Christ, who though he appeared so pitiably weak as to suffer and die on the cross, is nevertheless the One who enables us to enjoy God's presence, power, and protection. Many were the times that Charles Fuller preached on the wilderness wanderings of Israel during the next half century, using concrete details from the Old Testament to set forth Christ's person and work, and it was from the teaching of Mrs. Anna Dennis that he learned to do this.

It is interesting to notice the way he concluded this sermon:

Within a very few hours, we as a graduating class will be disbanded and our two years of study and fellowship will be over. We shall go out from these doors of the beloved Bible Institute and down Hope Street to Sixth, and from that corner we will scatter out in different directions to different parts of the world, some to be in the home land and others to cross the seas to lands of strange customs and unfamiliar faces. Everyone we hope and pray to be just where the Lord Jesus wants him. How we will need the presence, the power, and the protection of our Pillar of Cloud, the Lord Jesus, during the days that He may be pleased to tarry before we are caught up to meet Him in the air. No matter how dark and difficult the way (for we will find hard ways, and opposition, and buffeting, and misunderstanding; we will experience weariness and heartaches at times), we have always before us our Pillar of Cloud, just as surely as the children of Israel. We can be sure of His presence, His power, and His protection—He who is our shield, our deliverer, and our unerring, safe and complete guide. He will keep us for the Master's use[5] if we simply trust Him— "simply trusting every day, trusting through the stormy way; even when my faith is small, trusting Jesus, that is all. Trusting as the moments fly, trusting as the days go by, trusting Him whate'er befall. Trusting Jesus, that is all."

EARLY TASKS

The very year Charles Fuller graduated from Biola he became the president of the Orange County Christian Endeavour. As president he would visit a different chapter of Christian Endeavour each

---

[5] "Kept for the Master's Use" was the class motto.

week, at which time there would be a pot-luck supper. Raymond Crouch went with him to play the ukelele, whistle, and lead singing. Harry O. Anderson, a promising young evangelist, would often bring the message. From the monthly publication of the Orange County Christian Endeavour called the *Orange Juice,* we sense the strong evangelistic emphasis that characterized its leadership. Addressing its members for the first time in this publication, Charles Fuller cited the incident of a group of British soldiers during World War I who sacrificed their lives by drawing German artillery fire to themselves so that the main body of infantry could escape. In like manner, he continued,

The Son of God came, and went to Calvary, and there on the Cross He drew the fire to Himself in order to save us sinners. . . . Endeavourers, because He first loved us, may we not as individuals be more earnest in our prayer life, in Bible study, and in our consecration to Him. . . . As all roads lead to Rome, we want the paths of C. E. work to lead to the Cross of Christ that this year's work may count in young people won for Him and in those that are being drawn closer to Him. I am counting on you, *individually,* members of each society, to be loyal to C. E. and its Christ.

Charles Fuller's urge toward evangelism also exhibited itself in these early days by the way he and his wife would occupy themselves on camping trips in the summertime. They had always enjoyed the forests and mountains, but after his conversion Charles Fuller showed a great love for the people who lived in the out-of-the-way places—for the miners, the lumberjacks, and the sheepherders—who did not have much chance to hear the Gospel. In later years he realized that God had given him a love for such people because it would be through radio that he would be able to reach great numbers of them. In speaking to the class in evangelism at Fuller Seminary in February, 1962, he reminisced:

I didn't really understand why, shortly after my conversion, I had this drive or this burden placed upon me to go out into the mining towns and into the lumber camps and into the villages and into the cross roads. For instance, when Mrs. Fuller and I were vacationing in the Sierras, we made our headquarters at Huntington Lake, and then I would put on my knapsack, take some blankets, and go out to the camp where the hard rock miners were living who were blasting the aqueduct through Kaiser Peak to bring water from the Owens Valley to Los Angeles. I would distribute tracts to them and simply declare the claims of Christ. There wasn't any meeting hall, but I started things off out in the open by leading out in singing some familiar Gospel hymns. About five hundred finally gathered around and I gave them my testimony and a simple presentation of the claims of Christ.

While I was speaking, one fellow who was half-drunk said, "You're a blankety-blank liar." I said, "One more crack out of you, and I'll take you by the nape of the neck and throw you down the hill." When he repeated himself, five of the miners spirited him away.

Fellows, it was experiences like this that prepared me for my radio ministry later on. When I started preaching on the radio, I found that I was visualizing myself as speaking to individuals like these hard rock miners, living in some out-of-the-way place. When I'm speaking over the radio, I'm not thinking of those in apartment houses or in the thriving cities, but my heart goes out to those who are up in the canyon creeks and the mining gulches and in the remote places. And God prepared me for this in those early days as I would go out and talk to individuals in such places.

Here is another specific instance of this early evangelistic urge which he also related to the evangelism class:

Mrs. Fuller and I took one of our three-quarter ton White trucks and were driving up the northern part of the Sacramento valley toward Mount Shasta. It was very, very warm. We had spent that Sunday in two or three different places, stopping to give our testimony here and there and give out tracts. We drove through the town of Dunsmuir—very small, really a railroad center, where they put on the extra engines to boost the train over the Shasta grade on the Southern Pacific. As we drove through I noticed a group of about ten young people standing on the steps of the Methodist church. After we had camped two miles farther on, I said to Mrs. Fuller, "I think I'll walk back, and go down and say hello to the young people at the Methodist church." She protested that it was hot and we were tired and that it was too late, but I somehow felt led to go back. When I got there, their meeting had started and the leader asked me to say a few words. I told them a little bit about what I was doing. I also presented the claims of Christ in just a simple way and pointed out how we should present our bodies as a living sacrifice and to be real soldiers for Christ. Well, I gave an invitation, but there were no visible results.

So I went back to the camp and Mrs. Fuller asked, "Did you have any results?" And I said, "Not that I know of." And she said, "I told you not to go." I said, "Well, I just felt led to go, and I'll leave the results with the Lord."

Nine years later Mrs. Fuller and I were in San Diego, and we went to John Bunyan Smith's church, where an evangelist was holding a meeting. When the evangelist spotted me he said, "Charlie Fuller, you come up here and give a word." Well, I came up and gave a short testimony, and just before I started to go down a man in the audience stood up and said, "Is this the Charlie Fuller that was in Dunsmuir nine years ago? Well," he continued, "I've been wanting to tell you something for nine years. Do you remember that little meeting in the Methodist church on Sunday night?" And I said, "Yes." "Well," he said, "I was at that meeting, and afterward I got under conviction and went back to my room and got down on my knees and had a wrestling match with the Lord and accepted Christ as my Savior. And now I'm a salesman for a hardware company, and I travel up and down the Pacific coast, and wherever I go I try to contact a group of young people and tell them the way of salvation and instruct them as much as possible in the things of the Bible. And as a result several young people's groups have been begun."

Charles Fuller went on to tell the students what an encouragement this incident in these early days and its outcome nine years later had been to him throughout his many years of ministry. He concluded his remarks to the class by saying,

Paul said, "Woe is me if I preach not the Gospel." Not everyone has the specific gift of evangelism, but whatever your particular spiritual gift, you should be evangelistic. All we do is toward evangelism. There should be a definite purpose in preaching, and that is to realize that the people you are talking to are those that are alienated from Christ, dead in trespasses and sins, and walking according to the course of this age, energized by the prince of the power of the air, the spirit that now works in the children of disobedience. And people need to know that they are bound for everlasting separation unless they repent and believe the Gospel. So, that's been the heart of the "Old Fashioned Revival Hour" all these years.

4. Becoming a Pastor

DURING THE FALL OF 1921, Charles Fuller began a third-year graduate course at Biola designed to give additional training for those intending to be pastors. But for some reason he dropped out three months later. Perhaps his involvement as president of the Orange County Christian Endeavour proved too taxing, or perhaps he felt he had a good enough foundation now to go on studying the Bible on his own. At that time Dr. John W. Hunter, a Biola professor, wrote a letter of recommendation for Charles Fuller in which he said:

I consider him admirably fitted for the position of assistant pastor, or director of religious work, or young people's work in any large city church. Mr. Fuller is thoroughly grounded in the great fundamental doctrines of the Christian faith and he has also a good working knowledge of the Word of God in its application to life. He knows where to find those passages for comfort and help that so many of God's children need, and also where to find what God says to those who are not yet His children. He is a mature man for his age. His business experience has developed in him the ability to handle men. His work in his own home church has given him the opportunity of putting to the practical test the things he has been taught in the Institute. He is quiet and gentlemanly in his manner, and understands the art of being a good listener. His wife, who is talented along several lines, will be a great help to him in the work that I have referred to. Indeed, they are an exceptional couple. The fact that our Presbytery willingly received this young man, leaving it to himself to decide whether he would now take a theological seminary course or merely a course of reading under someone designated by them, proves that they recognize him as being an exceptional man.

The income from the twenty-acre orange grove which he had bought in 1919 continued to provide his support. Charles Fuller remained an elder and clerk of the session at the Placentia Presbyterian Church. In 1920 a fellow elder, Mr. O. W. Lillie, had resigned as teacher of the adult Sunday school class because of poor health and had nominated Charles Fuller to take his place.

None of the many references to Charles Fuller in the session minutes during the six years preceding the fall of 1919 convey any note of tension between him and the church. But it does seem that the spirit and outlook of Biola and the Fundamentalist movement— some of whose basic outlines were sketched in the preceding chapter —were now making their impact, so that his mood began to diverge from that of the church as a whole. And Elder Lillie, who thought very highly of Charles Fuller, also began to reflect his new mood. The minutes of November, 1919, state that "exception was taken by brother Lillie and brother Fuller for the aggressive work of the committee on Religious Education, this committee having made plans for boys' and girls' services &c." The next month's entry says, "Brother Fuller and brother Lillie took exception to the plan of the church in sending out missionaries on salary, stating that they believed in and were willing to support those that went out on faith." Two years later, in the minutes of March, 1921, we read:

The work of the C. E. Society was considered with special reference to a book[1] which had been distributed in the society by Mr. Fuller without the knowledge of the session and was being used to furnish topics for the meeting causing marked division and feeling in the society. The general state of the church was discussed and the need for cooperation amongst the elders was presented. It was agreed that from henceforth whatever was done would be done altogether. The objection was made by Mr. Fuller that there was too much social service in the church.

In its life and death struggle with Liberalism, Fundamentalism overreacted by tending to regard efforts to help the poor and underprivileged as a rejection of Christ, in that they encouraged the idea that men could save themselves and bring in the millennium by their own efforts. My mother used to recall how the Placentia church had a project of caring for the babies of the Mexicans who picked oranges for the growers. She remembered, regretfully, that in those days she and my father felt that the church should simply preach the Gospel and leave to other organizations the task of caring for

---

[1] I have not been able to identify this book.

people's physical needs. Those influenced by the Fundamentalist movement sometimes tended to forget that the Bible taught that Christians should also "do good unto all men" (Gal. 6:10).

There is no evidence that the Placentia Presbyterian Church was liberal. Mr. George Key, a charter member of the church and well acquainted with Charles Fuller in those years, wrote up the church's history for its golden anniversary in 1962. In this pamphlet he remarked, "The church was at times criticized for leaning too much toward the Social Gospel, but the church then, as ever since, felt it had an obligation toward the unfortunate." He then went on to show that this did not mean a denial of the Gospel, for at the very height of the Great Depression in July, 1932, when the church was fighting for its financial life, it nevertheless voted to support the John Brown Evangelistic Campaign that was being held in Fullerton (Charles Fuller's church also supported it). The newspapers of that time also show how the Placentia Presbyterian Church was always active in Christian Endeavour.

The Placentia Bible Class

But tension between Charles Fuller and the Placentia Presbyterian Church increased as he went on teaching the adult Sunday school class. By the spring of 1921 the 125-seat sanctuary, where the class met, was no longer adequate to hold all those who were coming to hear him. Besides the many Placentians who attended the class, there were those who drove in from Fullerton, Santa Ana, and even from Pomona. A number were converted through the ministry of this class.

Charles Fuller taught the Bible with an enthusiasm that had been growing ever since he had begun a diligent study of the Bible after hearing Paul Rader. Then, too, the orange industry was the main occupation of the people of that area, and Charles Fuller identified well with them. In 1921 he had also become a member of the board of directors of the same packing house which he had managed until 1919.

But the growth of this class presented a difficulty. The class met from 9:30 until 10:30 A.M., and there was an embarrassing contrast between the full sanctuary at that hour and the less well-attended main worship service at eleven. There was also the difficulty of shutting down all the socializing that naturally went on after such a class, so that the sanctuary could be readied for the worship service. To alleviate these problems, the class decided in April, 1921, to move from the church sanctuary to the meeting hall of the Placentia Round Table Club House two blocks away. The hall in this club house could accommodate one hundred seventy-five people. This decision was made, however, without consulting all the leaders of the church. An entry in the session minutes says, "At the meeting of the Bible class, held on the first Monday evening of April, [1921], . . . the class decided, at the suggestion of brother Lillie, to hold the regular Sunday morning sessions at the club house. This matter had not been previously presented to the session." Later on that year the session minutes report that Elder Ipsen, who was also superintendent of the Sunday school, complained that the removal of the adult class to the club house "was not in the proper form, the session not having been consulted." According to the minutes of October 13, 1921,

It was moved by Ipsen that we plan to build or secure a building adjoining the church for Sunday school purposes. Brother Fuller said the Bible class could not be brought into a building connected with the church. Inquiry was made by the pastor as to why all the elders could not take part in the group organizations of the church and why some made no effort to bring in new members either by confession of faith or by letter. Brother Fuller explained that the superintendent of the Sunday school and the pastor did not know what the Bible class was trying to do for the church and Sunday school through Bible class group organizations. The principle of cooperation among the elders was again considered and it was agreed again that what we do, we do all together. . . . The pastor made the following recommendations to the brethren: (1) that the superintendent of the Sunday school should be a member of the executive committee of the class and be given a notice of each of its meetings; (2) that the list of Bible class members and group organizations should be turned over to the superintendent of the Sunday school and pastor to be correlated with the church plans. These recommendations were approved by the brethren.

Two weeks later the entry for the minutes reads, "The Bible class at its regular meeting voted $300 [support] for an independent missionary." Then in February, 1922, after Charles Fuller had terminated formal studies at Biola, the class began to publish weekly "The Class Bulletin of the Placentia Bible Class. Placentia Round Table Club House, Placentia, Cal. Sunday Morning at 9:30. Charles E. Fuller, Teacher. O. W. Lillie, Assistant Teacher." Even though Charles Fuller continued as an elder in the Placentia Presbyterian Church and was still clerk of the session, there is no mention in the four pages of this bulletin of any connection with the church. Furthermore, three people were listed on the first page under the caption "Our Missionaries."

My conclusion from this evidence is that Charles Fuller had come to feel that this class was now doing some things that the church itself should have been doing all along. From his exposure to men like Paul Rader, Reuben Torrey, Thomas Horton, and the many capable leaders of what is known as the Fundamentalist movement, he had been imbued with a spirit characterized by such things as aggressive evangelism, enthusiastic Bible teaching, and the hearty singing of the Gospel songs made popular by D. B. Towner, Charles Alexander (Reuben Torrey's song leader during his evangelistic campaigns), and Robert Harkness (his campaign pianist). Charles Fuller's mood was also characterized by an interest in biblical prophecy and in the Zionist movement, which seemed to be the beginnings of a remarkable fulfillment of biblical prophecy. Then, too, he was influenced by the Victorious Life movement (stemming from the Keswick Conferences of England), which he had learned about from Charles Trumbull, the editor of the widely read *Sunday School Times* who had held several Victorious Life Conferences in Southern California.

It is easy to see that tensions within the church were bound to emerge when this young elder, so deeply involved in the main industry of the area, became himself an avid and highly capable representative of the chief characteristics of the Fundamentalist movement. Although quite orthodox, the Placentia Presbyterian Church did not completely fit the Fundamentalist profile, and therefore a clash between Charles Fuller and this church was inevitable.

When my father, in later years, reflected upon his zeal in these early days, he would remark that he wished he had had more wisdom and maturity. He frankly admitted that he had a youthful zeal which was somewhat deficient in love.

But in 1923 a new pastor came to the church, and after a year he made a move that cleared up this anomalous situation of the adult Sunday school class meeting two blocks away and making no mention of its connection with the church. He urged the Sunday school superintendent to organize a new adult class which would meet on the church premises. Charles Fuller recalled that the news of the formation of this new class came as a total surprise to him. He first learned of it at a Sunday school teachers' meeting in January, 1924, when the superintendent announced it. Charles Fuller asked whether this meant that his class would no longer be a part of the church's Sunday school, and the answer was yes. Being an elder in the church, he wondered whether he should resign from the class, but then he decided to let the class itself say whether it wanted him to continue as the teacher. Some of the members, however, when they learned that the church was starting its own adult class, decided to move back to that class. Therefore, those voting for Charles Fuller to stay on as teacher were people already inclined to be more loyal to him than to the church. George Key, in his history of Placentia Presbyterian Church under the section "Early Trouble," remarked that "part of the class returned to the church. From the rest, the Calvary Church originated. In fairness to the record it must be noted that these two elders [Fuller and Lillie] earlier had contributed a great deal to the young church both in time and money."

After the Placentia Bible Class voted to carry on as in the past, Charles Fuller and O. W. Lillie tendered their resignations as elders in the church on January 31, 1924. It is significant that on the following Saturday, two days later, the Placentia Bible Class advertised for the first time in the *Fullerton Tribune* alongside other churches. The advertisement read:

Placentia Bible Class, Sunday Morning, Round Table Club House, 9:30 A.M. Subject of the Lesson, "The Millennium and the Closing Events of the Age." The Placentia Bible Class stands for the fundamentals of the faith and it is evangelistic and missionary in scope. Cordial welcome. Charles E. Fuller, teacher.

Most of the churches that advertised in that paper were Fullerton churches; it was fifteen months before the Placentia Presbyterian Church began to advertise itself there sporadically. Thus the new

Placentia Bible Class was saying implicitly that the work they were carrying on was something so vital that all in northern Orange County should consider joining them.

THE FOUNDING OF CALVARY CHURCH

Now that the Placentia Bible Class was advertising itself alongside other churches, it found itself moving inexorably toward becoming a full-fledged church. Another step in this direction was taken when the women of the class organized themselves into a Dorcas society which sewed and collected clothing for the missionaries and the needy. The class also held special prayer meetings for its missionaries as they were about to return to the field, and it was Grace Fuller's task to read for the class the letters from these missionaries, which now numbered four.

Then in February, 1925, the class voted to ask Harry O. Anderson, a young people's evangelist, to come and hold a three-week evangelistic campaign. Harry Anderson had been a very successful evangelist ever since he graduated from Biola in 1915. He visited Placentia in March to help choose where the special wooden tabernacle with its sawdust floor should be located, and it was decided that the vacant land across the street to the east of the club house would be ideal. The campaign was to begin on the first Sunday afternoon in April, 1925. The newspaper reported that on Monday, March 16,

. . . about twenty-five men gathered at 7:00 A.M. with hammers and saws to construct a tabernacle for the Harry O. Anderson Revival Campaign which will be opened on April 5. At noon a sumptuous lunch was provided by the women of the class and a supper was spread at 4:00 P.M. All that could be done on the building before more lumber arrives was finished.

In the meantime Charles Fuller spoke on topics for each Sunday's lesson that would help prepare the class for the campaign. Included were topics such as "How to Have a Revival" and "The Three Foundational and Fundamental Facts in the Christian Faith." Committees for prayer meetings, finance, decoration, street meetings, ushers, music, and publicity were appointed.

By April 5 the tabernacle, seating several hundred people, was in readiness, and Harry Anderson began the campaign with a sermon entitled "God's Call to Placentia." He preached morning and evening each day for three weeks. After three days the paper reported that "Rev. Harry O. Anderson, evangelist, seems to be making a great hit in the tabernacle in Placentia where he has been preaching every day this week at 10 o'clock in the morning and 7:30 in the evening. Local residents have been surprised at the unusual attendance." He held a special children's meeting that first week, and immediately following it a large red, white, and blue balloon almost as big as a garage was readied with a sign attached to the balloon announcing the meetings. There was also a note on it which promised a reward to the one recovering the balloon. When a sponge soaked in gasoline was ignited and suspended beneath the balloon, it soared up and away. But then the campaign leaders became worried about where this balloon with the blazing sponge would land, and so they followed it in a car. This was indeed fortunate, for it settled finally on a garage and would have burned it up had they not been there to extinguish the blaze. In later years Harry Anderson remarked that he never again used this kind of a stunt for advertising an evangelistic campaign!

The campaign's special emphasis on reaching children was very successful, and it became evident that the Placentia Bible Class would have to organize a Sunday school to keep this children's work going. Two weeks into the campaign, the class took yet another step in becoming a full-fledged church by organizing the "Sunshine Sunday School."

There had been about forty decisions for Christ during the campaign. The newspaper reported that "people have been converted in the tabernacle, in homes, and even out in the orange groves." Night after night during the campaign the tabernacle, seating several hundred, had been filled with standing room only so that a makeshift enlargement of it was added midway through the campaign. People from Santa Ana, Orange, and Anaheim were saying they wanted to join the Placentia Bible Class.

For some time this class had urged Charles Fuller to make it into a church, but until now he had refused, saying that the last thing he wanted to do was to found a new church. But now that the class had its own Sunday school and had expanded through this large influx of new converts and older Christians, Charles Fuller realized

Above: *Pastor Fuller and congregation of Calvary Church, Placentia.* **Below:**
The Placentia Bible Class in front of Round Table Club House (about 1924).

that he already had all the responsibilities of a pastor. So at the last meeting of the evangelistic campaign on Sunday afternoon, April 26, 1925, he announced that the Placentia Bible Class would form itself into a church. *The Placentia Courier* that following week told the story as follows:

The Placentia Bible Class, organized some years ago, which has wielded such an influence in the religious life of the community and whose missionary effort has born fruit in so many lands, has outgrown its status as a Bible class, and last Sunday afternoon became a church organization. For some time there has been demand and an urgent need felt and expressed from many sources for a church organization where only and all fundamental doctrines of the Bible are upheld by those wishing to lend their united influence against the worldwide trend toward modernism and materialism. On next Monday night at the Tabernacle at 7:30 a meeting of interested persons will be held at which meeting incorporation papers will be signed and officers elected. Any one interested may see the statement of doctrine and upon signing the same be welcomed to join the new organization. The new church, which now has been finally named, will be interdenominational, fundamental, and evangelistic, the motto being "We Preach Christ crucified, risen, and coming again."

That week while the class was making plans to incorporate itself into a church, Charles Fuller made plans to become ordained so that he could be its minister. Since leaving the Presbyterian Church fifteen months before, he had cast his lot with the Baptists and particularly with those ministers in the Northern Baptist Convention who in 1921 had organized themselves into the Baptist Bible Union. This union had formulated a creed and by means of it had striven to purge from the convention and its foreign mission society all those who had any liberal tendencies. A leading spokesman for this union in the Los Angeles area was the Rev. Frederic Farr, pastor of the Calvary Church, Los Angeles. But many Baptist churches, even those which were strongly fundamental, did not want to enforce a strict creedal standard on other Baptists. As Baptists they honored the right of each individual to be answerable only to God in the way he understood the teachings of Scripture. Consequently, the Baptist Bible Union could not muster sufficient churches in the Los Angeles area for an ordination council. There were, however, a sufficient number of such churches two hundred miles to the north in the central valley of California near the town of Modesto. Frederic Farr was planning to lead a group of six young men, sympathetic to the stand of the Baptist Bible Union, northward to the Modesto area for ordination on May 4, 1925. Charles Fuller made arrangements to join this group. In its advertisement for May 3, the Sunday following the close of the campaign, the Placentia Bible Class called itself the Calvary Church for the first time, but it was careful not to call Charles Fuller its minister. He was simply "in charge" of the morning worship service. Charles Fuller conducted the services of the newly named Calvary Church that Sunday in the tabernacle. Then early the next morning he joined in a procession of three Model-T Fords whose occupants, led by Frederic Farr, were driving north for a mass ordination service. That evening representatives of churches near Modesto convened, examinations of the candidates were conducted, and Charles Fuller, along with the others, was ordained.

While he was being ordained that evening near Modesto, the members of his class were meeting to sign papers of incorporation and to appoint a board of directors, a board of deacons, and a board of trustees for the new church. Fifty people signed the church's statement of doctrine as charter members. Thus everything was in order for the service of that next Sunday, May 10, 1925, two weeks after the close of the campaign, when Charles Fuller as an ordained minister would lead the first communion service of the new Calvary Church, Placentia. That afternoon he would also take new members coming into the church upon confession of faith over to the Baptist Church of Fullerton where he would use that church's facilities to baptize them.

The Growth of Calvary Church

Filled with enthusiasm, the new church pushed forward to realize many opportunities for spreading the Gospel. They hired an architect to draw up plans for an L-shaped building. One wing would comprise a sanctuary seating four hundred people, and the other would consist of two floors for the Sunday school which would have eleven separate classrooms closed off from one another and each equipped with a blackboard. There would also be a social hall. Costing forty-one thousand dollars, the stucco church built in the style of early Spanish architecture was dedicated on February 21, 1926. It still stands today, enlarged by another wing which was added in 1954.

A notable feature of this new church was its zeal to extend its ministry beyond Placentia to at least the northern half of Orange County. It appointed an evangelist, Mr. William Pietsch, who was in charge of the Sunshine Sunday School and also conducted the evening evangelistic services, to head up an extension department and hold campaigns in the surrounding towns. Under the auspices of Calvary Church, he held a four-week campaign in June, 1925, in Anaheim, where a tent was erected in which five hundred people could be seated. He had a similar campaign in nearby Olinda during August. In between he held a series of evangelistic meetings at the tabernacle in Placentia.

The church also encouraged its own members to be evangelistic. A class to train personal workers was organized, and street meetings were held an hour before the evangelistic service on Sunday evenings. During the month of August a Gospel team from the church held several open-air meetings at Newport Beach. In September another team went to speak to the Indians studying at the Sherman Institute near Riverside and returned rejoicing with the report of forty-five decisions for Christ. The leader of the Midnight Mission in "Hell's Half Acre" in Los Angeles came and spoke to the new church, and a group responded with the commitment to be responsible for one night of meetings each month at that mission.

Charles Fuller was the prime mover behind this evangelistic emphasis which characterized Calvary Church from the beginning. The local newspaper said, "Calvary Church has a strong, aggressive evangelistic program and this, coupled with the establishment of Bible classes in various communities, will be a great factor in spreading the Word of God." The urge which in previous years had led Charles Fuller to use his vacation time to preach to miners and lumberjacks now manifested itself by inspiring a new church to be aggressively evangelistic. Calvary Church went to where people were rather than sitting and waiting for them to come to it.

While the sanctuary was under construction, the church also took steps to establish a strong Sunday school. It brought in Mr. Robert

Ringer of Arkansas, a specialist in organizing Sunday schools, for consultation. He recommended that Placentia and its vicinity be divided into six sections, and that a team from the church be assigned to each section to take a census and invite everyone to the Sunshine Sunday School who was not already attending a Sunday school. Enthusiasm for what lay ahead ran so high that as he left, Robert Ringer declared, "The spirit manifested in this movement here at Calvary Church is the best I have seen anywhere in more than fifteen years of Sunday school building in all parts of the country." The census turned up so many who were not in Sunday school that the young and optimistic church thought that all the churches in the Placentia area could be filled with them six times over. In December, 1925, the leaders of the Sunday school were even thinking that six to seven hundred pupils would be coming when the building was finished.

Before the end of 1925 two Biola graduates who had proved themselves elsewhere as experienced workers with young people were brought onto the staff of Calvary Church to head up the young people's work. Mr. Don Milligan came in the summer of that year to head up the boys' work and to be in charge of the intermediate and senior young people. Miss Edith McNutt came in December to take charge of the work for the junior-age children and to head up the girls' work. These two new staff members also organized soul-winning clubs for the older young people. By 1928 there were seven such clubs at Calvary Church and four more in the church of a neighboring community which was without a pastor. Don Milligan also organized some young men into a Gospel team which held meetings throughout Orange County.

This emphasis on reaching the youth soon bore fruit, for during a Sunday evening service nine months after the church was organized, sixteen young people consecrated their lives for full-time service. On the church's first anniversary there was a baptismal service in which a large number of young people made confession of faith. Many of these had been led to Christ through the efforts of their godly Sunday school teachers.

Right from the beginning there was also a strong emphasis on missions. At the Bible Class social for June, 1925, four missionary candidates just leaving for the Orinoco River mission in Venezuela gave their testimonies, and people were impressed with their joyous consecration and with their accounts of how God had provided so they could become missionaries. Of the sixty-three hundred dollars which the church received in offerings during its first year, thirty-five hundred dollars was used for home and foreign missions.

To underscore the church's commitment to evangelism, Charles Fuller climaxed its first year by having a week of evangelistic meetings in which he preached each night. After one year the Sunday school had doubled its average attendance to one hundred eighty. Church membership had climbed to one hundred forty-two, with fifty-seven of these having joined on confession of faith. At the church's first annual meeting the members applauded as it was announced that all the bills for building the church had been met and that there remained only a $2,000-a-year payment to amortize the balance of the debt. "This will enable the church," reported the newspaper,

. . . to continue their strong evangelistic and missionary program. Many have remarked that the spirit of harmony and cooperation, coupled with the unusual consecration and enthusiasm in the church, is the result of the teaching of the Word, the Bible, and prayer. When a year ago some expressed themselves as believing that Calvary Church was building beyond the needs of the community, and to the possible detriment of other churches already established, the expression is now voiced on all sides that Calvary Church has not built large enough for the future needs and that other churches in the town have grown and prospered also. Rev. Charles E. Fuller, pastor of the church, expressed himself in happy appreciation of the splendid year's work and is expecting great things for the year to come.

Not every dream of this church, however, was fulfilled during its first year. Sunday school attendance at Calvary Church has never reached six hundred even to this day. Neither was anything said after the summer of 1925 about the extension department. But Charles Fuller kept emphasizing evangelism. From the second summer onwards Calvary Church had a Daily Vacation Bible School which it conducted in conjunction with the local Nazarene church. A bus was provided to bring children from the surrounding towns each day. The Rev. Harry MacArthur who had special gifts in youth ministry was brought in to help organize the program. He

62

climaxed each morning with an interesting talk based on stereopticon slides. The pastor from the Nazarene church kept a large group of boys busy with shovels and hoes for an hour each morning building a relief map of Palestine in the vacant land to the south of the church.

Charles Fuller also worked hard to bring many outstanding Christian leaders from all over the world out to rural Placentia whenever they happened through Southern California. Among them were Mr. William Fetler, an evangelist to Russia; Mr. Cameron Townsend, who had been doing Bible translation work in Central America and would later found the Wycliffe Bible Translators; Dr. Charles Hurlburt, a missionary from Africa; Mr. Thomas Mosley, a missionary from Tibet; and Miss Marguerita Moran, a missionary to India. G. Campbell Morgan, one of the greatest Bible expositors, occupied the pulpit one evening in 1928. Charles Fuller also brought in a number of evangelists to hold campaigns in his church. Dr. John McNeill, the Scottish evangelist, came in 1926; Dr. Harry Anderson came for his second campaign in 1927; Dr. Paul Rood, the chairman of the World's Christian Fundamentals Association, held a campaign in 1929. Harry Vom Bruch came in 1930, and in 1933, just before Charles Fuller resigned as pastor, Mel Trotter held a campaign.

Charles Fuller's own preaching sounded the evangelistic note as he spoke on such topics as "The Burning Question of the Hour" and "Is Judgment Coming?" But under his pictures on church advertisements, he identified himself as a "Pastor-Evangelist, Bible Teacher." God had made it clear to him, by this time, that his special gift was to be evangelistic as he expounded and taught the Bible. The slogan he chose for the church was "A Place Where the Whole Bible Is Taught." His sermon topics for the eight years he pastored Calvary Church covered a whole range of biblical doctrines.

We have seen how the Bible had become a relevant and exciting book to him through understanding the dispensational system for setting forth God's purpose and movement in redemptive history. He was thrilled by the realization that God was bringing the events of history to a climax in His dealings with Israel and in the return of Christ to rapture His Church out of the world. In his sermons he argued that since God was in command of history and of men's lives and destinies, people should therefore turn to the Lord. He also urged people to align themselves with God's purpose for history by bending every effort to help get the Gospel out.

There were several occasions when he gave a series of messages on God's plan for the nation of Israel. He sometimes mentioned the Zionist movement as an indication that the period in which God would offer salvation to men on the basis of faith in Christ was nearing its end, and therefore people should make their peace with God now. It seemed to him that Mussolini was acting in many ways as the Antichrist himself would act before Christ came to destroy him and set up His millennial kingdom. Thus in the fall of 1929, Charles Fuller gave a series of messages on the following topics: "The Jews and the Battle of Armageddon"; "Mussolini, the Wild Man of Europe"; "The Future of Europe—the Resurrection of the Old Roman Empire"; and "The Bear out of the North," taken from Ezekiel 38 and 39, which he believed foretold Russia's destruction in attempting to conquer Israel after she had returned to Palestine.

Such topics were of great interest, and they helped to pack the church out on Sunday evenings. But Charles Fuller's ultimate purpose in stressing biblical prophecy throughout half a century of preaching was to show people how relevant the Bible is to what is happening today and thereby to awaken them to their need of turning to Christ without delay. His purpose was not in vain. For example, the newspaper reported that after the sermon on Mussolini, four people came forward to accept Christ.

On several occasions at Calvary Church Charles Fuller also preached on heaven. It was Paul Rader's message on the glories of heaven which had made a decisive change in his life, and he remembered how Reuben Torrey had recommended that ministers should preach much about heaven and the hope in store for the Christian. Those listening to his broadcasts in later years will remember how often he talked about heaven and how he would have the choir or quartet sing "Meet Me There" and "There's a Land That Is Fairer Than Day."

During Charles Fuller's eight years as pastor at Placentia, the church became seven times larger, growing from fifty charter members to three hundred and seventy.

5. Extending His Ministry

DESPITE THE EVANGELISTIC emphasis of the many activities of Calvary Church, Charles Fuller still did not feel he had found his niche. Something inside kept urging him to extend his ministry beyond the bounds of Calvary Church. He was free to do this because he had an independent income and took no salary from the church. In 1924 he had subdivided ten acres of orange property and used the profit to buy additional acreage, which further increased his income.

EXTRAPASTORAL COMMITMENTS

He had not been pastor very long before he began accepting invitations to preach at Bible conferences. In the summer of 1925 he spoke for a week at the Southwest Bible and Missionary Conference at Flagstaff, Arizona. Here some two hundred missionaries to the Indians and Indian Christian leaders gathered each year. God's blessing rested upon this conference in such an unusual way that the memory of it helped him in the difficult times of later years to remain confident that God had indeed called him to be an evangelist.

Then in December, 1925, Charles Fuller held a meeting at the Sherman Institute for Indians in Riverside, California. The newspaper reported that "there were a number of decisions when the altar call was given to the one thousand students attending. Mr. Fuller was invited to go back for a week's conference when he will speak twice a day to the Indians." He preached there again in March of the following year. Concerning these meetings the director of the institute, Mr. C. W. Cell, said, "Over four hundred of our choice Protestant Indian youth voluntarily attended Charles Fuller's series of Bible classes at our institute, and over one hundred of them took a definite stand for Christ."

One of the ways Charles Fuller was able to relate to these Indians was to recall the time when his Pomona College football team had played a team from this institute. The Indians, coming as they did from a life virtually untouched by civilization with its comforts which also weaken, were in so much better physical condition than even the star athletes at Pomona that the game had to be called off after the score had reached 100-0.

The blessings which attended these meetings away from Calvary Church encouraged Charles Fuller to give himself to this kind of work in a more official capacity. In November, 1926, he became a member of the Field Department representing the Bible Institute of Los Angeles. Biola published a brochure which billed him as a "Bible Conference Leader and Evangelist," and after quoting letters of recommendation from a number of Christian leaders, said, "Mr. Fuller is available for Bible Conference and evangelistic work and will gladly respond as far as possible to every appeal."

As a result he conducted a three-week evangelistic campaign in Ocean Beach, California, in January-February, 1927. The newspaper reported that "this is the first of his many calls for evangelistic work under the Bible Institute of Los Angeles." The church, in its own column in the newspaper, declared, "Mr. Fuller feels definitely led to go out and spread the Gospel in less-favored places. His opening meeting last Sunday night was greatly blessed of the Lord and seven souls were led to Jesus Christ."

Then after only one Sunday back in the pulpit of Calvary Church, he left again for two weeks of meetings in Walla Walla, Washington. The church reported wistfully in the newspaper that

. . . this will be Mr. Fuller's last Sunday with us for several weeks, as he will leave next week for Walla Walla, Washington, to hold a Bible Conference under the auspices of the Bible Institute of Los Angeles. We will miss our pastor but we are only too glad to share him in the work. It is our prayer that God will richly honor his ministry in Walla Walla and that souls may be saved.

In the spring of 1927 Charles Fuller resigned from Biola's Field Department in order to become a member of the school's board of trustees. And indeed, except for preaching at the Gideon Convention in San Francisco in June, he did not go on any more extensive evangelistic tours for the rest of 1927.

It might seem strange that one who had such urgings to extend his ministry to the people should now relinquish this work (at least temporarily) in order to have time to be a board member. But we must remember that Charles Fuller considered himself committed to teaching as well as to evangelism. Being on the board of trustees of a major Bible institute meant doing work which resulted in training tomorrow's leaders of the church. It was this same urge which would lead him, in the fall of 1928, to become a member of the faculty at the Los Angeles Baptist Seminary and teach classes in Bible exegesis,[1] and which, in 1947, resulted in his founding a theological seminary.

But the desire also to reach people could not be suppressed very long, for in February, 1928, he returned to the Northwest to hold a three-week evangelistic campaign in Touchet, Washington, under the auspices of Biola. It was miserably cold and wet during this campaign, and he came down with a severe attack of sinusitis. But God gave him strength to preach two to four times a day. The meetings were greatly blessed with conversions and dedications to service. But upon returning to Calvary Church, Charles Fuller had to stay out of his pulpit for two whole Sundays and then preach only once each Sunday for some weeks in order to regain his strength.

During this absence the church took up a collection for a special fund to spruce up his study. They carpeted the floor, hung paintings on the wall, and placed four potted ferns in the room. In doing this it seems that they were not only expressing appreciation for what he had done for the church but were also urging him to give as much time as possible to being a pastor. In May, 1928, Charles Fuller sent out a letter to the members of Calvary Church in which he thanked them for their continued support. He told them how much he appreciated being their pastor and then asked, "Will you not let this letter be my messenger to you in place of a personal call—which if time and pressing duties permitted I would gladly make. . . ?"

But it was not only the enervating campaign in Touchet, Washington, which was now limiting the time Charles Fuller had for Calvary Church. Biola was entering the worst crisis in its twenty-year history. All the board members of the school underwent a tremendous strain, but none so great as Charles Fuller, who had the courage to become the chairman of the board just when the school had to be rebuilt from the wreckage.

---

[1] Charles Fuller received his honorary Doctor of Divinity from this school in June, 1931.

This crisis centered around Dr. John MacInnis who had become dean at Biola after Reuben Torrey retired in 1924. A Presbyterian minister, he had been closely associated with Reuben Torrey for some years at the Montrose Bible Conference in Pennsylvania. Then in 1922 Reuben Torrey had brought him on to the faculty at Biola. But when John MacInnis became dean, he wanted to do things a little differently from his predecessor. He wanted Biola to work more in cooperation with the churches so as to be "constructive" in its influence. When he became editor of *The King's Business* in 1927, he stated that the policy of this magazine would be, henceforth, more to seek the "triumph of God's truth rather than the downing of an enemy."

This emphasis upon working for peace with the churches troubled some Fundamentalist leaders. But it was the publication in the fall of 1927 of his book *Peter, the Fisherman Philosopher* which unleashed a storm that almost destroyed Biola. Limiting himself to Peter's epistles and the New Testament's records of him, John MacInnis wrote to "indicate in a simple way that Peter's insights include a most comprehensive view of God and our world and can stand the test of the most searching thinking of our day."[2] He wanted to show that as a fisherman, Peter expressed theological truths in a way that the common man could easily grasp and regard as relevant and vital. For example, he interpreted Peter's statements in his first epistle that Christ bore men's sins upon the cross to mean that

. . . it was the sins of the people that put Him there. . . . [Jesus] openly attacked the sin of the race as it was manifested in his day . . . and men resented the exposure, and . . . [so] men actually attacked the innocent one and killed him. Peter clearly saw and stated that simple fact. The church has lost the full significance of this fact because it has allowed the actual thing that took place to be overshadowed by the theological explanation which grew up around it. The thing we need to clearly see is that Jesus literally carried up the sins of the

---

[2]John M. MacInnis, *Peter, the Fisherman Philosopher* (New York: Harper Brothers, 1930), p. x. The only copy of this book that is available to me is this 1930 edition which according to the foreword is no different from the original one published in late 1927.

world in His own body upon the tree. There was no artificial reckoning about the matter.[3]

Such a statement seems to discount Paul's teaching that when Christ died on the cross God imputed to Him the sins of the world, so that God could remain just in forgiving sins. To be sure, later in the chapter John MacInnis said that there was a deeper significance in the death of Christ by which it became possible for God to forgive sins. But this appeared to be only a concession, for was not this "deeper significance" a part of that "theological explanation" of the death of Christ which he had said was virtually incomprehensible to all but trained theologians, and which distracted from the "fisherman" understanding of the cross which even the simplest person could grasp and find intensely relevant?

Biola was soon beset by many cries of outrage. Four or five people closely connected with the school suggested to John MacInnis that he resign. On February 6, 1928, he did present his resignation to the board of trustees (Charles Fuller was not present because he was holding meetings in Touchet, Washington), but they refused it and urged him to carry on with his work. They did this because John MacInnis, a very sincere and godly man, assured them that he heartily endorsed the school's creed and that nothing in his book contradicted that creed in any way. A group of Fundamentalist ministers had also been asked to study the book, and their verdict was that "attacks on this book were wholly unwarranted."

But the book continued to rankle people. In recalling this incident in later years, my father used to quote Job 31:35, "Oh that . . . mine adversary had written a book," and note that it was not John MacInnis but his book which made people become his adversaries.

The *Moody Monthly* gave the book a very unfavorable review, as did Arno Gaebelein in his publication *Our Hope*. But the most damaging criticism came from Dr. Charles Trumbull, the editor of the *Sunday School Times,* the most influential periodical of the Fundamentalist movement. In May, 1928, he published a six-column editorial review of John MacInnis' book and concluded that "its central theme is unscriptural." He was disturbed that John MacInnis should regard Peter more as a philosopher than as an

---

[3] Ibid., p. 76.

apostle. The book argued that Peter, by his own powers of intuition and reasoning, and in close fellowship with Christ, had achieved the insight that God was ruling the world by a moral purpose. To Charles Trumbull, this contradicted a number of biblical passages which taught that revelatory spokesmen like Peter had not spoken from the impulse of their own spirit but had been "born along" (2 Pet. 1:21) by the Holy Spirit.

He also objected that for John MacInnis, Peter exemplified a "higher Fundamentalism" (the book's subtitle) in that he did not get involved in abstract theological concepts but had the rough fisherman's instinct to see through to the heart-stirring, simple meaning of it all. John MacInnis drew quotations from secular poets and philosophers and even some liberal theologians who echoed his understanding of Peter's down-to-earth, fisherman philosophy. Charles Trumbull objected that an interpretation of Peter which regards his teachings as essentially nothing more than what men can arrive at by their own efforts drags "the divinely given beliefs of the church down to the unspeakably low levels of the minds of men." Far from being a "higher Fundamentalism," John MacInnis' teaching was thus not even fundamental.

Charles Trumbull concluded his editorial with these strong words:

Not only a large number of Christian leaders and individual men and women throughout the Church in America, but undoubtedly some within the Institute itself among both teachers and students, and officers and members of the Church of the Open Door which meets on the premises of the Institute, are deeply distressed and are convinced that a crisis has come in the life of this institution. *The Sunday School Times* is in touch with much more information in the whole matter than it could give in these six columns. And so the staff of the *Times* are assured that they voice the heartfelt plea and prayer of a multitude when they urge confidently upon the Directors of the Bible Institute of Los Angeles that they recognize the true situation and cleanse the Institute of all false teaching. Only unequivocal and public action to this effect can restore the confidence of the Christian public in the school. . . . Many are praying for this action; may many more unite in this prayer, and pray without ceasing until the longed-for and gracious answer from God comes.[4]

---

[4] *The Sunday School Times* (May 5, 1928), p. 282.

It is easy to understand how such words appearing in so influential a journal challenged Biola's very existence. The cry of mortal anguish is unmistakable on the first page of the June, 1928, issue of *The King's Business* in which Keith Brooks, the editor, said that if what *The Sunday School Times* reported was true then the faculty of Biola was lying when it signed its creed and the school had apostatized. The page concluded:

Such an unjust and subtle attack will, we are sure, be deeply resented by hundreds who know the members of our faculty intimately, and we believe that those who stand for common honor among men, to say nothing of the "victorious life,"[5] will register strong protests. . . . The attack upon our Institute has resolved itself into a one-sided battle of mud throwing. If men must throw mud, they should remember that they cannot keep their own hands clean.

Charles Trumbull often spent summers on the west coast, and when he came to Los Angeles in the summer of 1928, he spent considerable time in conference and prayer with John MacInnis. But while conceding that he had misunderstood him at certain minor points, he continued to insist that basically John MacInnis' teaching was unsound. In the August 26 issue of the *Sunday School Times,* Charles Trumbull dropped Biola from the list of "Bible Schools that are True to the Faith." In September, 1928, he acknowledged John MacInnis' many protestations of being orthodox, but he concluded, "My conviction is that his book and his protestations do conflict, and that the two sets of teachings are mutually irreconcilable."

For a man of Charles Trumbull's influence to persist in such a judgment of the head of Biola (at this time the school had no president) could only mean that thousands of earnest Christians would entertain the darkest suspicions about the school's orthodoxy. The pressure mounted so during the fall of 1928 that finally the board of directors met around the first of December and voted six to four to reverse their decision and to accept John MacInnis' resignation. The four who voted to retain him then resigned from the board. These included the chairman, the first vice chairman, and the secretary. G. Campbell Morgan resigned from Biola's faculty as did

---

[5] Charles Trumbull was noted for championing the Keswick teaching regarding the Victorious Life on the platforms of many Bible conferences.

71

Keith Brooks from being managing editor of *The King's Business*. A Presbyterian minister who had championed John MacInnis and thus deplored the decision of the board said in a sermon the following Sunday that "the student body is reported as ready to revolt if the breach is not healed at once by the remaining directors who represent the majority." He also mentioned Biola's serious financial condition because a gasoline engine business had not proved as profitable as Lyman Stewart had hoped.

What a tremendous task of rebuilding the school fell to the remaining six directors, and especially to Charles Fuller, who then took on the responsibility of being chairman of the board. He was now the one primarily responsible for finding a new administration for the school, a new editor for *The King's Business,* and the replacements for the faculty and board members who had resigned. He also had to convince the Christian public that Biola had indeed cleaned house so that the school would continue to receive the support it needed. Obviously a man with such responsibilities was not going to be a very good pastor for some time.

Charles Fuller's first step was to call a special board meeting and draft the following statement, which appeared in the April, 1929, *King's Business:*

After much prayer and serious reflection concerning the book *Peter, the Fisherman Philosopher,* written by Dr. J. M. MacInnis, the former Dean of the Bible Institute of Los Angeles, the Board of Directors desires to make the following statement:

We reaffirm our belief in the great Fundamental doctrines of Christianity as set forth in the Statement of Doctrine of the Bible Institute.

Because we recognized that we were in error in commending the book *Peter, the Fisherman Philosopher,* the Board some time ago accepted the resignation of the author, and he has now absolutely no connection with the Institute; and being determined that our testimony to and teaching of the Fundamental doctrines of Christianity as set forth in the Institute's Statement of Doctrine shall be so clear as to be absolutely above all possibility of suspicion, we hereby express our disapproval of said book, and declare that its thought and teaching does not represent the thinking and teaching of the Bible Institute today; and further, as a first step in the execution of our determination to pursue a course which will put this Institute's loyalty to the Bible beyond question, we have already discontinued the use, sale, and circulation of the book *Peter, the Fisherman Philosopher* in the Bible

Institute or elsewhere, and all remaining copies, together with the type-forms, have been destroyed.

In respect to the future policy of the Institute, the Board hereby declares its determination to adhere strictly to the purpose for which the Bible Institute of Los Angeles was founded, namely: the teaching of the Bible as the inspired and infallible Word of God in order to train men and women for the task of proclaiming the Gospel of salvation through the blood of Christ at home and abroad.

The Board also hereby declares that only such teachers will be elected to or retained on the Faculty of the Institute as do solemnly pledge themselves without reservation that their teaching shall be in complete harmony with the doctrinal statement of the Institute and with this declaration, and that they will carry out this declared policy of the Board.

Adopted at a special meeting of the Board of Directors held March 20, 1929.

Charles E. Fuller
President, Board of Directors
Bible Institute of Los Angeles

The next step was to appoint not only a new dean but also someone who would fill the newly created office of president of the institute. The *Fullerton Daily Tribune* reported on May 14, 1929:

Through the efforts of the Board of Directors of the Bible Institute of Los Angeles, of which the Rev. Charles Fuller, pastor of Calvary Church, Placentia, is president, the first president has been chosen for the Institute in the person of Dr. William P. White, Pacific Coast representative of the Moody Institute of Chicago. . . . Rev. Fuller has made many trips throughout the United States in an effort to find a man to fill the place. . . . Dr. White, who has occupied the pulpit of Calvary Church, has been identified with Fundamentalism and is reported as being without a fad in his stand.

A week later the paper reported that

. . . Placentia pastor says new dean of Bible Institute to be announced soon. The reorganization of the Los Angeles Bible Institute, of which he is the president of the Board of Directors, is almost complete, the Rev. C. E. Fuller of Placentia has announced. Rev. Fuller returned Sunday morning from a hurried trip to Portland, Oregon, in the interest of the Institute. The name of the new dean will be announced soon, he said. On the readjustment, the Rev. Fuller said the Institute will be made clean-cut Fundamentalist. . . . Arrangements are being made to accommodate one thousand students this coming school year, Rev. Fuller said.

The new dean was Dr. Elbert L. McCreery who had been a missionary to Africa and then head of the pastor's course at the Moody Bible Institute.

In July, 1929, a second edition of the year's catalog was published which showed a full roster of the faculty for the forthcoming school year. Besides the new president and new dean there were three new faculty members. Dr. J. E. Jaderquist became the new editor of *The King's Business.* The July issue of this magazine had an article entitled "Restoring Confidence," which contained letters from such prominent Christian leaders as Charles Trumbull, Arno Gaebelein, Harry Ironside, Donald Barnhouse, William Evans, Courtland Myers, and Stewart MacLennan—all of whom expressed their confidence in the way Biola was now going. By June, 1930, seven new members of the board of directors had been added, among them Charles Trumbull.

Thus because of his great concern for training men for the ministry, as well as for evangelism, Charles Fuller had stood in the gap at Biola at a time when the school could easily have disintegrated, but through his efforts and leadership a solid foundation was laid which made it possible for the school to prosper thereafter.

Beginning a Radio Ministry

In February, 1929, during the height of Charles Fuller's travels to find replacements for the board, administration, and faculty at Biola, he spoke for ten days at the Cadle Tabernacle in Indianapolis for the Defenders of the Christian Faith Conference. On one of those days he was asked, with very little advance warning, to substitute for the regular speaker on a local Gospel radio program. He preached from Mark 4:35–41, which recounts how Jesus stilled the waves from the storm on Galilee, and set forth his message in four points: a Great Peril; a Great Plea; a Great Peace; and a Great Personage. The regular speaker was surprised by the many letters and phone calls that came in telling of the blessing people had received from this straightforward Gospel message. Charles Fuller was also surprised that his short, simple message should produce such a response.

From Indianapolis he went to Philadelphia to interview people and to preach twice on Sunday, February 10. After leaving Philadelphia—perhaps Monday evening, February 11—to begin the long journey back to Southern California, he was awakened in his Pullman berth as his train wound its way through the Allegheny Mountains. A sense of the great opportunity that radio afforded for getting out the Gospel overwhelmed him. He was weary from the heavy speaking schedule that he had just completed and wanted to go back to sleep, but it seemed that God kept impressing upon his heart that he should take the first opportunity that presented itself to begin preaching regularly on the radio. He was awed by the problems that would have to be overcome in order to fulfill such a task. How could he have a program with sufficient appeal to sustain a regular listening audience? How would he pay for a regular broadcast? Would people continue to respond enthusiastically to his preaching, or was his recent experience in Indianapolis just a fluke?

After tossing in his berth for some time, Charles Fuller finally told the Lord that he would go on the radio regularly if God would open the door. Having said yes to God, he slept soundly the rest of the night.

Charles Fuller had preached the Gospel from time to time on radio ever since 1924 when he gave Bible lessons two mornings a week over Biola's 750-watt radio station, whose call letters then were KJS. There had also been that Sunday evening in August, 1925,[6] while Calvary Church was still meeting in the wooden tabernacle, when he had taken some musicians from Placentia to Los Angeles to broadcast a program over KJS. Neither Charles Fuller nor the Christian public at large were very excited in those days about spreading the Gospel by radio. The first commercial radio station had gone on the air in Pittsburgh in 1920. As early as 1921, Mr. R. E. Carrier, the engineer at Biola, had persuaded Reuben Torrey and Thomas Horton—against strong misgivings—to extend Biola's ministry by constructing a radio station. The Biola radio

---

[6] It was this broadcast which my father used for counting the number of years he was on radio. Though he did not have a regular broadcast until early in 1930, yet he had spoken from time to time on Biola's radio station—whose call letters, after September, 1925, were KTBI.

station, the first devoted specifically to religious broadcasting, made its debut on March 10, 1922.[7] But for five years hardly anything was said about KJS in *The King's Business*. An exception was an advertisement appearing in the June, 1923, issue, which told of "soul winning by radio" among people in the backwoods, in distant homes, in the sickroom, on board ship—in other words, people who could not attend a preaching service.

In September, 1923, Thomas Horton wrote an article entitled "Restless over Radio," in which he cited several objections against using radio to preach the Gospel: (1) it would give some one preacher too much prominence; (2) it is costly and draws money away from other Christian enterprises; (3) it creates a "stay-at-home" habit; (4) it deprives a listener of that personal contact with the preacher himself; (5) decisions made for Christ through radio preaching cannot be followed up as well as those made in a church; (6) when radio is used for all kinds of commercial purposes and amusements, it is questionable whether the Gospel should also use it; and (7) should the Gospel be preached over the air waves when Satan is the prince of the power of the air? But Thomas Horton nevertheless gave a very cautious approval to the Christians' use of radio:

We have had splendid testimonies from all over this land, from Mexico and Honolulu concerning the messages given over the Bible Institute radio, and of souls who have accepted Christ because of them, but that does not *settle the questions* which have been suggested. . . . Should we not avail ourselves of this newest agency for broadcasting the Gospel, not allowing it to interfere with our emphasizing the obligation to assemble together, and recognizing the fact that the radio— with all of its advantages—is also another menace to the spread of the Gospel and the saving of souls?[8]

But by 1927, Christians' attitude toward radio was changing. That year Donald Barnhouse began preaching by radio from his Philadelphia church, and in 1928 he was heard as far west as Iowa on eighteen stations of the CBS network. (By 1932 he was on one hundred stations.) Then, too, in 1927 *The King's Business* began to

---

[7] John Wanamaker's station WOO in Philadelphia began on August 10, 1922. WMBI began on July 28, 1926.

[8] *The King's Business* (September, 1923), p. 901.

devote a whole page of almost every issue to its own radio station, citing letters that had come in reporting conversions and listing the programs appearing on its thirty-five-hour-a-week broadcasting schedule.

Thus Charles Fuller's vision to preach the Gospel by radio came when Christians were awakening to their responsibility to use radio. But a whole year passed after that night in a train winding through the Alleghenies before God provided an opportunity for him to broadcast regularly.

This opportunity first appeared when it was announced that Santa Ana's newspaper, the *Register,* would found a new radio station, KREG, whose purpose originally was "to emphasize the cultural, the educational, and the religious." On its inauguration broadcast, a director of the station said, "This station has no commercial aims and ambitions. It has nothing to sell and is sponsored by no profit-making concerns and interests." It seemed that a group of philanthropists were willing to underwrite the cost. In one of its editorials, the Santa Ana *Register* claimed that "KREG is the first such institution to be established in the United States. . . . Movies have failed to be educational, and radio so far, but it is hoped that this unique venture will be the reverse of all that."

Here was the opportunity Charles Fuller had been waiting for! Such a station would welcome broadcasts from his church because it wanted to emphasize the religious. The cost would be small since a group of wealthy men were going to sponsor the new station. And indeed, by December, 1929, KREG had promised to carry his Sunday evening service.

An article in the *Placentia Courier* for December 26, 1929, declared:

Sunday evening services of Calvary Church, Placentia, will be broadcast over the radio beginning Sunday, January 5th, according to the announcement made this week by Rev. Charles E. Fuller, pastor. The church is to have remote control hookup with KREG, the newly licensed broadcasting station of the *Register,* Santa Ana. Rev. Fuller has for some time spoken over the Bible Institute station in Los Angeles and is a firm believer in the effectiveness of this manner of reaching a larger number of people. Calvary Church will be the first church in Orange County to have the services sent out over the air after the new arrangement is completed.

Dr. Fuller shows Edward Carnell, the seminary's second president, a plaque commemorating the millionth electrical transcription of the "Old Fashioned Revival Hour," about 1956. Several hundred of these were made for each broadcast and shipped to radio stations around the world.

Charles Fuller (back row, far right) at Cadle Tabernacle, Indianapolis, in February, 1929, with Paul Rader (back row, fourth from left). Soon after this conference, while still in the east, he received his vision to preach on radio.

But the new station had trouble getting its signal heard clearly in the surrounding area. Its radio engineers had to devote all their energies to basic technical problems for several weeks before they could work out the details of broadcasting by remote control from Placentia, ten miles to the north. And during these weeks the new station also encountered economic problems. It turned out that sufficient money to run it would not be forthcoming from the philanthropists. Like other radio stations, KREG would have to be supported by commercial advertisers. So by the end of January, 1930, before he had yet broadcast on KREG, Charles Fuller realized that he would have to pay his own way in order to broadcast regularly.

So on February 6, 1930, he sent out the following letter to members and friends of Calvary Church:

An Investment That Will Pay Large Dividends for Time and Eternity

Calvary Church of Placentia, California, will begin broadcasting its regular Sunday evening services by remote control, over radio KREG, "The Voice of the Orange Empire," February 23, 1930. The hour is from 8 to 9 P.M., Pacific Standard Time. KREG broadcasts on 1500 kilocycles.

Calvary Church is presenting splendid programs of congregational singing, solos, instrumental numbers, and Gospel messages. This church is under contract for every Sunday night, for the hour 8 to 9.

We are sure that you will be glad and eager to have a part in broadcasting the Gospel over the air to thousands of shut-ins in hospitals and homes, and to many others who find it impossible to attend a Sunday night church service. There are scores who are longing for an inspirational service. Calvary Church desires to supply part of that need. This church stands for "The Faith once delivered unto the saints."

To broadcast requires financial assistance. We need your help. Calvary Church has created a radio fund and all money given for the radio and so designated will be deposited in that fund, which will be in charge of Mr. Walter Junkin, president of the Church Board of Trustees, and Mr. Howard Jerome, radio treasurer.

Enclosed you will find a pledge card. We are trusting that God will give us a large number of subscribers who will agree to give one dollar a month or more towards this radio fund. We feel you would like to become a sustaining member of the Calvary Church Radio Fund. If so, please fill out the enclosed card and mail to the address given. Your investments will pay large dividends for time and eternity. Help to bring cheer, inspiration, and heavenly manna to thousands. We are counting on you to sign this card and mail it immediately with your gift.

Remember, we begin broadcasting our first service Sunday night, February 23, from 8 to 9. If you cannot attend the church personally, tune in on KREG, and listen in every Sunday night.

Yours in an effort "to preach the Gospel to every creature,"

Charles E. Fuller, Pastor

According to the contract with KREG, it would cost Calvary Church one hundred eighty dollars a month to broadcast for an hour each Sunday evening, and there was naturally concern about whether there would be sufficient funds to pay for this new venture. But replies to the February 6 letter began to come in, and two days before the initial broadcast the Santa Ana *Register* reported that "there are now over one hundred regular radio subscribers to the radio fund and contributions have been received from as far east as Kansas and as far north as Washington State."

A few days before the last Sunday of February, 1930, the Fullerton newspaper reported:

Arrangements are complete and testings are being made of the Calvary Church broadcast system, over which the Sunday evening service, February 23, will be sent. Crews of the Pacific Telephone and Telegraph Company have been working every night on the wiring, and the church will be the first in Orange County to broadcast Sunday services regularly. Services will begin at 7:30 P.M. as usual. At 8 o'clock, the hour of christening the radio broadcast, Mrs. Robert Harkness, contralto, whose husband is composer of over a thousand hymns, will sing. Leland Green will play the marimba solo, and Rev. Fuller will deliver a sermon on "The Greatest Peril of the Hour." Rev. Fuller, who returned yesterday from a tour of the Pacific Northwest, says that the tragedy of empty churches faced him throughout the trip. He says that his only reason for going on the radio is that the simple Gospel messages may be sent to more people.

In another article the paper reported that "a large *Scofield Bible* will be given to the person hearing the sermon tomorrow or next Sunday the longest distance away, if he writes to the church before

March 15 giving excerpts of the sermon." But Charles Fuller's expectations about KREG's coverage were not realistic. He remembered how the 750-watt Biola station had been heard from Vermont to Hawaii, and so as he made this offer of the *Scofield Bible* during the first broadcast, he recalled the evangelistic campaign he had had with Paul Rader in McPherson, Kansas, a year and a half before and said he would be particularly delighted if one of his many friends there would write so he could send the Bible to him. Afterwards, someone who understood the technical realities informed him that KREG's signal reached no more than twenty-five miles from Santa Ana. Plagued with money problems from the beginning, KREG improvised by using a fishing pole to help carry the wire out of the studio window to the aerial on the roof. They later realized that about 75 of the station's 100 watts were being grounded through the steel of the newspaper building.

After two months of broadcasting on KREG, Charles Fuller contracted for an additional hour of broadcasting time each Sunday evening. Following the hour-long broadcast of the regular church service, he would broadcast a program called the "Happy Hour," a time of special music put on by the young people of the church. By now he was anxious to get some idea of how many were listening so he announced that a telephone would be installed at the pulpit and that in between the musical numbers of the "Happy Hour" he would attempt to answer any questions about the Bible that people would phone in. Charles Fuller recalled in later years that it was with bated breath that he waited to see if there would be any calls. But no sooner had he told people they could call than more calls than he could handle began pouring in.

During three weeks in May, 1930, he carried on these two hours of broadcasting on Sunday evenings, but then he stopped broadcasting altogether for the summer months. This was not because radio was curtailing attendance at his church. To the contrary, during the evening services which were being broadcast the attendance rose until there was hardly standing room. The primary reason for stopping that summer was that he felt he could get better coverage per dollar by broadcasting by remote control over station KGER in Long Beach, thirty miles away. A letter sent out on July 8, 1930, explains his strategy:

81

Calvary Church radio members:

We are delighted to make the following announcement. We will soon be broadcasting over a 1000-watt station. A contract has been signed with radio station KGER at Long Beach. On Sunday, September 14, we will begin to broadcast both our morning and evening services.

Radio KGER is considered by many as one of the best 1000-watt stations west of Chicago. This station covers an area populated by more than four million people. What an opportunity, therefore, to preach the Gospel, which is the power of God unto salvation!

A large percentage of the expense of this new arrangement has been promised by a party vitally interested in our church. However, we will continue to *need your support* during July and August and thereafter. Ours is a faith work. We feel you will greatly rejoice now that your money can be used on a station that has such a high reputation for its broadcasting qualities.

We are canceling our contract with radio KREG, Santa Ana. What we will save, therefore, during July and August, will apply on our new radio set-up. God is working. There are marvelous days ahead. Souls will be saved. Pray!

Yours for a better and bigger radio program,
Charles E. Fuller

Since both Sunday services would be broadcast starting in the fall, the church moved in a better piano and enlarged the organ loft. The Sunday school was scheduled to conclude earlier so that everyone could assemble in the main auditorium fifteen minutes before broadcast time. Thus announcements were made and the offering collected before the red light under the control booth flashed on at 11:00 A.M.

Charles Fuller came back from his vacation one week before the broadcasting was to resume. The paper said, "The pastor wished to speak once more to just the members of his congregation before the services go on the air."

The July letter had spoken of pledges for the support of a sizeable part of the expense of the broadcasts starting that fall. An orange grower in Pomona had promised, "If you don't get enough mailed in, I'll be responsible for up to sixty dollars a month to help you out." Two others had made similar promises.

But a few months after going on KGER a freeze came which made it impossible for the orange grower to fulfill his promise. Another had to renege because his investment in some oil wells failed. A third party who had made a promise moved to another part of the country. Accordingly, Charles Fuller went before the board at Calvary Church and said, "I guess we have to depend on the Lord now." He never forgot this lesson during the next thirty-eight years that he was on the radio. Even during the days when he was on some one thousand stations and the broadcast was costing about thirty-five thousand dollars a week, he depended only on the small offerings which came in from a multitude of God's people. Thus he was conscious of being cast only upon God and His guidance in carrying on the radio work.

He was much encouraged by the results from broadcasting both Sunday services over KGER. The church itself was filled for both services, and he estimated that fifteen thousand people were listening by radio. A letter had even come from as far as Walla Walla, Washington, telling of a large number gathering in one of the homes and attending church in Placentia via radio. "Mr. Fuller's voice came in as clearly and distinctly as though he were right in the room with us." The broadcast was also heard in Idaho and Iowa. Several months later when Charles Fuller visited Idaho, he was delighted at being able himself to hear the broadcast coming from Calvary Church.

From their experience gained the preceding spring on KREG, Charles Fuller and his staff had learned how to do a better job of programming. "Radio is something different, and I believe it can be used to reach a great many people with the message of the church," he said to the local Placentia newspaper in the fall of 1930. He continued:

There are many people who are unable to attend church, and from letters and telephone calls received we believe the present radio station hour is fulfilling a real need. It is our hope to present church programs of such quality that they will be sought out by those who handle the dials on radio sets.

My father often recalled that as he commenced preaching by radio he had the sense of doing just what he was suited for. Speaking of standing before a microphone (which he likened to a donut cutter because of the shape of the early models), he would say, "It just seemed the most natural thing in the world for me to tell the good news of Christ into a microphone which would wing my voice to an audience many times the size of what I could ever have visibly present." When he considered the vast multitudes who needed to hear the Gospel, the microphone was obviously the most efficient way to proclaim it.

Thus while chairman of the board at Biola, he heartily supported the ministry of KTBI, the school's radio station. But in 1931, as the effects of the Great Depression began to be felt, the board of Biola did not see how it could justify the expense of keeping KTBI on the air. Over Charles Fuller's protests they decided to sell the station and buy four hours of radio time a week in order to carry on a part of their radio ministry. But Charles Fuller was so excited about the influence of radio that he tried to make up for Biola's loss of KTBI (and also to extend his own ministry) by starting in the spring of 1931 a program called "The Pilgrim's Hour," aired on seven stations of the Columbia Broadcasting System from San Diego to Seattle. In its March, 1931, issue *The King's Business* reported:

Rev. Charles E. Fuller, Chairman of the Board of the Bible Institute of Los Angeles, has entered into a contract with the Columbia Broadcasting System for a half hour of Gospel music and expository preaching of the Word of God. . . . This broadcast is a step of faith on the part of Mr. Fuller to place the Bible Institute before its friends, and it is undertaken without any expense to the Institute, depending wholly upon the contributions of those interested in spreading the Gospel. Even though you do not send a check, if you wish to have this program continued, please send a post card of encouragement. Dr. W. P. White, President of the Bible Institute of Los Angeles, will be treasurer of the Pilgrim's Hour program. It is estimated that the number of listeners will run into the hundreds of thousands. If you are interested in having a part in this work, address your correspondence to The Pilgrim's Hour, P. O. Box 123, Los Angeles, California.

Thus during the spring of 1931 Charles Fuller conducted three broadcasts each Sunday, the morning and evening services of Calvary Church and a late Sunday afternoon broadcast to help Biola.

But this first attempt at network broadcasting was not a success. Apparently the 4:30 to 5:00 P.M. hour was too early to get much of a listening audience. Charles Fuller also felt he erred by not having enough informality and heart warmth in the program. Contributions to the broadcast were not sufficient to carry it on, especially in view of the oncoming summer months. So the program was discontinued at the end of April, 1931. Charles Fuller was now suffering great financial losses himself, and so he resigned from the Biola board in September, 1931.

But he continued to broadcast the morning and evening services of Calvary Church over KGER right on through the summer months of 1931, and then in September he even had the courage to launch a third broadcast, the "Calvary Church Radio Bible Class," from 8:00 to 9:00, Thursday evenings, over KGER. This new broadcast was significant because it was an extension of Charles Fuller's radio ministry that was somewhat independent of Calvary Church. The broadcast did not originate at the church but in the studios of KGER in Long Beach, located on the second floor above the Dobyns Footwear store. The room from which this broadcast originated allowed about fifty people to be seated in a semicircle around the musicians and the speaker. By then he had that many loyal supporters in Long Beach, and some of these came to the studio for this Thursday evening broadcast. They provided him with that visible audience which always made it easier for him to preach well to people listening by their radios.

On a post card announcing this new broadcast to his mailing list, Charles Fuller said, "Definite Bible study conducted by the pastor. Send in your card today for membership in this class." A few weeks later a newspaper article said that "this is the only broadcast of its kind offered on a radio program, and all who teach Sunday school classes are invited to tune in to this class and avail themselves of the opportunity offered each week." In other words, by means of radio Charles Fuller was seeking a ministry that would center not just around Calvary Church but would include Sunday school teachers in other churches.

Early in 1932 he dropped the words "Calvary Church" from the name of the program and called it simply "The Radio Bible Class." This indicates more of that trend in which Charles Fuller's ministry was shifting away from Calvary Church. He continued to originate the two broadcasts on Sunday from the church, but he was now finding more sympathy and support at Long Beach for his vision of preaching the Gospel by radio.

Churches need a leader who is basically a pastor. Charles Fuller, however, was never content simply to be a pastor. His heart was in heading up a mission to spread the Gospel by radio. But Don Milligan, the youth director, loved to visit people, and gradually the church shifted their allegiance to him.

In the fall of 1932 Charles Fuller realized that his days as pastor of Calvary Church were drawing to a close. He decided to make his exit with the grand finale of having evangelist Mel Trotter hold a three-weeks' series of meetings beginning in the middle of February, 1933. The evening after Mel Trotter's final message (March 5, 1933), my father preached his last sermon at Calvary Church, entitled "The Only Foundation," and then it was announced that the board of trustees had granted Charles Fuller an extended leave of absence. That week the newspaper reported that "the Rev. Mr. Fuller, after a period of rest, plans to do evangelistic work on the Pacific Coast, and is arranging to hold conferences in out-of-the-way places. At the present time, the Rev. Mr. Fuller and his wife, and his son, Dannie, are residing at Palm Springs." A later newspaper article reported that the board of Calvary Church had unanimously voted in the Rev. Don Milligan as pastor. It continued, "Voting to put the church program on a basis of strict economy, members of the board decided to discontinue the radio broadcast of the morning and evening services, as well as the midweek broadcasts of the Bible lessons." Charles Fuller's constant urge to extend his ministry had finally made it impossible for him to work from a church as his base of operations.

6. "Great and Mighty Things"

THE YEARS SPENT as teacher of the Placentia Bible Class and as pastor of Calvary Church had given Charles Fuller a chance to increase his knowledge of the Scriptures, to gain experience in preaching and teaching, and to make a beginning in radio evangelism. But during the last two years at Placentia, God began training him in another vital way for his life work as a radio evangelist. He had to go through the fiery furnace of testings and difficulties to learn to trust less in himself and be cast more completely upon God.

THE FIERY FURNACE

Throughout the rest of the 1920s and to the middle of 1931, my father had become increasingly prosperous largely through the speculative buying and selling of orange groves. Even before 1919, when he entered Biola, he had bought orange land and had been able to move from that small house in Placentia to a spacious, two-story ranch house on a thriving orange grove half a mile from the center of town. The exploratory oil well drilled at another grove had supplied the money for both my parents to study at Biola. In succeeding years they had made money by subdividing a part of a ranch which they owned near the town of Placentia.

By 1927 Charles Fuller was prosperous enough to build a home on the ocean front at Newport Beach. He bought a powerful Garwood speedboat and had it shipped by rail from the East. He named it "Dannie Boy" and loved to scare his friends as he took them for sixty-mile-an-hour rides, banging from wave to wave and making tight turns on the ocean beyond the breakwater. He also enjoyed swordfishing with his friend, Herbert Rankin, who managed a department store in Santa Ana.

But it was at this very beach house in June, 1930, where the tides of fortune began to change. That spring such a severe polio epidemic had broken out in Orange County that the health officer closed all the schools. Even the Sunday school at Calvary Church could not convene for several weeks. Fearful lest their only child would be

87

Above: *With friend Herbert Rankin after successful fishing trip at Newport Beach, California.* **Below:** *Family outing in speedboat in predepression days.*

stricken with this dread disease, my parents moved twenty miles south to their beach house. The winds blowing in off the ocean would not carry polio germs. But these winds brought me another illness which eighteen months later almost caused my death and made me a semi-invalid for the next six years.

One day my parents invited the older young people from Calvary Church to come down to their beach house for an afternoon of play on the sand and for an evening barbecue. There was a strong, chill wind blowing in from the ocean that June day, and my parents thought it best that I, not yet five years old, should remain inside. But I begged and pleaded to be allowed to join in the fun, and as parents of an only child are more prone to do, they relented and let me out on the beach that afternoon.

Many times in the years that followed I thought back to that day and wished that I had not been so insistent nor my parents so lenient. For I got chilled that afternoon and came down with whooping cough which kept me in bed for several weeks that summer. By September the whooping cough had turned into a persistent bronchitis. My mother recorded in her diary that by the end of the year I had had four relapses into serious bronchitis. A Los Angeles doctor took x-rays and found an infection in a bronchial tube close to the heart.

Today antibiotics clear up such infections quickly, but then the best thing the doctor could do was to prescribe that I spend two months in the desert sunshine at Palm Springs. So in January, 1931, my parents were still prosperous enough to pay eight hundred dollars to rent for ten weeks a house that was perched above the desert floor in the foothills near Palm Springs. It was a beautiful home with an unobstructed view across the desert to the purple hills and mountains beyond. Often when I hear the song "This Is My Father's World," I think of that view, for my mother taught me to sing this with her as we looked upon this spectacular vista through the bay window in the living room.

But the eight hundred dollars for the lovely home and the two months that my father had to be separated from my mother and me (except for a day or so now and then) did not produce much improvement in my health. It had rained for days at a time, and by March I had gained back only four pounds and seemed very little improved.

Even though the Great Depression had started in October, 1929, it had not yet affected my parents, and early in 1931 my mother wrote in her diary, "I am thankful that Charles does provide well for us." She was even looking forward to a new house that my father had been promising to build for her in Placentia. But during April of that year, some of my father's financial deals began to go awry, and the following entry appears:

Charles very anxious over finances. It looks as though we shall never get the money from Mrs. G., though promised for so long. Bills are piling up on every side, and we fear Charles' witness will be hurt. Charles gave a splendid message at church this morning. But he is very troubled over finances. We hope to sell a grove and thus to be able to meet our obligations. We are praying for wisdom. Tomorrow will be a hard day for Charles when he faces Mr. E. and tells him that he looks for nothing from the Kettleman Hills[1] deal. I wonder if we shall ever have our new house. Have been married nearly twenty years and still dreaming of it.

In this same entry the fear is also expressed that the "Pilgrim's Hour" broadcast would fail. Thus the clouds of adversity were gathering that April: there was indebtedness, my health was problematical, and the network broadcast up the Pacific Coast was not paying for itself and would soon stop.

In May of that year I had another attack of bronchitis, and to get me into the sunshine my parents took me to their cabin at the seven-thousand-foot level in the San Bernardino mountains. They hoped I could get enough sunshine and dry air to cure the persistent bronchitis. But after my father had established my mother and me there and had returned to Placentia, we were greeted by a four-inch snowfall—not the best therapy for bronchitis. Somewhat snowed in, we listened to the broadcasts from Calvary Church and heard my father say, "I am going to ask the congregation to sing 'Where Jesus Is 'Tis Heaven to Be' for a little group gathered round the fireside at Bluff Lake."

During the milder weather of the summer my parents kept me at Bluff Lake for many weeks, and my father took his vacation there.

---

[1] The Kettleman Hills are in central California where Charles Fuller had bought land that he hoped to lease for the drilling of exploratory oil wells.

But his financial deals became so entangled that he had no rest that summer. In August my mother wrote,

Charles went down to Los Angeles this morning to face many difficulties with Mr. A. and McF. and M. G., and the Kettleman deal. The financial strain is great and we may lose everything. . . . If we do we will start again and I will help Charles and mother him. He is so darling.

Two weeks later she wrote:

Charles very anxious about finances. The lease at Kettleman Hills is not yet made. M. attached everything and we lost the fifty-acre grove, having to pay $417.00 just for clearing the title. Now Charles is anxious because he is unable to pay F. So he went back to Placentia to see about business. I am praying that God will undertake in His way so that Charles may have peace of mind to preach the Gospel.

When my father returned to Bluff Lake from Placentia, she went out to meet him, and he reported that our home had been attached and that it might be sold at an auction. "Humiliating! How unnecessary. Charles was trying to sell it and had a prospect, but that possibility is all off now."

Back in Placentia in November of that year, 1931, my mother wrote,

I am writing this Sunday, the 29th, that when God has undertaken for us, I may look back and read of our terrible plight, that we may give all the glory to Him, our Deliverer. Truly we are up against a stone wall. We are at the Red Sea. We know not which way to turn, having reached our *extremity*, and our expectation is from Him alone. Our home is attached and may be put up for auction, unless the A. grove is sold soon. $3,000 crop money is tied up by Mr. A. Mother's bonds and securities are held by the bank to secure loans which Charles invested in Mrs. G's Kettleman Hills deal. $10,000 fertilizer bill. $25,000 owed at banks. Orange prices below cost of production the first part of the year, and jeweler is pressing Charles for payments on this terrible ring. I almost hate it! Cannot meet insurance premiums. If only we had not gone into the Kettleman Hills deal. If only we had prayed more and been cautious. If the lease could be made, an oil well might bring relief, but no one seems to want to lease. . . .

Charles says only a miracle can save him from financial ruin, but I believe God will perform a miracle, though we do not deserve it. We pray for peace of mind for Charles, that he may preach again in power, having time for prayer and study. Sales of groves and lease must come soon, or we lose even our *home*. . . .

I do not desire wealth but a good name, and I hope dishonor may not be brought on the cause of Christ through us, a minister of the Gospel, unable to meet his obligations. All the early part of this diary [the early months of that year, 1931] *self, ease, pleasure,* neglect of prayer and Bible study, and that is why we are in such a fix. [But] God has forgiven us, and I know He heard our prayers for deliverance.

A week later she again outlined all the financial tangle and remarked that the trial for the disposition of their house would occur the middle of December.

If the trial goes against us, our home place will be sold at auction from the county courthouse steps. Where we will go I do not know as the beach is too damp for Dannie now. Mr. A. will also take the $3,400 fruit money at the packing house which is tied up by the attachment. If only we could sell the grove we contracted to buy from Mr. A. Mother's money is all tied up, stocks, bonds, and $10,000 from the F. grove. Owe banks $50,000. The lease expires January 22nd and must be leased in another week! P. has given it up. *But God—* our expectation is from *Him!*

He may lead us—is leading us right up to the Red Sea, dipping our toes in. Surely the waters will part. Surely He will not forsake His servant and let it be said by the unrighteous, "He does not pay his debts." He will undertake marvelously and miraculously in ways we know not of. Bless His Name. We stand on Isa. 50:10; Ps. 62:5-8; Ps. 46:10; Ps. 25:9, "yielded man"; Phil. 4:6-7.

The result from the impending lawsuit was not quite so drastic that they had their home auctioned out from under them. Rather, they had to sign a harsh contract with Mr. A. and forfeit the crop money which was attached at the packing house. But Christmas, 1931, was a dark time. On that day my mother wrote, "No money to meet bills. . . . It is almost more than Charles can bear. He is *so* depressed, *so* burdened that he says he can stand no more." But the day after New Year's brought an even greater difficulty.

In her *Daily Light* for January 2, 1932, my mother wrote, "Dannie so ill, pneumonia. Depression [financial], but God." Six days later I almost died. On the morning of January 8 my father was in a lawyer's office in Los Angeles trying to find a way to remain solvent when my mother phoned to say that some mucus was caught in my bronchial tube and that as I was choking and coughing, I had grown so weak that a pulse beat was no longer discernible. They had just called the doctor and the fire department to bring oxygen. My father immediately left the lawyer's office to drive home, and as he went down the elevator, his legs almost gave out from under him. When he started to drive the twenty-eight miles back to Placentia he felt very rebellious and said, "Oh Lord, I have tried to serve you, but if you take our little boy I'm through! This is the one thing I just can't endure. I can't go on if you take him."

But then a few miles later his heart began to change and he said, "Yes, Lord. Thy ways are best—I yield to Thee and want Thy will done." And then he found himself singing the song,

> I will say, "Yes," to Jesus,
> "Yes," Lord, forever "yes";
> I'll welcome all thy blessed will,
> And sweetly answer, "Yes."

When he reached home the doctor had arrived and ordered an ambulance to take me to Los Angeles where a specialist with a bronchoscope might be able to remove the mucus plug. I lay in bed unconscious with a bluish color and deep circles under my eyes. My father said, "This is a time for prayer," and he, my mother, and Mrs. Sundstrom, a practical nurse and close friend of the family, knelt while he prayed, "I thank You for these six and a half years that we have had this little boy. He has been such a blessing in our home. We shall miss him so, but take him to Yourself, if that is Your will. You have given, and if it is Your will to take him away, then we give him back to You, our Father."

Then the ambulance arrived and took me into Los Angeles. But upon arrival there, the fluoroscope examination showed that the obstruction had dissolved away. Prayer had been answered, and God had seen Charles Fuller through a great crisis.

As soon as I had convalesced sufficiently, my parents felt their only hope for me lay in taking me out to the dry air and warm sunshine of Palm Springs again. But this winter, instead of living in a house on a hill overlooking the desert, we had a little shack on a back alley with only a small bedroom and a kitchenette. Here we stayed from February until April. After the evening service at Calvary Church, my father would often drive the one hundred miles to be with us and would stay a day or so before returning to his duties. All that year of 1932 he fought in every way possible to stave off bankruptcy. So much of his strength would be spent during the week on financial matters that when Sunday came and he stood behind the pulpit at Calvary Church, he wondered whether he could last through the sermon. Yet when he visited us at the desert, I remember how he used to sit in a canvas director's chair leaning against our shack studying his *Companion Bible*. I shall never forget one such time when I was playing a little distance from where he was studying. He startled me by letting out a whoop of delight because of some new insight he had just received from God's Word.

My mother poignantly remembered that when it came time to leave Palm Springs that April, 1932, there was no money to pay the grocery bill. She went to the grocer—my father had already left—and told him that although we were leaving town, the bill would be paid, and in a few months it was.

For awhile during 1932 my father tried to salvage something from his financial wreckage in Placentia. But finally he was convinced that the only way he could avoid bankruptcy was simply to bear his losses and take whatever he could get for any equity he had left in the orange groves or leases. Even now a Placentia barber remembers when Charles Fuller walked into his shop and said, "Ray, I gave up $200,000 in orange grove property today." Loosing himself so completely from his business involvements in Placentia meant giving up the Placentia home situated on one of the groves. Somehow he managed a down payment on a bungalow three miles to the west in Fullerton, and we moved there.

He also allowed all of my mother's inheritance from her father to be used to settle debts at the bank. This was a terrible blow to her, for it hurt her deeply to recall how hard her father had worked —for years as a country doctor in Oregon—to accumulate that surplus. Indeed, she had said in her diary that if they had to lose

Father and son on hike at Yosemite, summer 1937.

everything, she and Charles would just start over again and that she would help him by loving and mothering him. But when this inheritance was actually lost, there were moments when she would tearfully reproach him for having recklessly lost this money and talk of how she had better seek employment as a waitress at a drug store soda fountain. How well I remember my father replying, "I know. I guess I'm just a failure, but I sure have tried."

Even after this second winter at Palm Springs I was still sickly, and in the fall of 1932 I came down with bronchitis again, this time while my mother was recuperating from major surgery in a Los Angeles hospital. When I had improved somewhat, my father took me to visit her. She asked how I had been and he replied, "Just fine." Only after her recovery did she learn that I had been sick, and in her *Daily Light* for October 5, 1932, she wrote, "The year of the days of trouble. Charles brought Dan to me at the hospital. He looked so white and thin. Will God spare Dannie to us? He had been in bed ten days." X-rays taken that fall showed no improvement in my condition, and the doctor prescribed a third winter at the desert.

As the year 1932 drew to a close, my parents were not only fighting to remain solvent and to keep me alive, but they were faced with the fact that Calvary Church wanted a new pastor. Charles Fuller decided that he would resign at the conclusion of the Mel Trotter evangelistic campaign on March 5, 1933. He would carry on his three weekly broadcasts (Sunday morning and evening and Thursday evening) from the small KGER studio over the Dobyns Footwear store in Long Beach. His loyal band of Long Beach friends would crowd themselves into this studio to provide him with the visible audience that helped him preach better over the radio.

March, 1933, was not a very auspicious time to launch out alone on a radio ministry. The morning after his last sermon at Calvary Church, Franklin Roosevelt closed all the banks. Only those banks could open thereafter whose financial condition was sound, and there was a period of several weeks when people were very short of cash. Five days later, Long Beach suffered a severe earthquake which killed 115 people and inflicted $40,000,000 damage. United States Marines were guarding the city against looters, and only after arguing with a sergeant could Charles Fuller proceed to the KGER studio for his first Sunday morning broadcast from Long Beach.

Meanwhile my parents had the added expense and inconvenience of having me at Palm Springs for the third winter. But after returning to Fullerton I still languished, and so they decided to move to the Pasadena area which was drier and warmer, being twice as far from the ocean.

Now that he was on his own, my father needed to set up a nonprofit corporation to handle the contributions coming in for the support of his radio broadcasts. The preliminary meeting of the organizers for the new Gospel Broadcasting Association was held on May 8, 1933, at the Bible Institute of Los Angeles. Dr. John Forsyth, a Long Beach optician, who had been greatly blessed by Charles Fuller's ministry and had faithfully attended the studio broadcast of the Thursday evening "Radio Bible Class," was elected the chairman of the organizers. Among the other twenty-five organizers were the evangelist, Dr. Paul Rood; Dr. Louis Bauman, pastor of the First Brethren Church of Long Beach; Dr. H. A. Johnston, the physician from Anaheim whose Bible class had been such a help to the Fullers eighteen years earlier; and Dr. Stewart MacLennan, pastor of the First Presbyterian Church of Hollywood. The GBA became officially incorporated by the state of California on August 15, 1933.

Charles Fuller also needed now a mailing address for his broadcasts. During the two months in 1931 that he had broadcast the "Pilgrim's Hour" on a West Coast network, he had used the easy-to-remember address of Box 123, Los Angeles. It was remarkable that Mr. Howard Lucy, Biola's business manager at that time, could procure such a number for that broadcast. Biola had held the rights to this box for the two years since that broadcast had terminated, but they were now willing to let Charles Fuller take it over as the mailing address for the newly formed GBA.

All this time the desperate battle to remain solvent continued. About then a trust partner had gone into bankruptcy, and Charles Fuller had to shoulder his financial obligations to avoid bankruptcy himself. In July, 1933, the stock market reached its lowest point on the long slide which had begun in October, 1929. One morning in August, 1933, after my father had left home to go into Los Angeles to plot his next moves to remain solvent, my mother felt that she could stand the strain no longer. She told the Lord she simply had to have help, and in desperation she went into my father's study and started reading one of Charles Haddon Spurgeon's sermons on

97

prayer, which he had preached in London seventy years before. The sermon was on Jeremiah 33:3, "Call unto me, and I will answer thee, and show thee great and mighty things, which thou knowest not." Some months later she penciled the following remark at the beginning of that sermon:

When I called upon God in desperation in August, 1933, he answered me by directing me *unmistakably* to the library shelf on which this book stood and to *this* sermon. It brought great comfort and enabled me to trust God and to await the unfolding of His plans for us.

She said that God lifted her burden so remarkably that morning that when my father returned exhausted from another day of negotiations in a lawyer's office she was able to tell him, "Never mind how black things look now. God has assured me that He has great and mighty things in store for us for the future—things which we can't even imagine now." My parents felt that the "Old Fashioned Revival Hour," which had its faint beginnings that next spring, 1934, went coast-to-coast in 1937, and continues on today, was one of these "great and mighty things." Thus Jeremiah 33:3 became my father's life verse which he so often attached to his autograph.

Buoyed up by this word from God, which had come with such power in the doldrums of a summer marking the low point of the Great Depression, and with no end in sight to their own desperate financial plight, my father published the GBA's first letter, entitled "A Forward Step in Gospel Broadcasting," in September, 1933:

You would certainly be interested in reaching fifteen million people in Western United States and Canada with a ringing Gospel message. It can be done immediately—by *radio*—and here's the plan:

We have contracted for a half hour period on KFI, Los Angeles' 50,000-watt station, the key station for the National Broadcasting System in the southwest. Time: Each Saturday evening, 5:30–6:00. A helpful Sunday school hour presenting the method and manner of teaching Sunday school classes, as well as the message. KFI covers eleven western states and western Canada.

Again! After months of negotiations we have contracted for a half hour period on KHJ, the Pacific Coast key station for the Columbia Broadcasting System. Time: Each Sunday evening, 6:30–7:00, for a popular Bible Study class. The following radio stations will be included in the new hook-up: Los Angeles—KHJ; San Francisco—KFRC; San Diego—KGB; Fresno—KMJ; Sacramento—KFBK; Santa Barbara—KDB; Stockton—KWG; Bakersfield—KERN.

The heart of the matter: First, your check, money order, currency or subscription now. Second, the names and addresses of five friends. Your early response will encourage and help us to hold these open doors for God. Actual broadcast to begin in October, 1933.

Put your dollars to work for God *now*. The field is white unto harvest and the laborers few. The time is short. Occupy till He come. Pray Pray Pray.

Yours in His fellowship,
Board of Trustees of the Gospel Broadcasting Association

Many of Charles Fuller's friends tried to discourage him from carrying out such an ambitious venture, but he felt so sure God was leading him that he went right ahead. In later years my mother circled the words "October, 1933" on the above letter and wrote in the margin, "Depression." That such forward steps could be announced with a confident, urgent note at that time is a testimony to the power by which God's Word had gripped my parents' hearts. They took God at His Word and believed that He would see them through their financial difficulties. The scriptural teaching that people are lost unless they repent and believe in Christ so controlled Charles Fuller's thinking that all he could do was bend every effort to get the Gospel out. He assumed that other Christians felt the same sense of urgency and laid down specific steps they could follow in helping him evangelize by radio.

To take on the Pacific Coast network of the Columbia Broadcasting System as well as the powerful 50,000-watt radio station KFI, in addition to his broadcasts on KGER (Sunday morning, Thursday evening), meant far more than a doubling of costs, and so the only way that Charles Fuller could expect to carry on such a task was to try to multiply his list of supporters. Response from this September, 1933, letter was encouraging enough for him to go ahead with his plans. On Saturday, November 3, 1933, Charles Fuller began the broadcast of the "Sunday School Hour" over KFI from 5:00–5:30 P.M., thirty minutes earlier than he had hoped.

He was anxious to get on a 50,000-watt station like KFI because

5,000-watt KGER did not have a very good transmitter in those days, and there were some spots in the Southern California basin where its signal could not be heard. KFI, however, could be heard all the way up the Pacific Coast and, after nightfall, at least as far east as the Mississippi River. The plan was to have this program on Saturday evening to help Sunday school teachers get ready for teaching the next day. But more than this, Charles Fuller wanted to spur Christians to study their Bibles so they could become teachers and soul winners themselves. "As you know," he said in announcing this "Sunday School Hour" in the fall of 1933,

. . . my burning desire is to preach the Word; to get souls saved; and to get believers to study the Word. When a believer studies the Word prayerfully and with an obedient heart, two things are accomplished: he grows in grace and in the knowledge of God, and he goes to work. Now this work may lead him to teaching a Sunday school class, winning souls, praying, giving—as the Lord directs—doing his part to spread the Gospel. You see how the work is enlarged and enlarged. Oh! I want to get more and more people—thousands more—to know the joy and satisfaction of Bible study and work for God.

He then told how he would begin a series on "How to Study the Bible." After that he planned to spend possibly an entire year on a study of the typological significance of the Tabernacle in the Wilderness, and regarding this he said,

The study of the Tabernacle with its teaching of types is a great means of establishing the faith. There is nothing better for young people to ground them in the way of salvation. Fathers and mothers, Sunday school teachers, if you would hold your young people, get them grounded in tabernacle teaching. In my student days, I found it helpful above everything else and thrillingly interesting.

He promised to send out a multicolored printed replica of the Tabernacle and weekly lesson leaflets.

KFI gave Charles Fuller the coverage he yearned for, and in December, 1933, he reported that he had people on his mailing list even as far east as New York and Pennsylvania and in the South. Many Sunday school teachers were blessed by this broadcast. A lady from Chicago wrote,

As I went to the desk for my Sunday school quarterly, I wished I could dial on to someone teaching the Sunday school lesson for Sunday. At that moment my husband accidentally tuned in your station. It was exactly what I wanted. When he said it was coming from Los Angeles, it was all the more thrilling. It came in clearly—hardly missed a word.

His desire to help pastors was also realized as they sent him whole lists of their Sunday school teachers whom they were encouraging to follow the course of study provided by the "Sunday School Hour."

To help bind all these new listeners together, my father sent out the first *Heart to Heart Talk* in the fall of 1933. My mother had the gift of writing which he lacked, and writing what he wanted said in these talks became a major part of her ministry for the rest of her life. I was sick with bronchitis again that fall of 1933. During the daytime I was in bed in my father's study (so my mother wouldn't have to keep climbing stairs), and I remember their discussing the wording of that first *Heart to Heart Talk*. It began by stating the purpose of these talks:

These *Heart to Heart Talks* will come to you from time to time just as though you were sitting in my study and we were chatting together. There are many things which I would like to say to you over the Radio, but you know that time is limited, and we want to use every precious second for teaching of the Word.

That first *Heart to Heart Talk* went on to mention some of the verses which had comforted my parents during the past two years in which they had been going through such deep trouble. One of the verses was Jeremiah 33:3!

Charles Fuller was also anxious to extend the range of his Thursday evening "Radio Bible Class," and so on December 14, 1933, he hooked another Southern California station in with KGER so that this program could be heard everywhere in Southern California. All that fall he worked to carry out the plan of having a Sunday evening broadcast up and down the Pacific Coast section of the Columbia network. In anticipation of getting such coverage, he dropped his Sunday evening broadcast on KGER in December. But the Columbia network now had a policy of not accepting any paid-for religious broadcasts, and he had to begin anew his search for the wide coverage he believed God wanted him to have.

So there was a four-month period in the winter of 1933–34 when he was not preaching on Sunday evenings. This disturbed him since for the past seven years Sunday evenings for him had been a time for preaching. I remember how one evening early in March, 1934, he took my mother and me for a ride around Pasadena to help calm his uneasiness. As we started home, my mother comforted him by promising him his favorite dish by the fireside—clam soup and apple sauce. He responded by saying, "And then I'll listen to First Mate Bob to see how he's getting on with his new broadcast." (The "Haven of Rest" broadcast began in March, 1934.)

The battle to remain solvent continued right on through 1934. Early that year my mother recalled how badly my father needed a new suit. "Dear Dad was so shabby. We thought money was coming in with which we could pay for a *good* suit—Dad looks so shabby in a 'store suit'!" So they had a Christian tailor make him a suit, but then the money for it did not come in. My mother wrote a letter asking the tailor for an extension of credit, promising that my father would not wear the suit until it was paid for. The tailor replied, "Please tell Charles Fuller from me that this extension of payment is granted on this one condition: that he immediately begin to wear the suit." Later they were able to pay the bill, but my mother kept the tailor's letter as a reminder of how God was comforting them in those dark days when they were so distressed.

I also recall that on July 4 of that year I wanted very much to go to the fireworks display at the Rose Bowl. The admission was twenty-five cents per person, but my parents simply could not afford this. Yet these trials through which my father and mother were going equipped them to minister comfort to many thousands in the radio audience. In March, 1934, the *Heart to Heart Talk* said,

I pass on to you a little of the comfort wherewith Mrs. Fuller and I have been comforted. We have come to know God in a new way because of the trials we have been going through these past three years. We have known what it is to have much sickness; financial losses; to have those turn against us and seek to hurt us who we thought were true friends; to have our only child brought down to death's door on two occasions,[2] and to have gone before the microphone, after sleep-

---

[2] I do not know when that second time was.

less nights, so burdened and cast down I did not know whether I could preach—whether when I opened my mouth the words would come. Excuse these personal references, friends, I mention them only briefly as a testimony because I want to tell you that after going through all this and much more, Mrs. Fuller and I *know* that God is able— that His promises are true. We never could have known the sweetness of trusting God had we not come to the place where we ourselves could do nothing. We never could have known how precious it is to rest on Psalm 37:5, and having committed all to Him and waiting to see Him work, if we had not been sorely tested. . . . So friends, "Think it not strange when the fiery trials come," but take them as a schooling, and you will be able to look back and praise Him for these very testings which seem more than you can bear.

People in those depression days were comforted as the broadcast directed them to God's Word. One example was a person who wrote saying,

We have hit bottom in the past three years, but am not sorry, as it has been the means of my salvation. Had to look for help somewhere, and there was only one place to get it. Brother Fuller, you can take the credit for getting me interested in the Bible. Since I've started studying it, I want to learn everything that's in it.

The Beginnings of the "Old Fashioned Revival Hour"

Unable to buy time on any network, Charles Fuller procured the 6:30–7:00 Sunday evening spot on the 25,000-watt station KNX, "The Voice of Hollywood." He went on this station because it would soon increase its power to 50,000 watts and was even applying for the right to be a 500,000-watt station. It was also building a 520-foot antenna, and so next to being on a network, a half hour on KNX was the most promising way to get large coverage. The preceding summer the plan had been to make the Sunday evening program a "popular Bible study class," but when he launched this new broadcast on March 11, 1934, Charles Fuller called it the "Heart to Heart Hour" and began a series of prophetic and devotional messages from the psalms.

He was full of praise to God for opening the door on this promising station. KNX might never surpass KFI's coverage, but KNX was the only powerful station that would sell him an after-sundown time spot when radio signals traveled much farther. Then, too, KNX was an independent station whose decisions to sell time were not in danger of being countermanded by a network. The following statement made in the March, 1934, *Heart to Heart Talk* reveals Charles Fuller's thrill and awe at going on this new station:

> Friends, this is a tremendous step. . . . I am overwhelmed with the responsibility of going on this great station which is soon to be of 50,000 watts. The Word given forth will reach out into the homes scattered all over the United States, Canada, Alaska, and Hawaii. I am depending on you for prayer and help. I am not at liberty to tell all the steps which have led up to our securing this unusually favorable hour on this very popular station, when opposition to religious programs is increasing, but if I could tell you, you would marvel and realize that God has been working.
>
> I know not why God permits me to do this—others are far more gifted, and I feel like saying with Moses, "Lord, I am not eloquent." But the Spirit of God can use even me. Ever since He called me out of business, to teach the Word, it has been my greatest desire to exalt the Christ of the Book, and to give forth its riches in simplicity, but if I ever needed your prayerful support, it is now!

But going on KNX meant having the expense of two half-hour programs on two powerful stations, in addition to the cost of two programs over KGER. Some of his friends predicted that this new venture would swamp him. Still he felt impelled by a divine mandate to buy up the best opportunities for getting the Gospel out by radio.

Charles Fuller was convinced that through prayer God would work in great and mighty ways to get out the message that He had given His Son so men might be saved. Both from the teachings of the Bible and from personal experience he knew that Satan would surely oppose preaching the Gospel to so many people by radio. But he appealed for people to volunteer as "Prayer Warriors," and covenant with God to intercede for the broadcasts daily. He was very happy to announce in May, 1934, that one hundred prayer warriors had enlisted.

Prayer was surely needed that May of 1934, for one Thursday Charles Fuller came very close to canceling his evening spot on KNX (he had already cut back to fifteen minutes on KFI to economize for the difficult summer months just ahead). The next day he had to give KNX five hundred dollars or else cancel the Sunday broadcast. He had only three hundred fifty dollars. For a few minutes he looked at the phone and thought of calling KNX to cancel out. Then very regretfully he began to reach for the telephone, but before his hand touched the instrument, it rang. A dentist friend, Dr. Paul A. Dewhirst, was calling. He and his wife Elba had been converted through listening to Charles Fuller over KGER. He said, "Charlie, do you need any money?"

"Yes, I do."

"Well, then, come over and see me."

When Charles Fuller arrived at the dentist's home, Paul Dewhirst asked, "How much do you need?" "One hundred and fifty dollars," he replied. The dentist turned to his wife and said, "Elba, doesn't that beat the Dutch?" He pulled from his pocket a check already made out to the GBA for one hundred fifty dollars. Then he recounted how his wife had awakened him during the night and said, "We must give Charles Fuller one hundred fifty dollars tomorrow." Her husband replied that they had only twenty-five dollars in the bank. But she insisted, "I don't care; we've got to do it." The next morning a patient came unexpectedly into his office to pay up an eight hundred dollar dentist bill. And immediately Paul Dewhirst made out a check for one hundred fifty dollars and phoned Charles Fuller, without knowing anything of the terrible crisis that he was facing that very day.

Charles Fuller was thus able to carry on that spring of 1934, and the response to the KNX broadcast was so encouraging that he reported,

Because of the volume of prayer, and your sacrificial giving, the Word is reaching out as we never dared hope it might. . . . The letters which pour in tell us of a great heart hunger, of many conversions, of many believers being awakened to their great privilege of service for their Master, and there is a great, renewed interest in Bible Study over the land because of these broadcasts.

Surely God was fulfilling His promise to work as men prayed. In her diary for May 11, 1934, my mother again detailed the desperate

105

situation of their own personal finances and how only God could deliver them. But then she concluded that in recent months, "God has shown us great and mighty things in the radio ministry."

It was very difficult that summer of 1934 to get enough funds to stay on KNX. The GBA set aside a day in August on which it invited people to come to its offices (then located on the eighth floor at Biola in downtown Los Angeles) during whatever time they could spare to join in prayer for God to enable the GBA to hold onto KNX. One hundred fifty people came during that day, and enough funds did come in not only to continue but to contract with KNX to broadcast for an entire hour for four Sundays in October. In the August, 1934, *Heart to Heart Talk* the words "old fashioned revival" appear for the first time:

Don't forget the four Sundays in October when we plan for an old fashioned revival to be broadcast each Sunday evening, 6:30–7:30 from the Women's Club House, La Brea and Hollywood Blvd., Hollywood, California. We are asking all our friends to come. Harold Alexander, the Singing Circuit Rider, will lead the singing. The place seats one thousand people. Pray that we may have a great outpouring of the Holy Spirit and that the blessing of these meetings may reach out to the most distant listeners.

From that point on, Charles Fuller called the Sunday evening broadcast on KNX "The Radio Revival Hour."

As the time approached for the first of these hour-long radio broadcasts to originate from the one-thousand-seat auditorium, the hope was expressed that many radio listeners within a hundred-mile radius would try to be there in person, and especially that there would be a large number of young people to do the singing under the direction of Harold Alexander.

But when Charles Fuller and his wife arrived at the Women's Club House that evening, only fifty people had come, and these seemed almost swallowed up in the cavernous place. Harold Alexander was there to lead the special group that was to sing. But he had been waiting for more to arrive, and with only a few minutes left before air time, he pleaded with any of the fifty who could possibly carry a tune to gather around the microphone and provide the singing for the hour-long program. In the next *Heart to Heart Talk* Charles Fuller confided he was glad they weren't on television because "there sure was some pretty fast moving at times to make things run smoothly." Mrs. Fuller described that first broadcast as follows:

We were all pretty nervous. None of us were singers, but we did our best and sang lustily, "with grace in our hearts to the Lord." I went over to the radio technician backstage and asked him to build up the singing as much as possible. We were determined that this program was going to be informal and spontaneous, and it certainly was! Mr. Fuller preached that night with great freedom and conviction. After the broadcast we hurried home to Mrs. Barnhill, to ask her how it had sounded over the radio. We were so relieved when she said that it sounded as though a large group were singing and that she considered the sermon good!

Attendance did not come up to expectations during the remaining three Sundays at the Women's Club House, and at the end of October, 1934, it was announced that the broadcast would again originate from the KNX studio in Hollywood. People were encouraged, however, to come to the studio:

We urge you to be with us and help us sing. We are a friendly lot there and you will find a warm welcome. I wish more of you could meet with us in the studio, for sometimes the best part of the services comes after we go off the air. Last Sunday night several gave their hearts to the Lord there in the Club House, and one man who had been out of fellowship was reclaimed.

Thus, for the time being, the idea of having a large visible audience for "The Radio Revival Hour" was discarded. But response from the invisible radio audience to an hour-long broadcast was so encouraging that Charles Fuller could not bear to cut back to a mere thirty minutes. The 6:30–7:30 spot was his if he could continue to pay for it, and he believed that God wanted him to have this hour-long, after-sundown spot on powerful KNX. Therefore he presented the following argument to his supporters:

Though our contract for an hour-long broadcast was for the month of October only, we feel that under the circumstances we should keep this valuable evening hour for the glory of God. I have told you before how difficult, how nearly impossible it is to get an hour for speaking after 6 P.M. on any large station. The only explanation I can give for our having this opportunity is that it must be God's plan for us. The way seems just to have opened without our pushing it at all. Do you not feel we *must hold this hour for Christ?* . . . God is plainly opening these doors, and we should be failing Him if we did not use these opportunities, so I do covet your prayers that every broadcast might be what He would have it.

His radio listeners responded to this challenge sufficiently for him to continue broadcasting for a whole hour on Sunday evenings. Thus that first Sunday in October, 1934, when only fifty people showed up at the Women's Club House, was the first hour-long broadcast of what was later called the "Old Fashioned Revival Hour." For the next twenty-three and a quarter years, Charles Fuller broadcasted an hour-long old-fashioned revival service each Sunday.

The earliest recordings of the broadcasts are from the last two Sundays of 1935. Merely written words cannot convey what the tone of voice and the tempo of words do as one listens to these recordings. But one or two excerpts from these earliest records indicate something of Charles Fuller's great desire to get the Gospel out, and those who remember him will be able to recapture more than the written words can give.

Now at this Christmas season I know there are some out in radio land who perhaps do not know just where to turn or what to do. I am going to ask the choir to sing a favorite number of mine, "He's the One," a song I'm sure you love. Give me a song book, Mr. Miller,[3] and I want you to notice the words of the first verse as I read them:

> "Is there anyone can help us,
> One who understands our hearts,
> When the thorns of life have pierced them till they bleed?
> One who sympathizes with us,
> Who His Wondrous love imparts
> Just the very, very blessing that we need?"

---

[3] Mr. Miller was the director of the choir of the Fountain Avenue Baptist Church of Los Angeles, and during these years this choir donated the music for the "Radio Revival Hour."

Then the chorus says,

> "Yes, there's One, only One,
> The blessed, blessed Jesus,
> He's the One.
> When afflictions press the soul,
> When the waves of trouble roll,
> And you need a friend to help you,
> He's the One."

Listen, my friend, out in radio land tonight. You have tried a thousand ways to find peace and comfort. Perhaps your heart is breaking tonight with a load, with trouble—you are in despair and disheartened. I want you to know that in all the eternal realm, there is only One throughout eternity that you can trust. You can trust Him right now, and He is willing to come in and be a friend, an advocate, a paraclete, one who stands by—Jesus will become your friend. I want you to know that through the many, many trials Mrs. Fuller and I have gone through—that God has graciously permitted us to go through—and we have rejoiced in them—we have found time after time how sweet it is just to turn to Him, to go to Him, and He strengthens, cheers, comforts, guides, and directs.

Later the choir sang "Christ Receiveth Sinful Men," and after the first verse, containing the words, "Make the message clear and plain," Charles Fuller broke in and said,

That is exactly what we are trying to do—to make the message plain and simple, just the a-b-c's of the Gospel, because when I stand before the judgment seat of Christ someday, I want to be free of the blood of every man God lets me come in contact with. I appreciate the privilege of speaking all over western America, and I want to give out the Gospel in no uncertain terms. So choir, sing it again. I know there is some boy, some girl, some father, some mother, out in radio land tonight who needs Christ, and we want to sing it out that "Christ receiveth sinful men."

During the months after October, 1934, a response came in that at last corresponded with the outreach by radio for which Charles Fuller had been relentlessly working. "We have heard from people in high and low stations in life," he said on the first anniversary of the "Radio Revival Hour" in the fall of 1935.

. . . From the palatial home letters written on monogrammed note

109

paper, and from the miner's cabin written on a smudgy piece of a paper bag, from black and white, from doctors and lawyers, laundresses and laborers, from sick beds in hospitals, sanitoria, asylums, from ships on the sea, from the floor of the Grand Canyon, from lonely sheep herders on the Canadian plains, from beacon light keepers, from the Bible Institute boys who picked up our program while spinning along in their car on the Florida highways, from the lonely American boy in Sonora, Mexico, who listened in with Mexican laborers all crowded into the little adobe hut—(the Mexicans loving the music though they could not understand the words), from prisoners in San Quentin, from families snowbound during the long winters of the North, from lonely prairie farm homes, and many other places. Letters have come from heart-broken, heart-hungry humanity, some contemplating suicide, yet hundreds have come, cheery and full of thanksgiving that they have received comfort and new hope and strength from hearing God's Word again, and hearing the songs they used to sing "back home" with Mother. Many say that the Bible is to them a new book since they have learned to study it, and we shall never know of the conversions resulting from the sowing of the Word over the "Radio Revival Hour."

This increased response required moving the GBA office from the few rooms on the eighth floor at Biola to the second floor of a small office building in Pasadena. From the beginning it was the GBA's policy to draft, prayerfully, a personal letter "to every seeking, questioning letter."

The greater coverage provided by KNX also made Charles Fuller feel that he was wasting his energies to drive every Thursday evening to Long Beach just to broadcast his "Radio Bible Class" over the small coverage provided by KGER. (He continued his Sunday morning broadcast over KGER, however.) His energies could better go into the broadcast of the "Sunday School Hour," which he had moved to KNX and was now sending out from 5:30–6:00 on Saturday evenings.

But no sooner had Charles Fuller given up his midweek Bible class on KGER than he began to feel very uneasy, for now six whole days were going by (Sunday evening to the next Saturday evening) without his being able to preach on the radio. So in the spring of 1935 he asked his listeners whether they would send support for a midweek Bible class over KNX. Apparently they gave him sufficient encouragement, for in the fall of 1935 he began to broadcast "The Prophetic Lamp Hour" on Tuesday afternoons, 3:00–3:30 over KNX (he could not procure an evening hour on this station week nights). Then a month later he announced that he would also broadcast "The Radio Bible Class" on Thursday afternoons from 3:00–3:30 over KNX, and so by November, 1935, my father was broadcasting five times a week, four times on KNX and once on KGER, for a total of three and a half hours.

Charles Fuller enjoyed preparing sermons and preaching five times a week. He loved to study the Bible and then proclaim its message on the mighty voice of radio. In the spring of 1936 he said:

Certainly I am in no way responsible for making the "Radio Revival Hour" the great success and blessing it has been for the past twenty months, aside from the fact that I have been preaching the Word and "Thus saith the Lord." I am not gifted as many men are for preaching—but I love God and His Word, and I have a burning desire to see men brought to Christ while there is yet time. I'd rather preach the Word than anything in this world, and my constant prayer is that I may be able to make it so simple and plain that everyone can understand, and as I pray, or as I preach, that the Holy Spirit may open the eyes of sinful men and women to behold the beauty of Christ—and that is what He has been doing.

Early in 1936, however, he dropped the "Sunday School Hour," because Saturday evening, just before supper, was not a good time, and the Thursday "Radio Bible Class" had virtually the same objective as the Saturday evening program.

The radio signal from KNX was clearly heard in the Pacific Northwest and in western Canada, but because it bounced back off the ionosphere just above San Francisco, it was impossible to hear just five hundred miles away in California's second great population area. So in December, 1935, KNX hooked in with the San Francisco station KSFO, and to reach listeners in the Bay Area, Charles Fuller increased his cost of radio time by sending his Tuesday and Thursday afternoon programs out on this new station.

But during the summer of 1936 changes were in the wind for the

111

At home beside radio with cocker spaniel, Toffee.

world of radio. The Columbia Broadcasting System wanted to have KNX, with its large coverage, instead of KHJ for its Los Angeles affiliate. KNX came under CBS management on June 1, 1936. Since CBS permitted no paid-for religious broadcasts, Charles Fuller knew that his days on KNX were numbered. Always quick, however, to make the necessary moves to stay on the radio, he had begun earlier that spring to make electrical transcriptions of the "Radio Revival Hour" which he could then mail out to various independent stations across the country. Thus, if he had to go off KNX, he could actually have better coverage (especially for the summertime) as recordings were played on local stations in many states. By July, 1936, recordings of the "Radio Revival Hour" were heard on seven stations in the Pacific Northwest, in Montana, on powerful WHO in Des Moines, and on KOB in Albuquerque. He was also negotiating to get some outlets in Canada, Alaska, and Hawaii.

It was a good thing that he had dropped his Saturday evening program by then because now he and some singers had to spend every Thursday evening in a hot, soundproof studio making a recording of the program to be sent out. Often parts of the transcribed program had to have several "takes" before they were deemed ready for broadcasting. All in all, it was very exhausting. An electrical transcription was a new development in radio at that time, and Charles Fuller took pains to explain it to his listeners:

A transcription is a recording of a program, on a disc, like a phonograph record, which when released from a radio station, sounds exactly like a program being given in person. Listening, you would never know that we were not, at that moment, standing before the mike talking to you—that is, if you had not heard the announcer say—as required by law—"this is electrically transcribed." I made a transcription of an afternoon Bible lesson, just before Easter vacation in order to see how it would work. So when Mrs. Fuller and Dan and I were taking a little trip to Arizona we drew up by the roadside, about fifteen miles out of Prescott, one Thursday afternoon, and as we sat looking out over the desert to the blue hills beyond, we listened to our own voice, telling the story of God's great love to sinful man. It was indeed a strange and thrilling experience, and caused us to marvel at modern invention, and to thank God that this part at least could be used for His glory.

Charles Fuller gradually increased the number of stations playing his transcriptions, since he expected KNX to notify him at any time that his contract with them would be terminated. Heretofore, no broadcast, secular or religious, had gone out on so many stations by electrical transcription, but God had opened the way to use this new technology as a means for keeping the message going out when the KNX door closed.

But now that he relied on a dozen or more stations to gain the coverage that KNX had previously made possible, his radio expenses increased several times over. And to make matters worse, he was approaching the dreaded summer months. The way to meet these increased costs, he knew, was to develop a corps of supporters in the areas where his transcription stations were located. More people were now listening to him by transcription in these places than had listened over distant KNX. The air waves were becoming filled with stations, and people were now more interested in listening to their local stations than in finding out the farthest signal their radio could pick up. Thus the way to get these new listeners behind him was to hold public meetings in cities such as Portland, Oregon; Seattle, Washington; Boise, Idaho; Salt Lake City, Utah; and Albuquerque, New Mexico. Air transportation was now coming into its own, and he could hold meetings at such places during the week and still be back to broadcast on Sundays. Charles Fuller went to these cities during the summer and fall of 1936. After his trip to the Northwest he wrote:

We were surprised by the fruitfulness of our trip north. . . . Souls were saved, and with the personal contact it seemed that in every meeting interest was aroused in Bible study, soul winning, and other Christian work. I feel led to go out and hold short series of meetings in other nearby states this fall, coming home for the Sunday broadcasts. In this way I hope to get close to the hearts of the people, and arouse them to the need of the hour for prayer, and carrying the Gospel out into the neglected places. If you do not feel your heart burning within you, ask God on your knees to give you a burden for the lost, and He will do it. Oh *I need* your prayers, and if we together pray and work, God will bless and reward our efforts.

That fall of 1936 Charles Fuller also urged people to pray especially about what should be done when they went off KNX. He now had at least five hundred prayer warriors, and early in October he asked them to be praying "about a radio hour on another station."

Then word came that a new network, the Mutual Broadcasting System, was being formed. Since CBS had shifted from KHJ over to KNX, the MBS was making KHJ its Los Angeles outlet and was lining up affiliates all across the country. Late in November, 1936, Charles Fuller reported that "it looks as though we will be on a network after January which will reach farther than KNX and have more intensive coverage." He continued:

After the change, we are making plans for a better Sunday night program—more varied, interesting, and more spiritual—but continuing our policy of singing the *old songs* and giving only the *old Gospel*. We are not called to discuss politics or plans for fixing up the world, much as it needs fixing. We are called to preach *Christ* and men and women are hungering to hear. We are praying—God is working. You have assured me you are going to continue to stand by financially and with prayer, so I am eagerly looking forward to increased opportunities for reaching the lost before it is too late.

In order to get his foot in the door of the new Mutual network, he put his Tuesday afternoon program on an early evening time over four stations in California. Since expenses would be increasing soon, he dropped the Thursday afternoon Bible class program. At the end of December, 1936, he was able to report that

. . . we have been contacting Mutual's officials for some weeks and they have approved our program. But since approving it, they have determined that their future policy will be *no more releases for religious programs.*[4] There are two other coast-to-coast networks whose policy is the same—no time to sell for religious services. So you see with this opening we have a great opportunity indeed to eventually cover the land with a fundamental Gospel service, and if we do not take it, *this door may be permanently closed.* We are beginning cautiously, taking the barest skeleton possible, expecting to add other

---

[4] In later years the MBS relaxed this policy for awhile.

stations as income permits—as the new listeners become interested and get under the burden to help. We believe everyone listening now will be able to hear the entire program on this new network by the second Sunday night in January, 1937.

Thus plans were made to go onto fourteen Mutual network stations up through San Francisco and across to Chicago for the evening of January 10, 1937. After the last broadcast held in the KNX studio on the Sunday before, Charles Fuller had the group that had gathered there in Hollywood for the past two and more years stand and sing "God Be with You Till We Meet Again." Though the "Radio Revival Hour" now had a door opened to much greater outreach than before, it was hard to say farewell to the KNX ministry, for as the *Heart to Heart Talk* said the week following the last broadcast on that station, "God has given us such a marvelous harvest of souls, far above anything we asked or thought when we started our ministry there [more than] two years ago."

Sustaining a Coast-to-Coast Broadcast

Charles Fuller was somewhat nervous during that first Mutual network broadcast early in 1937. He was on at that time of the week when the greatest number of people listened to their radios, and he wanted the singing, the reading of the letters, the announcements, and the sermon to be well programmed without losing the sense of informality and heart appeal which he knew were vital for gaining and holding a radio audience.

The greater problem, however, was the cost of station time which was now more than twice what it had been on KNX and the several transcription stations. This problem was complicated by the fact that Mutual had sold time to but one religious broadcast, the "Radio Revival Hour," on the condition that no direct pleas for contributions could be made. About all Charles Fuller was now supposed to say was, "Your prayers and help are greatly needed." Previous experience had shown that it took about two months before response to a broadcast over new stations would become evident. So even though he was having to pay out two-and-a-half times more each week than before, there would be several weeks before contributions would increase at all. Early in February, 1937, Charles Fuller said,

116

The thing that heartens me most of all, when the obstacles in the way of the "Radio Revival Hour" seem almost unsurmountable, is the fact that so many hundreds of you are praying daily for this work—praying that we might have wisdom, that other doors might open, that financial support might come, but most of all that as we preach the Word the Holy Spirit may use it mightily as He works in hearts. Shall we enter into a compact, dear friends—you and I? I shall continue to preach from the dear old Book—the simple Gospel story of salvation to the lost, and comfort and strength and living on "higher ground" to God's children—only this. On your part, you agree to pray earnestly, believingly, and continually, and to give something to this work regularly, as God prospers you. Working thus together, this ministry cannot but continue for His glory.

Two weeks later he reported that the offerings had picked up as a result of this special call to prayer, and now he told his supporters of the pressing need to buy up more of the Mutual network affiliates and to extend the broadcast to the Eastern seaboard. "We are confronted with the necessity of taking more stations very soon, to reach the Atlantic coast, in order to hold our place on the network." By April 1 it was possible to add some additional stations which made the program heard as far east as Windsor, Ontario.

But as the radio coverage increased, Charles Fuller was conscious of more Satanic opposition against sending out the message of Christ to so many millions of people.

Friends everywhere, I ask you to pray as I preach. In all of my ministry never have I felt the conflict with Satanic powers as I do now when I stand before the microphone, preaching the shed blood of Christ as sinful man's only way of approach to God. The Word goes out over the air which is Satan's realm, and his opposition is certainly keen. But God gives us victory as we continue in prayer. Do pray that the Word may be used to bring conviction of sin.

Charles Fuller believed that in preaching the Gospel, there were recurrent battles with Satan and his demons that must be fought. The *Heart to Heart Talk* often made reference to this. Once a radio listener argued that "if this is God's work He will supply the need, and you need not have such a struggle to meet station time, and to hold this place on the network." But my father replied:

This friend does not know the Bible teaching regarding the believer's warfare with Satan. . . . Satan, the "prince of this world" (John 12:31) . . . has greater power than man, and he makes it his business to hinder Christ's servants in carrying on their work for God. Paul says in 1 Thess. 2:18, "We wanted to come to you, but Satan *hinders* us." Satan also buffets God's servants (2 Cor. 12:7). This, however, results in good for God's servants, as it keeps them humble, and drives them to prayer.

Would not Satan bring this program to nought if he could? Does he not hinder in every possible way? Indeed he does, as I know from constant experience, and the conflict is terrific!

So dear friends, as we realize . . . that Satan does strive to hinder and buffet us, let us use the spiritual weapon of *prayer* to an *all-powerful* God. . . . I thank God upon every remembrance of you good soldiers, who are standing with me in this conflict.

That April, 1937, contributions again dropped alarmingly, so much so this time that it seemed necessary to cut back only to the Mutual stations in California for the summer months. The Mutual managers promised Charles Fuller that he could keep his Sunday evening spot during the summer, even if he had to cut back, but they also added that there would be no chance of keeping it after October unless he would go on many more affiliates by then. He knew that he could save money by making such a cut, but then he would lose the supporters in the Midwest who would be absolutely essential for supporting the new stations he must take in the fall. So he hung on tenaciously to his dozen or so network stations during April and May.

But there came a "black Thursday" in May, 1937, when after opening the mail that had come in that day and projecting the amounts likely to come in on Friday through Sunday, there seemed no possible way he could hold on to these stations for even another Sunday, to say nothing of the difficult summer months that lay ahead. "On one Thursday morning in May," he related,

. . . I almost gave up, when the mail was especially low, and when we did not have even one-half enough to meet the next Sunday night's broadcast. I actually lifted the telephone receiver to call our radio agent and tell him to notify the network officials that we would have to fold up for the summer. But as I started to give the number, I felt checked—and remembering that hundreds of friends were praying—

118

*Participants in first coast-to-coast broadcast of "Old Fashioned Revival Hour,"
October 3, 1937.*

Staff and audience in Mutual Studios, Hollywood, in 1940.

*The quartet in early days of
the broadcast: Rudy Atwood,
pianist; William McDougall, first
tenor; Arthur Jaissle, bass; Al
Harlan, baritone; Robert Gordon,
second tenor.*

the girls in the office, we at home, you out there—I just hung up the receiver. I said, "Lord, You haven't forsaken us. Forgive me for the lack of faith. I'll just trust and wait."

Well—after that very blue Thursday came three days which brought the average up and gave us enough to pay for that following Sunday night. Monday morning started the week very low, but enough came in for that week—and so it has been going from day to day, and now I firmly believe that though the summer will be hard sledding, we shall be able to hold the network through July and August, and then go into the autumn with far greater impetus and vigor because we did not have to quit.

Indeed, summertime had been difficult for Charles Fuller ever since he had been on radio. Things usually looked blackest in early July, and so as he approached the Fourth of July that year, he said, "I just dread to think of a firecracker because of what I have to go through each year trying to meet radio bills at this time."

But the Lord brought the broadcast through that summer without having to cut back, and now plans were made to go ahead with the expansion the Mutual network had said was mandatory for the fall. Late in August, 1937, however, a terrible crisis came. One day Mr. Rudy Alber, the radio agent, walked into my father's office in Pasadena and informed him that he had just learned that a tobacco company wanted the "Radio Revival Hour's" Sunday evening time spot. They had told Mutual they were ready immediately to sign a contract to go coast-to-coast on all of Mutual's affiliates beginning the first Sunday in October. Now Mutual was saying to Charles Fuller that unless he was willing to go coast-to-coast in the fall, he would lose his most prized Sunday evening time spot. The radio agent had driven over from Hollywood to break this news. He regarded it as an utter impossibility to jump from the present sixteen to ninety or more Mutual stations. So he had come to make a personal visit to his friend and, now that the end had come, to tell him how much he had enjoyed working with him.

But a different train of thought ran through Charles Fuller's mind as he heard this latest piece of news. He had marveled at how God had brought him through the difficult summer, and he believed that he was now on the verge of seeing more of the great and mighty things that Jeremiah 33:3 promised. After looking out the window and thinking for a moment, he stood up and announced to his agent, "Rudy, you tell the Mutual Broadcasting System that the 'Radio Revival Hour' will sign a contract today to go coast-to-coast on their network."

Rudy Alber looked at him in astonishment and said, "Do you think you can make it, Charlie?"

"No," he replied, "but *God can.*"

A few days later, however, Charles Fuller became convinced that he simply could not take on so many new network stations all at once. The present supporters simply could not increase their giving fivefold, and while so many new stations would surely gain new listeners and supporters, there would be that inevitable time-lag before they would pay for themselves. Another plan had begun to take shape in his mind, a plan which constituted a step of faith but which was more realistic. He instructed Rudy Alber to tell Mutual that he would relinquish his 7:30–8:30 evening time spot to the tobacco company if Mutual would give him an earlier hour on Sunday along with the firm assurance that he could keep that hour while he gradually took on the whole network.

Thus in the jargon of radio, the broadcast became a "martyr program" by relinquishing its time to another advertiser. But this move was made to gain some important advantages. The earlier time would not conflict so much with evening church services and would give a better time on the east coast than the 10:30–11:30 p.m. spot. Then, too, by being a martyr program Charles Fuller was obligating the Mutual management to return some favors to him for allowing them to gain an additional advertiser. The management had become very friendly during the nine months he had been on part of their network, and they had been impressed with the letters they had received from managers of their affiliates who had asked, "When will the 'Radio Revival Hour' be broadcast on my station?" They were also impressed with Charles Fuller's shrewdness and toughness as a negotiator. When Rudy Alber broached this latest proposal to Mutual, one executive exclaimed, "That Fuller man knows just what he wants, and does he hold out for it! I am going to do everything I can to work with him."

The plan finally arrived at for the first Sunday in October, 1937, was for the "Radio Revival Hour" to go coast-to-coast on a skeleton network of thirty Mutual stations. Then as contracts expired that various other Mutual affiliates had for Sunday evening, the broadcast would expand until it had a major part of the Mutual network. The Mutual officials promised that as soon as everything could be worked out, the broadcast would be given the 6:00–7:00 p.m. hour, Pacific Standard Time.

Thus the "Radio Revival Hour" was a coast-to-coast broadcast for the first time on October 3, 1937, when it was heard on thirty Mutual stations, one of which was in Boston on the east coast! This was such a momentous occasion for Charles Fuller that he had all the participants and the studio audience photographed. Since from that night on the broadcast would be heard "live" three thousand miles to the east, he decided that the theme song for it should be "Jesus Saves," because its words, such as "Spread the tidings all around," "Tell to sinners far and wide," "Give the winds a mighty voice," were so appropriate to a coast-to-coast broadcast. He was so excited about broadcasting coast-to-coast that he exclaimed, "I think my heart will miss a beat or two for joy when the chorus rings out from Boston to Hawaii with the strains of 'Jesus Saves.' If you can think of a better song to use for our first one on October 3rd, write and tell me about it." He also changed the name of the broadcast to "The Old Fashioned Revival Hour." In one of his announcements given a few Sundays later he explained why he wanted the broadcast to have this name:

Each Sunday by God's grace we have an hour to broadcast the old songs and the old Gospel which is the power of God unto salvation. Our one message is Christ and Him crucified, and we endeavor by God's grace to beseech men and women to be reconciled to God in Christ Jesus, never closing a broadcast but what we give every one an opportunity to accept Christ as their personal Savior—this is truly an *old-fashioned Revival Hour.*

In preparation for this first coast-to-coast broadcast, Charles Fuller felt the need for more varied and better music. He invited the Goose Creek Quartet of the Country Church of Hollywood and Rudy Atwood, their pianist, to become part of the musical staff of the "Old Fashioned Revival Hour." Four years previously, the Country Church of Hollywood had been founded by Dr. Josiah Hogg. This church had become well known all over Southern California through a unique broadcast aired each morning at 8 o'clock. Dr. Hogg had a quartet and a pianist, Rudy Atwood, whom he had assembled while heading up the Paul Rader Tabernacle in Los Angeles, a counterpart of work Paul Rader himself was doing in Chicago. On this program Dr. Hogg would play the part of "Parson Hopkins" and Rudy and each of the quartet would be typical members of a rural community back in Tennessee who would be conversing just before it was time to "go to meetin'." Then the program would shift to the meeting itself with hymns and message.

Thus Rudy Atwood and the quartet appear in the photograph of that first coast-to-coast broadcast. Rudy Atwood continued as pianist for the "Old Fashioned Revival Hour" even beyond the time of Charles Fuller's death in 1968, and the quartet sang for the program for more than twenty years, although no one of its original members remained for all that time.

According to the plan which had been hammered out between Charles Fuller and the Mutual officials, the broadcast was to add sixteen stations by the end of October and had to be willing to take on an additional forty stations *whenever* new contracts could be worked out with them. As it turned out, however, contracts with these forty stations were made very quickly—much sooner than Charles Fuller had felt he could handle them. By the first Sunday in November, he announced that he was now broadcasting on *eighty-eight* stations coast-to-coast! This meant that during a period of about six weeks his radio station time doubled and then trebled, from fifteen hundred dollars to forty-five hundred dollars a week. It is no wonder, then, that in the October *Heart to Heart Talk* he said:

Dear Friends, I do wish you could all gather with me this morning for a prayer meeting, for my heart is so burdened for the "Old Fashioned Revival Hour." Since KNX was sold on January first, and we were forced to change to the Mutual network, we have had just one crisis after another to meet. In our weariness we have asked God for a respite—but He has shown us that as the days darken and the end of this dispensation approaches, the battle with Satan and his forces will grow even more fierce, so we must be good soldiers, putting on the whole armor and going forward with much prayer, hoping for no rest except as we rest in Him. We can expect only the most bitter opposition from Satan because this message of redemption is going right through his realm—the air. We must, in the future, meet all his thrusts with spiritual weapons, as we have done in the past.

We are now at another crisis—financial need—and only prayer and trust in God will carry us through. He has given us the opportunity—never dreamed of even fifteen years ago—of reaching four or five million persons at one time . . . *right where they happen to be.* . . . We have this opportunity, but we cannot hold it unless we have more income at once. The daily income is not sufficient to meet station time. . . .

"Commit thy way unto the Lord, trust also in Him, and he worketh" —(Ps. 37:5). We are standing on this promise. Will you stand with us in prayer, and let us all together praise God that since we have committed this ministry to Him, and are trusting in Him, that *He is working.*

We can also understand the plea he made on the radio on November 7, 1937:

In order to hold our place in competition with the great coast-to-coast programs backed by unlimited finances, we, on a faith basis with no backing other than God, must obtain our goal of 108 radio stations *right away.* Some twenty more stations must be added just as soon as possible. This goal can be accomplished, if every *new listener* would immediately step forth and stand in the gap and say count on me and do it sacrificially, as our faithful and true older listeners have done over the past months.

He then illustrated the kind of giving he meant by citing the example of one very poor listener who had convenanted with God to send in twelve cents a month. Charles Fuller continued:

Once this goal of 108 stations is obtained, it will not be necessary to add additional stations to hold our place. We are so near to a wonderful victory—a victory is right around the corner. Let's all get under the matter and put it across this week. Thank you. God bless you. I'll report the victory as soon as it's accomplished.

These were suspenseful days. There was one time period that fall of 1937 when the radio expense had trebled, and as the deadline came for paying the Mutual network, there was only four dollars and twenty-four cents left. One incident illustrating how tense my father was during those weeks was one evening when he himself drove down to the Los Angeles post office and opened up Box 123 to bring home the mail packets. When he returned home, he spread them all over the living room rug to estimate whether, when the enclosures were counted the next morning, there would be enough to pay for the following Sunday. But when our Siamese cat began to investigate and sniff the mail packets, tipping some of them over, my father picked the cat up and threw it half-way across the room. As only a cat can, however, it nimbly landed on its feet.

In November Charles Fuller reported:

This week of November 7th to 14th has been terribly hard—the offerings falling below what was necessary for station time, and the need constantly pressing us to take a few more stations in order to hold our place on the network. We felt ourselves in a vise. Satan's bitter attacks were there, and yet your encouraging letters poured in, telling of the great hunger for the Word. We felt we must curtail—yet we *must not!* So we called for a day of prayer on November 15th, and I am writing to you on that day. As Mrs. Fuller and I knelt in prayer this morning we were thrilled with the knowledge that our prayers were just a little part of a great wave of prayer from all over the land, and Canada and Hawaii. For our comfort He gave us these verses of Scripture.

"He led them on safely" (Ps. 78:53).

"Behold, I send an angel before thee, to keep thee in the way, and to bring thee into the place which I have prepared" (Exod. 23:20).

Friends, we are almost over the top for God. In a few weeks we shall have more listeners—more supporters—and it will not be so hard. We long to hold all we now have, and to take the few more stations necessary, so that the Gospel songs and messages from the Word may *continue* to ring out in all the homes where expectant and needy hearts wait—little homes at the crossroads lighted by kerosene lamps (I always think of these as I preach) as well as the richer ones. . . . *Continue in prayer*—and give as you can even though the amount must be small. How we shall all rejoice in the *Victory* won— when we go on into the typical teaching of the Tabernacle, which is so rich and faith-strengthening.

The previous year when Charles Fuller had to expand rapidly by playing electrical transcriptions on several stations, he had seen how effective holding public meetings in other parts of the country was in building up a corps of regular supporters. So that fall as the Mutual network pushed him to expand so rapidly, he lined up a meeting in Des Moines for the early part of December, and then several meetings in Chicago in the middle of January.

Now that he was on a live network, he could originate the "Old Fashioned Revival Hour" from another part of the country and still be heard "live" all across America. The meeting in Des Moines was sponsored by a group of Bible-believing churches in the area, and Charles Fuller was greatly encouraged by the five thousand people who came to the meeting. As a twelve-year-old listening to this at home in South Pasadena, I was impressed by my father's saying that if he called to our cocker spaniel, Toffee, he bet the dog would jump right into the radio speaker. Another meeting was held the following evening with the auditorium again filled. Some drove as far as two hundred seventy miles to attend.

Both the response at Des Moines and the gradually increasing letter response led Charles Fuller to say after returning home:

From my heart I thank every one of you who has shaken my hand (in Des Moines) or has written in. If the "Old Fashioned Revival Hour" ever needed friends she needs them *now*—and *she has them.* Your warm assurance of continued support encourages me beyond words, and I believe that by God's help and yours we are going on to victory. But friends, the next thirty days are still days of crisis. . . . Had I known the titanic struggle that would be involved in this coast-to-coast expansion I should never have had the courage and faith to attempt it. But you have stood by wonderfully, and together we have pulled through a long hard summer and autumn, up the steep hill of achievement for God—often slipping back, but then overcoming *by prayer* the buffeting and hinderings of satanic forces until we see, just ahead, a time in January when we can be "on our feet."

As soon as the holidays passed, Charles Fuller headed east to Chicago, where the Moody Memorial Church and its pastor, Dr. Harry Ironside, had been diligently working to prepare to originate the broadcast from there. Then the next evening the Chicago Christian Business Men's Committee had invited my father to be their speaker for their seventh anniversary rally, which would be held in the 3300-seat Civic Opera House. Every seat was taken for both meetings, and so the Chicago trip also helped establish the broadcast. His was the only coast-to-coast program in the heart of Sunday evening that was sending out the message of salvation through faith in Christ. Radio surveys showed that only one program on Sunday evenings had a larger listening audience than the "Old Fashioned Revival Hour." Hundreds of conversions were being reported each week through the mail. But though the uphill climb was now not quite so steep, it was still very much uphill, and Charles Fuller continued to schedule as many meetings as possible in cities across the network to consolidate a firm basis of support under the one hundred eight stations.

On Good Friday of that year he had a meeting of fourteen thousand people in the Olympia Auditorium in Detroit. I was with my parents on that trip and was seated on the front row for the meeting. I remember my father preaching on the text, "When I see the blood, I will pass over you" (Exod. 12:13). Though at that time I was still uninterested in spiritual things, I was impressed with the sense of the power of God coming down on that meeting as the altar call was given and three hundred came forward, many with a manifestly deep conviction of sin. Often when I hear the song, "There Is a Fountain Filled with Blood," I recall that day in Detroit, for that was what the whole congregation sang during the invitation service.

The following Sunday morning my father was the speaker for the Easter sunrise service held at Soldiers' Field in Chicago. It was a cold, windy, overcast morning, but forty thousand people came, which was the largest number yet to attend a sunrise service there. My father spoke from a podium in the middle of the field, wearing his overcoat and a fedora hat. (He wanted to avoid catching laryngitis since that evening he would originate another broadcast from Moody Memorial Church.) The people were so far away that it was impossible to see hands raised in response to the invitation. So he asked all those who wished to accept Christ as their Savior to wave their programs, and a flutter of white could be seen throughout the stands. There were spaces on the programs where those receiving Christ could fill in their names. Several hundred such programs were turned in to the committee, and all were carefully followed up.

Above: *Leland Green leads the choir at Mutual Network Studio, with Rudy Atwood at piano and George Broadbent at organ.* **Below:** *Easter Sunrise Service, Soldiers' Field, Chicago, 1938. Charles Fuller, speaker.*

This is the way my mother recounted that memorable meeting:

Of course I was praying for Mr. Fuller as he spoke, as many others were doing. In fact, there had been some all-night prayer meetings there in Chicago. The committee was very much pleased with the definiteness of the message, and I, too, thought it was very good. It was the Word of God given simply, and the Holy Spirit was using it that morning. As I came out through the long tunnel, after the service, I heard a woman say to her companion, "Well, I don't think he was much of a speaker. He used the same word twice in one sentence, and his vocabulary was not brilliant—in fact, it was rather limited."

I smiled to myself as I looked at her. She was nice-looking, and I should like to have remarked, "No, if you came to hear a brilliant orator, that man from California certainly disappointed you! But if you were a sinner needing a Savior, you might have found the way to Him this Easter morning." Some people like to hear man lauded and praised, and it was displeasing to some of them to have Mr. Fuller tell them they were dead in trespasses and sins—dead, if they were outside of Christ. But it was the power of God which brought conviction to those hearts, that Easter morning.

But now, just as Charles Fuller began to feel that he had built up the supporters who would maintain a 108-station broadcast, the Mutual network officials told him they would renew his contract in the fall for his prime Sunday evening time only if he would take all one hundred twenty-eight of their stations by the end of 1938. His radio agent advised him to go on a less vulnerable, less expensive Sunday afternoon time on Mutual. But Charles Fuller said no and urged his supporters to join with him in this:

Shall we give up our Sunday evening hour? I say no!!—and I think I can hear emphatic nos coming from all over Canada and Alaska. And straight across our land, I hear you say, "No—keep the Gospel ringing out over the entire network, and keep this valuable hour which has five times the listeners of any afternoon hour."

I know there are enough Christian people who believe that America needs the Gospel, and when they get the vision of the need, they will buckle on the armor for the battle, and pray and give that God's work will *not* have to step aside for mere entertainment.

The listeners responded favorably enough to this challenge for Charles Fuller, even in June, 1938, to take on seven of these additional twenty stations. As the new supporters produced by these new stations became established, then another third could be added in the fall, and the final third in December.

But at this point the difficulty began to loom up of maintaining through the summer a broadcast that was now coast-to-coast. The "Old Fashioned Revival Hour" could not, as many commercial programs, go off during the summer months. Never underwritten or sponsored, it could continue only as it maintained people's interest sufficiently for hundreds each week to send in small contributions. At that time it was the only coast-to-coast religious program to stay on all summer. There was simply no other way for it to survive. Radio officials marveled that such a broadcast not only planned to stay right on through the summer but was even adding seven new stations at the beginning of the summer.

In order to get through that hard summer, Charles Fuller continued to hold meetings. He went up to northern California during June, and as my parents traveled to the Pacific Northwest on their vacation, they held meetings almost every night, originating the broadcast on Sundays from such places as Portland and Seattle. From Seattle my father wrote,

God has been graciously blessing our summer meetings, in answer to your prayers. The heat has been intense, but in spite of that the dear people have driven for miles and have packed the building—fans waving, faces wet and shiny, friendly and eager—and have I enjoyed preaching to such audiences!—sometimes giving the invitation as late as 10:00 P.M. and God has given us souls at every meeting.

We are greatly impressed how this simple, spiritual, homey program is reaching the hearts of people, young and old, rich and poor, unsaved as well as saved. We *must* hold this hour for God.

That summer Charles Fuller knew that to stay on prime Sunday evening time he must also improve the music on his program. During his trip to Seattle he wrote Leland Green, asking him to be in charge of the choir and, like the quartet and Rudy Atwood, to be on the permanent staff of the program. My father had known Leland Green since the early days in Placentia. In 1921 he was converted under my father's ministry. He had sung and played during the first broadcast over KTBI in 1925 and contributed greatly to the musical program of Calvary Church. In 1926 he accompanied Charles Fuller to the Southwest Missionary Conference at Flagstaff, Arizona, where he provided the music by singing solos and playing several different instruments. While he was playing at one meeting around the campfire under the stars, he told God he wanted Him to use his musical talents. My father gave him some help with his education before he lost everything in 1931, but Leland Green persevered through college during the depression, choosing to work nights in a menial job as a janitor when he could have earned money more easily and quickly by playing in a dance band. From 1934 onwards he taught music in the high school in Garden Grove, California. Later he taught in Pasadena where, after receiving his doctorate in music, he became coordinator of music for all the Pasadena schools.

Leland Green had been singing solos and playing the vibraharp for the "Old Fashioned Revival Hour" ever since the first coast-to-coast broadcast in 1937, and he accepted Charles Fuller's invitation to assemble a group of top-notch, dedicated Christian singers who would receive some remuneration each Sunday and thus be more dependable. From then on the choir music improved greatly, as Leland Green with his fine singers and musicianship sought nonetheless to keep the message of the song foremost and to reach people's hearts. Like Rudy Atwood, he remained with the broadcast even after Charles Fuller's homegoing in 1968.

Back from the Northwest, Charles Fuller soon left again to hold a public meeting in the Hippodrome at Waterloo, Iowa, which was to climax in the live broadcast of the "Old Fashioned Revival Hour." The mild rain which had been falling that day had not kept people from crowding out the 10,200 seats, nor had it fallen hard enough to make any noise on the corrugated roof. But about ten minutes before they were to broadcast, the rain came down in such torrents that many could not even hear what was being said over the public address system. Charles Fuller picked up some earphones to see if the choir's singing could be heard, but to his dismay there was only the roar of the rain.

He knew that unless the rain stopped, five million or so people would not be able to hear the broadcast that night. To those sitting near enough to the loudspeakers, he said, "I want everyone to join with me in prayer that God will stop the rain." As he was repeating this message and getting everyone to join with him in prayer, the satanic suggestion came to him, "Suppose when you pray the rain does not stop. You'll be laughed right out of town." But he felt led of God to pray that the rain would stop, and so he prayed very simply, "Father, in Jesus' name will you please stop the rain so this broadcast may go out clearly for Thy glory." And no sooner had he finished praying than the noise of the rain stopped. This was such an obvious answer to prayer in a time of extreme crisis that some faces turned white with the realization that God was indeed there at that meeting. And when the broadcast was completed and the invitation given, some actually ran down the aisle in their eagerness to accept Christ and to make their peace with God. Just as the meeting ended, the rain again came down in torrents and continued throughout the night.

The meeting the following night was in Cedar Rapids, but when Charles Fuller approached the auditorium there, he was alarmed to see long lines of people waiting to get in. He thought that somehow the building had not yet been opened for the meeting, but what had really happened was that through the grapevine, word of the miracle that had occurred in Waterloo the night before had reached Cedar Rapids. As a result, so many had come to the meeting place that it had already been filled for an hour. Again when the altar call was given that evening the response was immediate and large. Some who had reputations of being hardened sinners made their peace with God, and there was talk of the God of Elijah being at work in Iowa.

The success of these meetings in the summer of 1938 made it possible to increase to one hundred twenty stations in the fall, and so the program was well on its way to reaching the number needed by the end of the year in order to stay on the network. This latest increment of stations put the "Old Fashioned Revival Hour" on at least one station in every state in the nation, as well as across all the population belt of the southern part of Canada. But in September of that year the Mutual network added another thirty stations, and so it was obvious that the broadcast would have to continue adding stations during 1939 in order to hold its prime

Sunday evening time. "When this word came to me," Charles Fuller said,

> . . . I confess it almost took the heart out of me. I thought, "Our supporters have been sacrificing and doing their *very* best; I cannot ask them to undertake any more." But as I have continued to pray these words kept coming to me, "God is able," "God is able." This is as far as I get.

But the knowledge that God is able gave him faith to keep on scheduling meetings to gain the support necessary to expand to one hundred fifty-two stations by October, 1939. Plans were made for a heavy series of meetings the following May in Amarillo, Minneapolis, Boston, New York City, Louisville, Chicago, Grand Rapids, Philadelphia, and Washington, D.C.

Early in 1939, however, the doctor told Charles Fuller that he had a tired heart muscle. He would have to be relieved of the stress he had been under in maintaining a coast-to-coast broadcast on Sunday evenings. So he rented a house at Palm Springs and after each Sunday's broadcast drove out there alone. He took long walks in the sunshine and rested a great deal. For a while he doubted whether he could carry that heavy schedule of meetings in May. The following message appeared in the *Heart to Heart Talk* of February, 1939:

> I ask you dear friends to pray for my physical health. I have a wonderful constitution, and for years have carried a load of work that would have broken the average man. In the last fifteen months I have traveled about 60,000 miles by train, plane, auto, and boat—holding meetings—and God has given a rich harvest of souls. I had hoped to go East in May to meet the friends in Philadelphia, Boston, New York, and Washington, as well as in some of the smaller cities. But I am not sure that I shall be able to do this. A physical check-up recently showed an urgent need for slowing up and rest, and I am trying to get some rest each week. We do need your prayers both for physical strength and for this ministry.

Charles Fuller's health did improve sufficiently for him to take on the meetings scheduled for May, 1939. Eight thousand people crowded out Mechanics Hall in Boston for both an afternoon service and then for an evening service which originated the weekly broadcast. Just as my father was about to leave the building, he was stopped by a man who said that he had been a professional gambler. Two weeks before he had been in a gambling den. He had just made fifteen hundred dollars and was gathering up the gains of the day when he felt gripped by Charles Fuller's message which was playing in the room. Normally he would have turned it off, and his gambling friends wanted it off, but the songs he heard reminded him of his mother, who had sung them, and he listened to the sermon through to the end. He had become deeply convicted of sin and of his need for Christ to be his Savior. Right there in that gambling den he had accepted Christ, and pushing the fifteen hundred dollars he had won back across the table he said, "Boys, you can take it. I am through with all this." He had walked out, and now, two weeks later, he told Charles Fuller that he had started to live a new life and was confident that he would meet his mother in heaven.

The next Sunday evening the broadcast was to originate from New York. The New York World's Fair was just opening that week, and in conjunction with this fair the Christian Business Men's Committee was planning to hold services every night of the fair in the Calvary Baptist Church of New York City. They had planned that the meeting which originated this broadcast would also be the opening meeting of the summer-long series. But as the New York City meetings approached, Charles Fuller became convinced that Calvary Baptist Church would not be large enough to accommodate the numbers who were planning to attend. On his own initiative, he booked Carnegie Hall for that coming Sunday afternoon and evening. My mother had reached New York ahead of him, and she recorded in her diary their feelings when she met him at the Pennsylvania station:

Dad met Dan and me in the Penna. station. I knew he was discouraged. Offerings were very low at home for the radio work, and there was little cooperation here in New York City for the meetings. We had decided to rent Carnegie Hall. Would anyone come? We will surely have pulled a boner if our prediction of needing a larger auditorium is not fulfilled. We pay the $300 rent out of our own pocket.

That evening Charles and I went to prayer. *Daily Light* gave great comfort. It had been raining all day. We prayed for crowds, souls, peace with the brethren, and good offerings. Retired trusting God, Psalm 37:5.

Earlier that day my mother had written in her *Daily Light,* "Must we drop our Chicago station? And some other Mutual stations? What then? New York unfriendly. Rainy, homesick. But God. My strength fails—true."

My parents were staying across the Hudson in New Jersey at a friend's home, and my mother's diary continues in recounting how the next afternoon

. . . we drove along the Hudson River to Carnegie Hall. Would anyone come? At the door a surly guard said, "No room here, or on first balcony. Take the elevator way up." We went around to the stage door and saw that even the highest balcony was fast filling. Praise the Lord! The congregation sang "Only a Sinner Saved by Grace" and "There Is a Fountain Filled with Blood." The singing of the crowd accompanied by the great organ brought tears to our eyes. Charles spoke wonderfully. We shook hands afterwards for an hour or more. Someone gave me lilies of the valley.

My mother went onto the stage and I took the elevator up to the highest balcony to witness that afternoon meeting. People who remember my father's platform style know that one could never be quite sure what he would do next. During that service he said, "When a singer gets to sing in Carnegie Hall, he feels that he has arrived. Now here I am in Carnegie Hall, and I don't want to lose my opportunity to sing." So he asked the pianist to accompany him while he sang, "What can wash away my sins? Nothing but the blood of Jesus"—in all probability the first and last time anyone ever sang that as a solo there.

As crowds from that afternoon meeting subsided and we were about to leave, my parents were greatly encouraged to find that as early as 6:00 P.M. people were taking seats to be in readiness for the meeting that would originate the broadcast at 9:00 P.M. Many were turned away from Carnegie Hall, which was filled long before 9:00. An overflow meeting was hastily arranged in Calvary Baptist Church, the place that others had felt would be quite adequate for those attending Charles Fuller's New York City meetings. That evening my mother put the following note in her *Daily Light*: "Carnegie Hall filled twice. Souls. Power of God. Good weather. Praise God. Glorious answer."

Charles Fuller then flew west for ten days before returning to hold other meetings in Chicago, Louisville, Philadelphia, and Washington, D.C. From Washington he wrote:

The beloved hour is still going, and though things do look dark for our continuing, yet I am ready to fight on to the last ounce of my strength, and to pray in faith believing, that this valuable hour may not be handed over to commercial programs, but may be kept for the preaching of the old Gospel.

The difficult summer months were just ahead, with twenty more stations than the preceding summer to carry and with the knowledge that he must contract for thirty more by the first Sunday in October. But these meetings in the East had gained many new friends for the broadcast. Additional meetings that summer in Detroit, Winona Lake, Topeka, and finally at a mass rally at the World's Fair in San Francisco also gained more loyal supporters. Furthermore, that previous fall Charles G. Trumbull, editor of the *Sunday School Times,* had written an article about the "Old Fashioned Revival Hour" entitled "The Miracle Broadcast of America." One hundred thousand people read this paper twice a month. When Charles Trumbull endorsed the broadcast in such glowing terms, many hundreds of Christians were moved to join in support of this work which was reaching many millions each Sunday evening.

Thus because "God is able," and because He keeps His promise to do great and mighty things for those who simply call upon Him, the "Old Fashioned Revival Hour" took all one hundred fifty-two Mutual stations that fall of 1939 and so sustained its coast-to-coast broadcast in the heart of Sunday evening to at least ten million people.

7. The International Broadcast

CHARLES FULLER BROADCAST the Gospel continuously for almost thirty-eight years. Through the intercession of many thousands of prayer warriors, this radio ministry, begun in the Great Depression, has been heard coast-to-coast and internationally ever since 1937, despite the upheavals of World War II, the postwar recession, the Korean War, and then the gradual encroachment of television into the popularity that radio had been enjoying. That this preaching could go on for so long to such a vast audience is indeed remarkable, but even more so as we trace through some of the major battles and triumphs that were involved in broadcasting from 1939 until Charles Fuller's homegoing in 1968.

THE YEARS ON THE MUTUAL NETWORK

We have seen how the public meetings held during the summer of 1939 provided enough additional supporters for Charles Fuller to sign a contract for 152 stations starting in October, 1939. The following memo from Rudy Alber, the radio agent, indicates the prominent position which the broadcast now occupied:

Beginning with the first Sunday night in October [1939], the "Old Fashioned Revival Hour" will be using the facilities of 152 radio stations, which means the Gospel Broadcasting Association will have the largest single release of any radio broadcast in America. This means that the "Old Fashioned Revival Hour" has now topped such commercial broadcasts as Amos 'n' Andy, Texaco Corporation, Ford Symphony Hour, and other top-notch commercial broadcasts. This is truly a testimony to God's work, and He is certainly blessing the "Old Fashioned Revival Hour" in a wonderful way.

I might point out that on the Mutual network, which is directly connected by telephone lines, we are using 106 stations. The other 46 stations, while they will be releasing the broadcast the same night, are at a different time and are individually transcribed releases with the exception of the North Central Broadcasting network comprising 17 stations. Out of the 152 stations, therefore, 28 of them are individual releases, and the balance are by direct network.

137

The number of letters coming in during the fall of 1939 required the services of twelve full-time secretaries, four more than the year before.

But soon after the broadcast added these additional stations, there was an alarming drop in the offerings. Europe had just been plunged into war. America was still feeling the effects of the depression, and there was much uncertainty. An indication of the battle that Charles Fuller experienced during that time comes again from the pages of my mother's *Daily Light,* where on October 28, 1939, she wrote, "1 A.M. Charles so oppressed. Will the O.F.R.H. go under? Charles has gotten up to rewrite his message for tomorrow. Can't stand it, he says. Prayer. We have made mistakes. Satanic opposition. Offerings so low."

The burden weighed so heavily on Charles Fuller that his physician again ordered him to spend the weekdays of that winter and spring of 1939–40 at Palm Springs taking long walks in the sunshine. The plans for another round of meetings for New England in the spring of 1940 were canceled. But during these dark months Charles Fuller felt upheld by the intercession of the many prayer warriors and supporters who had been gathering around him for the past seven years and more. In the March, 1940, *Heart to Heart Talk* he had a word especially for the many elderly folk who prayed for the broadcast:

We have many radio friends who are on the sunset path of life, looking forward eagerly to an abundant entrance into the Heavenly Home, after long, busy lives of service on earth. Now this Heart to Heart Talk is for you!

It is hard for you to be set aside—many with the feeling of not being needed any more, and some of you, I know, are bedridden. As you have walked the rocky, thorny uphill paths of life you have learned to pray, and now so many of you pray daily for this ministry. I know because you have written us, and I've come to depend on your prayers. Sometimes when I feel a little bit discouraged I am strengthened as I remember the great band of faithful folks who are praying for me. God bless you everyone and may His presence be increasingly real and comforting to you, as you look forward to the day when you can be at home with the Lord.

The many prayers of God's people achieved a very specific and crucial result just at that time. The Mutual network continued to increase its number of stations, and again there was the question of whether to keep the Sunday evening hour as secure as possible by adding these newer Mutual stations. One day during March, 1940, as Charles Fuller had gone a short distance on his daily constitutional of a half dozen miles at Palm Springs, he suddenly felt a strong conviction to turn back and call his radio agent to come at once the one hundred miles from Los Angeles and confer with him about a matter that he believed God was laying heavily on his heart. When Rudy Alber arrived, my father told him he felt deeply convinced that he should immediately notify the management of the Mutual network that he would take all the remaining available stations on their network beginning with the first Sunday that next October, 1940. To Charles Fuller's surprise, Rudy Alber said he also had had the same conviction, but that he had been reluctant to speak about it because he knew how low the offerings had been.

"Go right back to Los Angeles," said Charles Fuller, "and send an airmail special delivery letter to the network at once, telling them what to do." Mr. Alber did so, and the next day the letter reached the Mutual management in New York City. That very morning the officials of the network had held a meeting in which they formulated the policy that anyone occupying the 9 to 10 P.M. hour Sunday evening, Eastern Standard Time, must take all the available stations all across the network if he wished to have this best time of the week. And then, before the meeting adjourned, the letter from Rudy Alber arrived! Since the Mutual network was experiencing such demand for this prime time, the "Old Fashioned Revival Hour" might well have lost this spot if the letter had come even a day or two later. But people were praying, and God had led His servant to take this specific action needed to stay on that coveted Sunday evening hour.

Thus with the contract with the Mutual network renewed for another year, the GBA was committed to raise offerings each week to support two hundred fifty-six radio stations beginning on the first Sunday of October, 1940, a gain of one hundred stations since the preceding year. But then more contributions to the broadcast began to come in, so that a year later the broadcast could be heard over three hundred forty-one stations, and then in the fall of 1942, over four hundred fifty-six stations. In 1941 there were twenty-three full-time secretaries to handle the mail. The office force had outgrown its old quarters and had now moved to a new building in Pasadena which had been specifically designed and built as a headquarters for the broadcast.

Why did Charles Fuller keep increasing his number of stations, so that by 1942 the "Old Fashioned Revival Hour" was by far the most widely heard broadcast in America? He no longer needed to take so many stations to keep his Sunday evening hour. For two years now he had been on every Mutual station, but even so, these accounted for a little more than half of his four hundred fifty-six outlets. He had gone on so many stations by 1942 because the amount of money contributed to support the broadcast had grown by that amount. As World War II increased in intensity in the spring of 1940 with the invasions of Norway, France, and Russia, as America's own young men began to be drafted in the fall of 1940, and then as America herself was plunged into war at Pearl Harbor and suffered such losses there and in the months following, people became more eager to help get the Gospel out than ever before or since. As they said good-by to loved ones whom they might well not see again, they came to put less value on material things and were seeking God more earnestly.

Charles Fuller, heard by millions right in the heart of each Sunday evening as he pleaded for the souls of men to a world-wide audience, stood as a symbol to many in those dark days of what had eternal value. The following excerpt from a column entitled "Washington Day by Day" appeared in three hundred newspapers in those war days and gives an idea of the impact the "Old Fashioned Revival Hour" was having:

In a world with war and crime writing the annals of greed and violence in the blood of countless victims, it is restful to hear an old-fashioned preacher preach old-time religion in the good old-fashioned way. Coming out of California every Sunday evening, this Gospel hour of the radio breaks through the din and clamor of swing-whoopee, croonings, and news broadcasts to almost startle a weary world with its unretouched truths.

This earnest, pleading Baptist preacher who exhorts a bizarre world in a manner simple and devoid of sophism is the Rev. Charles E. Fuller. His millions of devoted listeners contribute money for buying radio time on several hundred stations—a whole hour each week—indubitably a stupendous sum.

The radio sets of blasé Washingtonians pick Evangelist Fuller's soul-searching messages from the gentle autumn breezes that blow out of the night across the Potomac lush-lands and over the low-hung islands which dot historic Chesapeake Bay. The congregation's singing of such time-tried hymns as "There Is a Fountain Filled with Blood," "Let the Lower Lights Be Burning," and "Sweet Hour of Prayer," comes like a ground swell from a new and better world, and by the air waves reaches comforting hands across all the North American continent and to the islands of the sea, bringing the new-old story of religion to the weary heart not only here in sophisticated Washington but to mansions and hovels, homes and brothels, prisons and cocktail lounges the country over. It steals into rooms made restless by the unquiet slumber of sick life, hovers over the cabins in the cotton, and filters into the lumbermen's camps in the great North woods.

Because the "Old Fashioned Revival Hour" stood as such a symbol of hope in a war-torn, uncertain world, people's contributions to the GBA steadily increased from the fall of 1940 onwards until a peak was reached in 1944. We recall that Charles Fuller's consuming passion was to make it possible for everyone to have a chance to hear the Gospel, and so as more offerings came in, he used the money to buy more station time. Not content to be heard "live" just once on Sunday in America's population centers, he would buy two and even three more hour-long spots in such areas, so that people could hear a transcription of the broadcast before church in the morning, after church, late afternoon, and after church Sunday evenings.

To satisfy his consuming desire to get the Gospel out, Charles Fuller also tried to launch a Spanish version of the broadcast in the spring of 1941. He appointed a Spanish-speaking preacher and got Leland Green to assemble a group who could sing in Spanish. This broadcast was recorded and broadcast to Latin America over the General Electric shortwave station in Schenectady, New York. Twenty stations in Central and South America picked up this shortwave broadcast and rebroadcast it. But this venture had to be dropped after a few weeks because church leaders in those countries brought pressure on their local stations to stop relaying this Protestant broadcast.

As the war continued, the ministry of the broadcast became increasingly important to the many men who had recently gone into service and were now scattered far and wide. Many letters were now coming from servicemen in which they told how the "Old Fashioned Revival Hour" provided the spiritual continuity between their homes and their presently uprooted lives. Reports began to come in of Christian servicemen setting up "listening posts" in their barracks or on ships where the radio would be tuned to the "Old Fashioned Revival Hour" and room provided for men to stay and listen. Many were the letters which came from young men who heard the Gospel in these posts and were converted, blessed, and comforted in their homesickness and uncertain future.

Charles Fuller felt he should make a special effort to minister to these men. As letters came to his office from army camps and ships all over the world, he knew he had the potential of being a sort of clearing house whereby Christian servicemen could make contact with each other. As he learned of a certain strong Christian stationed on a ship or military installation, he could tell others writing from that base the names of that Christian and others with whom they could have fellowship. He also asked his radio audience to help by sending in names of servicemen, at various posts who could exercise Christian leadership or who needed it.

To help in this tremendous task, Charles Fuller called on Mr. Dawson Trotman, the founder of an organization called The Navigators. For about a decade Dawson Trotman had had a remarkable ministry among sailors whom he had contacted at the naval base near his home in Torrance, California. Not content simply to win men to Christ, he emphasized the importance of teaching a new Christian to depend on the teachings of God's Word, to pray, and to witness to others. He stressed that a Christian's purpose is to "know Christ and to make Him known" and to "reproduce reproducers." Thus when thousands of men began to enter the service in the winter of 1940–41, Dawson Trotman had a group of highly trained key men who were either stationed on ships and military bases or who were able to travel from base to base where they could help organize and strengthen groups of Christians.

Dawson Trotman had made a particular emphasis on the importance of memorizing Scripture. He had produced packets of memory verses and when someone had thoroughly memorized one set of verses, he was allowed to proceed, successively, to additional sets until he knew verses covering the essentials of the Christian life and the steps necessary to win others to Christ. He helped Charles Fuller by giving him names of key men in service installations who could nurture the Christians who wrote in to the broadcast. Charles Fuller in turn passed on the names of servicemen that he had learned of through his radio mail, and so these two had a partnership of ministering to military personnel.

To reach servicemen Charles Fuller also bought an hour's time on a 100,000-watt shortwave station in Iceland in the summer of 1942 so that the increasing number of troops in the British Isles could hear the Gospel. In the August *Heart to Heart Talk* he told his mailing list about this new outlet and said, "This station reaches England at an early evening hour, which is most desirable. Mothers, write your boys 'over there' to be listening for the 'Old Fashioned Revival Hour'!"

We have seen how Charles Fuller's health forced him to curtail the holding of public meetings after being at the San Francisco World's Fair in August, 1939. But by the fall of 1941 he had regained his strength sufficiently to hold rallies in various cities. Now that the program was more firmly supported, his purpose in holding these rallies was not only to keep people interested in the broadcast but also to understand better how his listeners were feeling and thinking during these dark days and thus be able to minister more adequately to their needs. In September, 1941, Rudy Atwood and the quartet accompanied him to hold a mass meeting in the War Memorial Opera House in San Francisco. Then in October there was the memorable meeting in the Boston Gardens where fifteen thousand people came on Sunday afternoon and seventeen thousand in the evening for the origination of the broadcast. One thousand churches sent delegates to these meetings. Mr. Allan C. Emery, the beloved Christian wool merchant, was the chairman of the meeting. Dr. F. Carlton Booth, who was later to be professor of evangelism at Fuller Seminary, was the song leader and director of the three-thousand-voice choir. Dr. Harold J. Ockenga, the pastor of Park Street Church, who would help Charles Fuller found a seminary in a few years, was on the platform and led in prayer.

In the afternoon meeting Charles Fuller said,

I don't know how many people I talk to on the radio. I'm not interested in figures—I'm interested in souls. Some people say I reach twenty million people. I don't know. All I know is that I preach the greatest message in the world. There may be greater orators, but nobody can preach a greater message, because I preach from the world's greatest Book.

We cover 90 percent of the globe. We get letters from New Zealand, India, England, the Far East, from Nova Scotia, and from Capetown, South Africa. We have discovered that "listening posts" have been established in the army camps where many of the soldiers gather to listen to the broadcast. I don't say this for myself. It is the old Gospel, the simple Gospel that pulls.

Then he introduced Mrs. Fuller. "I want you to meet the woman I call Honey." As she stepped up to the microphone he said, "Don't you think she's good-looking?" The audience laughed and applauded. Mrs. Fuller said that she knew the prayers of many in the auditorium were responsible for enabling her husband to bring God's message to a dying world.

Charles Fuller went on to tell how some commercial firms had tried to get his Sunday evening hour away from him by offering to pay for it thirteen weeks in advance. "I can only pay for it one week in advance because that's all the money I have." (So far Mutual was content to receive week-by-week payments.) Then he added that he considered every dollar given to him as part of a sacred trust and that not one cent would be spent for anything but the furtherance of the Word of God. "How many of you want to see a few more radio stations added to the radio hour hookup?" he asked. A large part of the audience raised their hands. "That's fine," said Charles Fuller. "That'll cost you each one dollar."

Then he again preached his sermon used in the Detroit Rally of 1938, "When I see the blood I will pass over you" (Exod. 12:13). "God's wrath will not reach to those who are trusting in Christ and His shed blood for the forgiveness of sins. God's wrath will pass over them. That's all that matters. The Bible doesn't say anything about passing over the homes of the rich, or the heads of corporations." Then he continued, "And oh, how beautiful is the picture of Him who passes over and withholds God's wrath because He bore God's wrath for your sin and for mine."

At the conclusion Charles Fuller gave the invitation for people to accept Christ. "If you want the joy of being a child of God simply by exercising faith in Jesus Christ, raise your hand. God bless you

144

down there. I see you, and God bless you. Oh, to have the blessed knowledge that your past sins are washed away. How about those in the first balcony? I see you. Raise your hands way up high. Show the Lord you mean business. I can't see all of you on account of the lights, but God bless you all. Any more up there? Yes, I see you. Thank God!" While the audience sang hymns, many came forward to be counseled regarding their newly found faith.

Similarly warm and well-attended meetings were held in the spring of 1942 in the Municipal Auditorium at St. Louis, in the Uline Ice Arena in Washington, D.C., at the New York State Fair Grounds, in Convention Hall in Philadelphia, and in the Cleveland Arena. The following excerpt from the St. Louis *Daily Globe-Democrat* gives some indication of the tone of those meetings:

Evangelist Fuller made no mention of the war, confining himself to a simple but eloquent plea for all to accept the teachings of the Divine Master and publicly acknowledge their faith in Jesus Christ.

But nevertheless the influence of the war on the minds and hearts of thousands in his audience was obvious and pronounced.

As young men in uniform stepped forward, handkerchiefs by the hundreds came into view, dabbing at the eyes of both old and young. Men of military age and many far beyond it, stared grimly ahead or took occasion to wipe their eyeglasses. When Evangelist Fuller called upon his audience to join in some of the better-known hymns, there was a burst of song which rocked the auditorium roof. The crowd was distinctly in the mood for religion and gave vent to its feelings without stint.

In the June, 1942, *Heart to Heart Talk* Charles Fuller commented on people's increased interest in spiritual things, which he had especially noticed from these meetings:

In the past seven months I have traveled something over twenty thousand miles preaching the Gospel, and I find that because of conditions in this war-weary and sin-sick old world that people are thinking more than ever of eternal things, and in the hearts of the unsaved there is a greater hunger and a greater openness to the Gospel than I have ever seen before. Another thing—the rubber shortage and gasoline rationing mean that more people are at home now with ears to the radio, *listening.* Oh friends, what a doubly rich opportunity God has given us to reach by radio, *just where they are,* our soldiers

145

and sailors, the unsaved, the indifferent people, and that great army of those who need the comfort of the Scriptures in these days.

Knowing that the number of stations carrying the "Old Fashioned Revival Hour" had reached the saturation point, Charles Fuller decided to put his Sunday morning broadcast of the "Pilgrim's Hour" also onto one hundred thirty-five stations of the Mutual network, so that he would be on two, hour-long, coast-to-coast broadcasts each Sunday. In the August, 1942, *Heart to Heart Talk* he explained:

Because the rubber and gasoline situation is keeping more people at home, we feel that the opportunity to reach a tremendously larger listening audience by radio cannot be overlooked. Therefore, arrangements have just been completed for the Pilgrim's Hour to be released on the Mutual network.

We have seen that after Charles Fuller left Calvary Church in 1933, he continued to broadcast Sunday mornings at 11 o'clock over the Long Beach radio station, KGER. Loyal friends in the Long Beach area packed themselves into the tiny second-floor studio over the Dobyns Footwear store in Long Beach, and then around 1935 they moved to the more spacious 250-seat Times Building Auditorium. Charles Fuller continued to broadcast this Sunday morning service over the single radio station KGER, even when his evening broadcast had become the largest single radio program in the United States. One might well ask why, when he had the heavy responsibility of a coast-to-coast broadcast on Sunday evenings, he would make a fifty-mile round trip to Long Beach each Sunday morning to hold a public service which was broadcast over only one local 5,000-watt station. The answer is that his Long Beach friends were his oldest and most loyal supporters, and preaching there and having fellowship with them on Sunday mornings gave him a lift which helped ready him to preach with greater boldness to the many millions who would hear him later on Sundays.

As he became better known because of his coast-to-coast broadcast, greater numbers of people began to crowd into the Times Building for this Sunday morning service. One of his most loyal supporters, Mr. George Workman, came to him one day with the suggestion that he move to the one-thousand-seat downstairs hall of the Long Beach Municipal Auditorium. Charles Fuller did not see how he could possibly fill that hall each Sunday and how the Long Beach people could raise the three hundred dollars rent such a meeting place would cost each month. George Workman, however, felt that the Municipal Auditorium, located on the waterfront and right next to the amusement park, was a much more strategic place for reaching the unsaved than the Times Building. War clouds were gathering and the greater numbers of lonely servicemen now walking up and down the pike offered a marvelous opportunity for evangelism. To back up his faith, George Workman presented Charles Fuller with a three-hundred-dollar check to cover the rent for the first month. The move was made, and in 1939 the first broadcast originated from the building where for the next nineteen years so many thousands would assemble Sunday after Sunday to be the visible audience for a broadcast reaching a vast unseen audience. George Workman's faith that one thousand seats could be filled each Sunday morning proved accurate. The servicemen also began coming to these broadcasts, and their presence established one of the prominent characteristics of the Long Beach meetings thereafter.

When the "Old Fashioned Revival Hour" went coast-to-coast in 1937, Charles Fuller began to call his Sunday morning broadcast over KGER the "Pilgrim's Hour," using again the title for the West Coast network broadcast that had failed after being on for only two months in 1931. While the "Old Fashioned Revival Hour" came on the air to the strains of "Jesus Saves," the theme song for the "Pilgrim's Hour" was "Guide Me, O Thou Great Jehovah, Pilgrim in a Barren Land." When the "Pilgrim's Hour" began to originate from the Municipal Auditorium, Charles Fuller called on Leland Green to help him with that broadcast also by assembling a male quartet and later a choir.

It was at the public broadcast of the "Pilgrim's Hour" on October 19, 1941, that Charles Fuller first used the song "Heavenly Sunshine," which was to become such a trademark of the "Old Fashioned Revival Hour." That was the Sunday after his meeting in the Boston Garden. While still in New England, he had had lunch with Mr. and Mrs. Cutler Whitwell. For the past two years this couple, as representatives of the "Old Fashioned Revival Hour," had been going into New England towns without a Gospel witness and holding evangelistic services, often opening up churches that had been closed and boarded up. Years before, Mr. Whitwell had been a prominent executive with the Standard Oil Company of California, but had felt led to resign that post and go out by faith to preach the Gospel. During the late 1920s he had been dean of men at Biola, and his wife Florence had taught Bible lessons for children each morning over KTBI. It was during this time that they had become close friends of the Fullers, and on this Monday noon in the fall of 1941, after the strenuous meetings in the Boston Garden the day before, these two couples were enjoying a time of fellowship together at Ye Old Oyster House in Boston. Mr. Whitwell was telling of the conferences he had been holding in New England, and he mentioned that he had found particular blessing in using the hymn "Heavenly Sunlight." The words of the chorus of that hymn by the Rev. H. J. Zelley are "Heavenly sunlight, heavenly sunlight,/Flooding my soul with glory divine;/Hallelujah! I am rejoicing,/Singing His praises, Jesus is mine." They sang the chorus for the Fullers, and Cutler Whitwell recorded in his diary that "Charles heard it and said, 'I want that for the "Old Fashioned Revival Hour".' I said, 'I'll send you the song book with it in it.' " As Charles Fuller drove up the Maine coast the next day that song kept ringing in his ears. But he did not have an accurate memory of the words and tune, so what he kept singing over to himself became his own version of Zelley's hymn.

That next Sunday morning at the broadcast of the "Pilgrim's Hour" he decided on the spur of the moment to see how "Heavenly Sunlight" would go over with his Long Beach friends. What came out was his version, which he called "Heavenly Sunshine," and it had the following words: "Heavenly Sunshine, Heavenly Sunshine/Flooding my soul with glory divine/ Heavenly Sunshine, Heavenly Sunshine/ Hallelujah, Jesus is Mine." The response from the Long Beach audience was so enthusiastic that he began to use the chorus Sunday after Sunday. And so it was that this chorus became a trademark for Charles Fuller's ministry. It should be mentioned that the copyright owners of Zelley's hymn generously allowed him to use and publish his own version of their song.

We have noted that the "Pilgrim's Hour" went onto one

hundred thirty-five stations of the Mutual network at noon on Sundays out of response to the markedly increased interest in spiritual things which Charles Fuller and many others were noticing during that dark year of 1942. But the increase in giving which made this possible in 1942 continued to grow during the fall months of that year. Consequently he took another step to blanket America with the Gospel. He contracted with the Mutual network to rebroadcast the "Old Fashioned Revival Hour" over one hundred thirty-five of its affiliates late Sunday evenings so that war-workers coming off the swing shift could still hear the broadcast. This arrangement continued until May, 1944, and so for seventeen months Charles Fuller was broadcasting three hours each Sunday over the coast-to-coast Mutual network. By computing the station count on the basis of the number of times that either the "Pilgrim's Hour" or the "Old Fashioned Revival Hour" were heard on each station that carried them, he was on over one thousand stations during these months at a cost of around thirty-five thousand dollars a week. According to *Advertising Age,* January 24, 1944, the total amount of money the GBA paid just to the Mutual network during 1943 was $1,566,130, one and one-half times more than the runner-up, a secular company, paid for its broadcasts on that network.

It should be emphasized that the money to support the broadcast week by week did not come chiefly from a few large donors. It came instead from the small offerings of many thousands of people. People gave in that year as they have never given since, because there was, as we have seen, an acknowledged religious awakening in America. In May, 1943, *Coronet* magazine published an article entitled "America Goes Back to Church," which said in part:

If you're inclined to wager that America's largest radio audiences tune in on Charlie McCarthy or Bob Hope, ignore your hunch and save your money.

For while these comedians are indeed aces of the air, a couple of preachers operating on shoestring budgets are giving them a run for their money. These men of faith number the stations over which they broadcast by the hundreds—their followers, by the tens of millions.

They are Walter A. Maier of St. Louis . . . and Charles E. Fuller of Los Angeles. Their broadcasts find outlet over some four hundred stations and are supported entirely by listener contributions.

Maier preaches on the National Lutheran Hour, which can be heard every Sunday afternoon over 434 stations.

Fuller is the founding father of the "Old Time Revival Hour," which has so many outlets there probably isn't a radio set anywhere in the United States which can't pick up his hymn-singing and sermons on Sunday nights.

It was indeed the small, and often sacrificial, gifts of many people which made such broadcasts possible during 1943. An example of this which so impressed Charles Fuller was that of a very poor woman who lived in the Pecos region of Texas where she and her family eked out a bare existence through dry farming. She had enjoyed the "Old Fashioned Revival Hour" for years and wanted very much to send a contribution for its support. She had no money to send, but one Sunday afternoon after listening to the broadcast she got down on her knees and prayed that God would provide some means, however small, which she might send in as an expression of gratitude to God for the blessing the broadcast had been to her. A wind storm was then raging, and looking out the window she saw something fluttering in the breeze which looked like more than a mere torn piece of paper. She went out, picked it up, and discovered that it was a dollar bill which had been embedded in the clay formation of that region but which the wind had loosened. Thanking God for the answer to her prayer, she sent the dollar with a short note on butcher paper telling of her experience. When Charles Fuller received this, he exchanged her dollar bill for one of his own and carried her dollar bill in his wallet for the rest of his life. He often showed it to audiences in public meetings and estimated that over the years fifty thousand dollars had been given out of the inspiration that it provided.

The following letter is also a sample of how people so loved the broadcast that they were willing to sacrifice to help support it:

Dear Rev. Fuller,

I prayed God to provide some way so that I could have a little part in the "Old Fashioned Revival Hour" which I love so much. I knew that we had one crate of berries sold, but how could I get the rest to make up the $2.00 I wanted to send? But today someone came and wanted some berries, so he took four crates. I am sure that if I did not love the "Old Fashioned Revival Hour," I could not have gotten out in the hot sun and worked to pick those berries, but I did. Finally I gave out, but the man helped finish the job. How thankful I am I can have a part in this glorious spreading of the Gospel which means so much to us.

The increased giving of 1943 which was used to buy more station time did achieve the desired results, for in the April, 1943, *Heart to Heart Talk* Charles Fuller was happy to announce that "reports of conversions continue to pour in in greater numbers than ever before, for which we do praise God. This is the result of your faithfulness in prayer and support."

DIFFICULTIES FOR EVANGELICAL BROADCASTERS

While great gains were being registered for the "Old Fashioned Revival Hour" during 1942–43, storm clouds of opposition from the Liberals were beginning to gather on the horizon. The July, 1942, *Heart to Heart Talk* gave the first indication of this:

At this time the "Old Fashioned Revival Hour" needs the prayers of its friends, for serious problems have arisen. There is now organized opposition to all Fundamental radio programs in the United States, and this organization is bringing pressure to bear on the radio stations, asking them to refuse time to all religious programs which are not approved by a committee (though these programs are paying for their time). They plan later to have time given free of charge for approved religious programs, and the "Old Fashioned Revival Hour" would not be on that approved list! Why? Because the hour is Fundamental and too evangelistic in its teaching. This is a powerful organization, and what a tragedy it would be if it could accomplish the ends which it is now trying to attain! So we ask all our friends to pray regarding this matter, that God will undertake to frustrate these plans.

For some time a conference called "The Institute for Education by Radio" had met annually to grapple with the problem of how radio, with its vast potential to mold public opinion, should conduct itself in a democratic society. When Fundamentalist programs like the "Old Fashioned Revival Hour" and the "Pilgrim's Hour" were heard three hours coast-to-coast each Sunday and had a greater

151

listening audience than either Charlie McCarthy or Bob Hope, some feared that radio was giving Fundamentalism a much greater chance to influence public opinion than it deserved. Thus in May, 1941, this conference formed a committee to work at drafting certain recommendations for changes in policy for religious broadcasts. Of the five recommendations presented at its May, 1942, conference, the first and third would have sounded the death knell for evangelical broadcasts like the "Old Fashioned Revival Hour." The first recommendation was "that religious radio programs, received in the homes of individuals of different religious faiths, should be addressed to a cross-section of the public—to Protestants, Catholics, Jews, and nonbelievers—and not to members of any one faith." The third was "that the broadcasting of religious programs should be provided by radio stations in keeping with their responsibility to serve 'the public interest, convenience, and necessity.' Religious programs, like educational broadcasts, should be presented on a sustaining basis, without payment for time."

The National Broadcasting Company and the Columbia Broadcasting System had been adhering to such policies for some time. They had opened a few half-hour spots during the daylight hours on Sunday for certain very prominent Protestant, Catholic, and Jewish spokesmen to conduct religious broadcasts. For example, Bishop Fulton J. Sheen had represented the Catholics and Harry Emerson Fosdick had been speaking coast-to-coast since 1929 to represent Protestants. While the particular convictions of such men could be detected in their radio messages, they did not try to convert their hearers with the fiery zeal and outspokenness of a Charles Fuller. In May, 1938, the fifteenth anniversary of the beginning of the first continuing religious broadcast,[1] Ralph Sockman and Daniel Poling joined with Harry Emerson Fosdick for a memorial

---

[1] The credit for the first broadcast could well go to D. L. Moody, who along with Ira Sankey in 1876 transmitted a religious service over Alexander Graham Bell's newly invented telephone. The first wireless transmission of a religious service was on January 2, 1921, when the first licensed commercial radio station, Pittsburgh's KDKA, broadcast the worship service of the Calvary Episcopal Church. To Paul Rader, the evangelist who had such an influence on Charles Fuller, goes the credit for being the first one to sense the opportunity radio provided for evangelism. From June 17, 1922, onwards, Paul Rader and a brass quartet kept moving between several of Chicago's radio stations preaching and playing whenever a vacant spot of

broadcast during which Fosdick said, "Whatever may be the future uncertainties, it is sure that we have an opportunity in religion on the air to make an incalculable contribution that will outflank, overpass, and undercut sectarianism in religion." By "sectarianism" Fosdick meant a particular set of religious beliefs that would be espoused by only one of the many different religious groups in America. Charles Fuller's biblical message of salvation by faith in Christ's shed blood alone was surely an example of what Fosdick meant. Charles M. Crowe, writing in the *Christian Century,* expressed the same sentiment when he declared, "The 'Old Fashioned Revival Hour,' the 'Pilgrim's Hour,' the 'Haven of Rest,' and others of the same stripe have long been distasteful to liberal church leaders . . ."[2] Crowe wanted religion on radio to be presented by programs "with the counsel of an interfaith advisory committee, rather than any denominational or federated church group. . . . They must be warmly human, down-to-earth, realistic, sincere, artistic, broadminded, non-sectarian, non-controversial."[3]

The National Broadcasting Company and the Columbia Broadcasting System, in fulfilling their responsibility to serve "the public interest, convenience, and necessity," had looked to the Federal Council of Churches, as the representatives of Protestantism in America, to nominate the ministers who should speak during the half-hour spots which they made available on a sustaining basis. The federal council had recommended Harry Emerson Fosdick and Ralph Sockman, and so over the years Liberalism received millions of dollars worth of free radio time to set forth its teachings coast-to-coast, while those representing biblical Christianity had received nothing. It seems clear that the vast power and prestige of the Federal Council of Churches was in support of the two recommendations set before the Institute of Education by Radio in the spring of 1942.

---

time would be offered to them. But it was the Calvary Baptist Church of New York City that first broadcast its church service regularly over its own radio station, WQAQ, beginning March 4, 1923. Barry C. Siedell, *Gospel Radio* (Lincoln, Nebraska: Back to the Bible Broadcast, 1971), pp. 49, 57, 61 ff.

[2] Charles M. Crowe, "Religion on the Air," *The Christian Century* (August 23, 1944), p. 973.

[3] Ibid., p. 975.

It was just at this time that the National Association of Evangelicals had been organized by Bible-believing churches and Christians from a large number of denominations. Dr. Harold J. Ockenga, the first president of the NAE, appointed Dr. J. Elwin Wright to head a delegation to attend the 1942 Institute for Education by Radio to speak for the millions of evangelical Protestants who were not being represented at all by the Federal Council of Churches. Their desires had not been reflected in the ministers the federal council had chosen to use free coast-to-coast radio time made available by NBC and CBS, and now this same federal council was behind recommendations which would even ban evangelical radio preaching that had been paying its own way.

The Elwin Wright delegation succeeded in killing the recommendation that religious radio should refrain from preaching specific beliefs. However, the recommendation that religious broadcasts should not appeal for funds but should have certain free radio times given them could not be defeated. This recommendation was then passed on to the networks and radio stations of America, and this was the cause for the note of alarm that appeared in the July, 1942, *Heart to Heart Talk*.

The passing of this recommendation put considerable pressure on the Mutual network to follow the other networks in banning all paid-for religious broadcasting. For Mutual to have programs on its schedule that powerful organs like the *Christian Century* and the Federal Council of Churches regarded as outlets for sectarian and controversial points of view obviously detracted from its public image. Then, too, the *Christian Century* darkly suggested that some evangelical broadcasters were not overly scrupulous in the way they handled the large sums of money they were receiving to pay for their coast-to-coast time spots. While discounting the magazine *Variety's* claim that religion was such "Big Biz" for radio that the one hundred or so religious radio programs paid $200,000,000 a year for their time, the *Christian Century* nevertheless declared in an editorial that

. . . so much of this flood of contribution does not, after all, roll into "church coffers" but goes into the pockets of individuals and irresponsible exhorters, free-lance evangelists, and independent peddlers of spiritual nostrums who have no more "church" behind them than a microphone with which to send forth their appeals and a post office box in which to receive their proceeds.[4]

A few months later Charles Crowe wrote that "the network religious radio program racket, capitalized by independent superfundamentalist revivalists, will not be eliminated until Mutual goes the whole way and bans paid religious programs altogether, as other networks have done."[5]

Indeed, there may have been religious broadcasters who were not fully scrupulous in handling contributions, but Charles Fuller was above reproach. Ninety percent of the contributions that came into the GBA went to pay for radio time. From the remaining 10 percent came Charles Fuller's salary, the salaries of the thirty or so clerical workers, the cost of postage, mailing, and the upkeep of the office building, equipment, and so forth.

Jealousy may also have played a part in Liberalism's criticisms of evangelical radio broadcasters. The Liberal radio preachers were not popular enough to stay on the radio by paying their own way. Thus Charles Crowe complained that

. . . in spite of the fact that radio affords the most powerful medium of mass influence in history, with opportunity to reach a vast, heterogeneous audience untouched by conventional church activities, its use by religious leaders has been lamentably unintelligent and ineffective. . . . Regardless of how popular the preacher may be, these programs often lack the common touch, the dramatic, mass appeal which is the genius of radio.[6]

Naturally he was speaking here of the Liberal broadcasters, for such criticisms certainly did not apply to evangelical broadcasters like Walter Maier, Percy Crawford, Paul Myers (First Mate Bob), M. R. De Haan, Charles Fuller, Theodore Epp, and others. God had enabled these men to adapt the preaching of the Gospel to the particular opportunity radio afforded so well that masses of people were blessed enough to pay to keep such programs on the air week by week the year around. But if enough people liked these programs

---

[4] "Religious Broadcasting Needs a Check-up," *The Christian Century* (December 15, 1943), pp. 1461 f.
[5] Crowe, op. cit., p. 973.
[6] Crowe, op. cit., p. 974.

to support them, then should they not have been allowed to continue paying their way in a free society?

The Mutual network was very sensitive to the arguments, pro and con, for keeping the "Old Fashioned Revival Hour" and the "Pilgrim's Hour" on. But the economics of the situation was what finally prevailed. On the one hand, they could not well afford to give up all their paid-for religious broadcasts, for during 1943 these brought in about $3,300,000, or 25 percent of Mutual's gross income. On the other hand, Mutual felt that in order to be competitive with the other three networks, it should now ban paid-for religious broadcasts from the prime times of Sunday evening and afternoon. Sponsors of commercial broadcasts on Sunday evening complained that a time spot following the "Old Fashioned Revival Hour" did not have the audience on the Mutual network that it would have on NBC or CBS because only religiously inclined people would, in the main, be tuned to a Mutual station at the beginning of such a time spot.

Mutual's decision, then, was to allow paid-for religious broadcasts only on Sunday mornings. In this way it would still receive some income from its religious broadcasters, but now during any of its prime Sunday evening and afternoon time spots it would be as competitive as the other networks for a broad range of listening audience. The Mutual network reached this decision in the fall of 1943 and informed Charles Fuller that after the middle of September, 1944, he could no longer have his hour in the heart of Sunday evening. It gave him first choice for a half-hour spot for the "Old Fashioned Revival Hour" or the "Pilgrim's Hour" on Sunday morning.

It was then that Charles Fuller made the crucial and far-reaching decision to reduce the "Pilgrim's Hour" to a half-hour broadcast that would originate "live" from the Mutual studios in Hollywood at the 9 A.M. PST spot. As for the "Old Fashioned Revival Hour," rather than keeping it on Mutual by paring it down to a half-hour, he decided to maintain his carefully developed and proven format for a sixty-minute broadcast. So he instructed Rudy Alber, his radio agent, to negotiate with independent stations for hour-long spots on Sunday afternoons and evenings. No longer having a network to carry his program live, he sent to these independent stations recordings which would be played at whatever time spot had become available.

Indeed, Charles Fuller felt keenly the loss of going off the prime Sunday evening time on the Mutual network which he had enjoyed for seven years. Yet this shift did yield one very positive compensation. All the time he was on the Mutual network, the "Old Fashioned Revival Hour" originated from a studio, first in Los Angeles and then in Hollywood, which could never seat more than two hundred people. My task was to be an usher who would make sure that every last seat was filled from the large numbers of people who would line up outside the studio each Sunday, hoping to be able to witness a broadcast. When every last seat was filled, those still in line would be shunted over to an adjoining studio. Mr. and Mrs. Fuller would come in to greet these people, but they could only hear the broadcast over a loudspeaker.

But now that the broadcast of the "Old Fashioned Revival Hour" would soon be off the Mutual network, Charles Fuller decided to remedy this situation by originating the broadcast from the Municipal Auditorium in Long Beach, the place where he had been broadcasting the "Pilgrim's Hour." This building not only had the one-thousand-seat auditorium downstairs but also a five-thousand-seat auditorium upstairs, and so here there would never be any problem of providing enough room for people who wanted to attend. In fact, people could now be actively encouraged to attend a broadcast whenever they visited Southern California.

One of Charles Fuller's great characteristics was to see how positive benefits could be realized out of apparently adverse situations and then to act decisively in a bold and imaginative way. So, not long after Mutual told him he could no longer have the Sunday evening hour, he announced that the public meetings of the "Pilgrim's Hour" at Long Beach would end in May, 1944, and in their place, from four to five each Sunday afternoon, there would be a public meeting in which the "Old Fashioned Revival Hour" would originate. By that time Rudy Alber, his radio agent, had been able to contract for a number of hour-long spots on good stations across the country. He had even been able to put together a network of a number of independent stations up the Pacific Coast and through Idaho and Montana that would carry the "Old Fashioned Revival Hour" "live" from 4 to 5 P.M. on Sundays.

Consequently, four months before going off the Sunday evening hour on Mutual, the "Old Fashioned Revival Hour" started being heard on a new set of stations at new times. In this way the transition from the Mutual network to times on independent stations would not be so abrupt and a greater portion of the listening audience would not lose the program. This transition period provided time to advertise the new stations and times and also to encourage people to attend the broadcast as it now originated from the Long Beach Municipal Auditorium. In the June, 1944, *Heart to Heart Talk* Charles Fuller said,

> The "Old Fashioned Revival Hour" is now being released at 4:00 P.M. Pacific War Time each Sunday from the upper hall of the Municipal Auditorium at the end of American Avenue in Long Beach, California. Here the broadcasting facilities are excellent and there are five thousand seats, so when you make your next trip to California, be sure to save Sunday afternoon for a visit to the broadcast, where you will receive a warm welcome. We are so thankful that we have been able to combine the special features of both broadcasts[7] in one, for we have not only our fine quartet with "Rudy" at the piano, and our able director, Mr. H. Leland Green, with a large chorus, but Mr. George Broadbent will be at the organ as usual, and Mrs. Fuller will be reading the letters which so many are glad to hear. We are having a fine musical program each Sunday beginning at 3:30—a half hour before we go on the air, so when you come be sure to be in your seat by half past three.

When the "Old Fashioned Revival Hour" moved to Long Beach, the half-hour version of the "Pilgrim's Hour" moved to a Mutual studio in Hollywood, where it now originated at nine o'clock on Sunday mornings. For years Charles Fuller had depended on this morning broadcast and especially the visible audience of loyal supporters to inspire him for the "Old Fashioned Revival Hour" later in the day. But now these friends were attending the afternoon broadcast of the "Old Fashioned Revival Hour" at Long Beach, and he missed their presence for his morning broadcast. In fact, the only visible audience he had for the broadcast of the "Pilgrim's Hour" from the lonely Mutual Broadcasting studio in Hollywood was Rudy Atwood and the faithful quartet, who provided the music for that program.

Producing the "Pilgrim's Hour" now drained energies that could have been used better for the afternoon broadcast. Nevertheless he

---

[7] I.e., the "Pilgrim's Hour" and the "Old Fashioned Revival Hour."

kept up this half-hour broadcast "live" on the Mutual network Sunday mornings for three years because he wanted to keep his foot in the door in the hope that Mutual might change its policy back to where he could at least have an hour-long afternoon spot on this network. But Mutual did not change its policy, and Charles Fuller dropped the "Pilgrim's Hour" entirely at the end of 1947. For his remaining twenty-one years he originated only one broadcast on Sundays.

The Broadcast from Long Beach

Times were difficult for the "Old Fashioned Revival Hour" in the fall of 1944 after it had broadcast for the last time on the Mutual network. To be sure, the program had been aired for four months on a large number of the independent stations by which it would henceforth carry on as a coast-to-coast broadcast, but even so, many people wrote in that fall complaining that they could no longer find the broadcast. The November, 1944, *Heart to Heart Talk* told the listeners how they could help:

If the "Old Fashioned Revival Hour" is not being as clearly heard in your locality as before, will you please let us know, and be sure to tell us the station over which you are trying to hear it? It is our desire to give all our friends the best possible service, and in reaching you clearly we will also be able to reach the unsaved better. Do continue to pray much as we work toward extending our network coast-to-coast. This network is not yet complete, but we trust that in the near future it will be heard clearly across the land.

Rudy Alber was working marathon hours negotiating with stations far and near so that the "Old Fashioned Revival Hour" could again have good time spots and cover all areas. The situation did gradually improve as each week new stations were added and old listeners learned where they could now find the program. Then, too, it soon became evident that retaining the broadcast's hour-long format by going on independent stations had been a wise decision because there was only a slight dip in the number of letters that came in that next year. Likewise the decision to originate the broadcast from the Long Beach Auditorium was wise because it led to an improvement in the quality of the program.

Servicemen talk with a good friend after Long Beach meeting.

With two of the faithful ushers at the Municipal Auditorium, R. W. Cooper (left) and Walter Herring (right).

Quartet members John Lundberg, Jack Coleman, and Art Jaissle "join in" as Charles Fuller sings "Meet Me There," at public broadcast at Long Beach.

Above: *Municipal Auditorium on the ocean front at Long Beach, California, where broadcast originated every Sunday for almost twenty years.* **Middle:** *Dr. Fuller gives invitation at close of the broadcast as counselors assemble in front of platform.* **Below:** *Audience at broadcast of "Old Fashioned Revival Hour" at Long Beach.*

Now there were about thirty-five hundred people attending the broadcast every Sunday, in comparison to the mere two hundred who had packed themselves in to the previous studio broadcasts. As this larger group came together, a spirit of enthusiasm and anticipation was generated which helped both singers and speaker to do their best. While Charles Fuller found it very difficult to counsel with individuals, he came fully into his own on a platform before a large audience. This large visible audience in Long Beach aided him greatly to communicate more effectively to the vast unseen radio audience. The Long Beach Auditorium was where he had been originating the Sunday morning broadcasts of the "Pilgrim's Hour," which were so characterized by a spirit of spontaneity and informality, and Charles Fuller now injected more of this spirit into the "Old Fashioned Revival Hour" broadcast than he had felt free to do back in the Mutual studio.

People began to assemble for the broadcast at Long Beach an hour or more before it actually was aired. Leland Green and his thirty choir members, Rudy Atwood, and the organist, George Broadbent, would commence rehearsal at 2:30 P.M., and people loved to come early to watch that. Rudy Atwood's back was at an angle to the audience so that while he could watch Leland Green direct the choir, the audience could watch his fingers fly up and down the keyboard. Then about fifteen minutes before broadcast time Charles and Grace Fuller would come out onto the platform to get acquainted with the people. He would ask all those who were there for the first time to raise their hands, and then he would ask them to call out the states and countries they were from. As he was able to distinguish various places from the ensuing babble, Charles Fuller would repeat, "Arizona, Georgia, Maine, Panama, England," with the result that people got a sense of how they were indeed about to engage in a service extending throughout the world. Then he would have them practice the hymn they would all sing during the broadcast. Broadcast time was now approaching, but just before the red light flashed on, Charles Fuller led the Long Beach audience in prayer for God's blessing on the forthcoming hour.

Soon after the broadcast commenced, the audience would stand and sing the chorus "Heavenly Sunshine" as they turned around and shook hands. Later they would sing "Sweet Hour of Prayer" or "What a Friend We Have in Jesus." A wonderful spirit of prayer

162

prevailed as Charles Fuller then asked God to comfort the lonely and brokenhearted and to bring people to salvation through Christ.

Then, never to be forgotten, were the public invitations to accept Christ which now could be given during the last three or four minutes of the broadcast, while the choir sang "Just as I Am" or "Softly and Tenderly Jesus Is Calling." It was indeed remarkable that during the next thirteen and a half years that the broadcast originated from Long Beach, there was never a Sunday when Charles Fuller did not have a number responding to the invitation to accept Christ. These were invited to come forward after the program was off the air, and a group of counselors, several of whom had been Charles Fuller's loyal supporters at Long Beach for years, talked with the inquirers and helped them find Christ.

Several large military installations were nearby, and since there was an amusement park next door to the auditorium, there were always numbers of servicemen strolling along the walkway in front of the auditorium. Some of the faithful co-workers would circulate among these service people and give them flyers inviting them to attend a world-wide broadcast which would soon originate right there on the ocean front. The Christian Service Center in Long Beach, manned by Dawson Trotman's Navigators, also brought groups of servicemen to the broadcast each Sunday. The ushers reserved two hundred and fifty seats right at the front of the auditorium for service personnel. Before the broadcast went on the air, opportunity was given for Christian servicemen to give a short testimony. Something of the spirit of those war days still comes through from the May, 1945, *Heart to Heart Talk* in which Charles Fuller said,

It would cause you to rejoice to see from ten to twenty men and women from different branches, and from all ranks of the service, jump to their feet and line up before the loud-speakers to tell that great audience what God has done for them. There are waves of applause as men with service ribbons showing action on all fronts tell of God's keeping and sustaining power. . . . One sergeant shaking with nervousness said it was harder for him to face that audience than to face enemy fire, but he just *had* to say a word for Christ who had saved his soul and who had stood right by him through the worst that the enemy could give.

163

Many a serviceman found Christ at the public broadcast at the Long Beach Auditorium during those closing days of World War II and also during the Korean War a few years later. The following letters provide two examples:

Dear Dr. Fuller,

We have listened to the "Old Fashioned Revival Hour" for years and have been strengthened in our faith and often comforted by the program. But especially do we love it now, for our marine son, stationed out there in California, attended your Sunday service two weeks ago and went to the altar and there accepted Christ as Savior. We had prayed for him so long, and you can imagine how happy we were to have the answer to our prayers. We were listening alone that day, and though we did not know that our son was there, yet we felt especially impressed by some of the songs. Our son called us by telephone late that night, and gave a real earnest testimony and was very happy. How wonderful is radio, that we out here on the prairies of Dakota, could hear the same service that led our soldier-son to Christ away out there in California!

Dear Bro. Fuller,

When I've been listening and hear you ask for hands for prayer, and then hear you say, "God bless you, soldier boy, God bless you, sailor lad," I would think of how happy I would be if that were one of my boys.

Last May my oldest son—in the Navy—was sent to Long Beach, and his ship docked there for a long time. He wrote me he would be there in your service July 18. I had been praying for him for so long, but then I began to plead with God for his soul. On July 18 I fasted and prayed, and he wrote me on July 19 how good it was to be there and that never before had he had quite such feelings in a service. I still prayed. On Sunday August 1 he wrote me he had gone to your service and that day had gone forward and made his surrender to God. I only wish you could see the letters I get from him now! I can tell he is really a new creature in Christ Jesus. . . . He is still at Long Beach. Every time he can he goes to your services and they mean so much to him.

Many servicemen also found Christ or were helped spiritually as they heard the broadcast in various parts of the world. A serviceman stationed in Miami during World War II wrote,

Dear Bro. Fuller,

Your program has just gone off the air, and I can say I really enjoyed every moment of it. I have listened to you under almost every circumstance in the last three years. I have been in your studio at least a dozen times, have had the car radio on while traveling cross-country, and in the last year since I have been in the navy I have heard your program in almost every part of the world.

One program some months ago I shall never forget as long as I remember anything. We were sailing on a large troop transport ship in the Southwest Pacific. Everything was very calm, and your program had just come on the air. The men were listening very quietly, when all of a sudden the bell rang out for manning our battle stations. In the rush the radio coming over the loud-speaker system was not completely turned off. My battle station was directly under one of the loud-speakers connected to the radio, and very faintly I could hear your choir singing. In a very short time antiaircraft guns began their barking, and for about five minutes (which seemed like ages) my mind was drawn from your program to combat with the enemy, and I forgot it completely. But when the roar of the guns ceased, I stood quietly and then I heard the quartet singing, very softly and plainly, "Take Time to Be Holy." An instant later, someone turned the radio up so it came on again loud and clear over the loud-speakers in the ship, and instead of the usual loud discussion of the attack by all hands, everything was just as quiet as if we had been right in the studio with you. Immediately after your program the chaplain gave a five-minute talk to the men, and several gave their hearts to Christ. Some of these men are in eternity now, and how thankful we are they are spending eternity with Christ. It may interest you to know that my father is a minister of the same Gospel which you preach.

A similar event occurred during the Korean War. The cruiser St. Paul was standing along the firing line off the coast of Korea. It was Sunday, and although the ship's guns were relatively silent, every one of the thousand men aboard was at his battle station. This posed a problem for the chaplain, for no services could be held that Sunday. For purposes of morale, several of the armed services radio shows were piped through the loud-speaker system. These were largely musical excerpts from well-known stateside radio shows. But suddenly an idea occurred to the chaplain. A quick word with the captain, together with a hurried trip to the radio shack, and precisely at 1600 hours (4 P.M.) a voice cracked through the loud-

165

speakers: "Now hear this. During the next hour you will hear the only church service that it is possible to bring you today." There followed a spirited singing of "Jesus Saves" by the Old Fashioned Revival Hour Choir. In the wardroom, on the bridge, all over that ship, even down in the powder magazines came the message of Christ and His power to save.

Here is how a lady in the Women's Auxiliary Corps came to find Christ through the broadcast from Long Beach. In 1949 she wrote,

This is a few lines to let you know that it was just five years ago this month that I tuned in accidentally to your program while waiting in the city of Detroit, Michigan, to be called into active duty in the Women's Auxiliary Corps. That night what you said about eternal judgment and hell didn't suit me, and I promptly switched the dial. However, the next Sunday night I tuned again just to hear the music and singing, thinking to turn the dial when you started to preach; but when I tuned in Mrs. Fuller was reading the letters. I heard her say, "Rev. Fuller does not tell people what they always want to hear, but he tells them the truth." So I listened on while you preached on the first chapter of Romans. Never in all my life had I heard such a sermon. Every false foundation was swept away from under me, and I was completely changed.

Upon going home on my first furlough I found that my family had been converted through your broadcast. That first Sunday I came home on furlough I found my home a transformed place. Now the "Old Fashioned Revival Hour's" music was heard, whereas before all religious music had been strictly banned. As you prayed during our meal, Bro. Fuller, my father and mother bowed their heads and prayed with you. Shortly after this my elderly aunt became interested in your program, and she also got soundly converted. She fired so many questions at me about the Bible that I became aware of my lack of knowledge of things spiritual, and so I decided to quit the army and attend Bible school. Just now I am here on the Pacific Coast doing preparatory work prior to going to China to take up orphanage work in Hong Kong. Oh, I know of so many people who have been saved listening to your broadcast I couldn't begin to mention them all.

After World War II, the difficulty of retooling American industry to produce peacetime goods provided the broadcast with an unusual opportunity for acquiring better time spots on stations with greater coverage. By the fall of 1946 the demand for goods was still far greater than the supply, and naturally there was little point in spend-

166

ing money to advertise products that could not be supplied in any adequate quantity. Thus it was easier for the "Old Fashioned Revival Hour" to get better station times. In the October, 1946, *Heart to Heart Talk* Charles Fuller said,

Commercial programs are giving up much radio time because they cannot deliver merchandise. This gives great opportunity to get better hours on the radio, and we are doing considerable shifting. Also there are some very desirable stations now available, which have been closed to us.

A month later, he reported that he had two hundred and fifty offers for station time.

Then, too, as countries overseas began to rebuild themselves, radio transmitters were constructed which opened new doors to radio evangelism. The most important of these for the "Old Fashioned Revival Hour" was Radio Luxembourg in Europe. This powerful station was clearly heard in the British Isles. British radio itself was entirely controlled by the government, which opened up only one or two hours a week for religious programs conducted by the Church of England. But now Radio Luxembourg enabled the "Old Fashioned Revival Hour" to be heard clearly in England, Ireland, and Scotland from eleven to twelve Thursday evenings.

At first the radio station's surveys estimated that 450,000 people in the British Isles were listening at that time. By 1957 they estimated that the figure had almost doubled. Something of the British people's hunger for God's Word can be sensed from the following letter from Yorkshire in June, 1957:

Dear Brother Fuller,

How lovely and fresh it is to tune into Luxembourg every Thursday evening and listen to one who still believes that the *whole* Bible is God's Word. How we thrill to hear you say, "I stand on the authority of God's Word and believe it all." How this poor old world is being saturated with those who are preaching unbelief. Just the other day a minister said that he could not understand anyone believing all the Bible. . . . Keep right on, Mr. Fuller. We are praying for you every day, praying that God might spare you and allow you to preach the Word until Christ Jesus comes again to receive His own.

A similar note was sounded by a coal miner who wrote in 1957:

Dear Mr. Fuller,

For twenty years I have worked in the coal mines in England. Life is hard but not so hopeless for me as for some, because my parents brought me up to be a Christian, and I married a good Christian. Hearing your program the last seven years—every week—is the best thing in our lives, the brightest hours. We are thankful you came to preach in England. The program comes on pretty late. I go to sleep first and set the alarm for 11 o'clock, since I can't afford to miss the "Old Fashioned Revival Hour."

The miners in Wales also loved the broadcast, as this 1954 letter shows:

Dear Brother and Sister Fuller,

I am writing to express my thanks for the wonderful and truly Gospel messages which are given over the air every Thursday and which come to us in the mining valley of South Wales, Glamoryan. You can tell in this village that people are listening by the lights in their windows, and your messages bring that greater Light. I have followed your messages over our small radio set over the last two years. Your exposition of Paul and Job and the final climax of his hope that "I know that my redeemer liveth" have been a great blessing. Last night my wife and I listened to your good discussion on the Tabernacle in the Wilderness. Joy filled my heart when Brother Fuller gave out the invitation, hands going up all over the auditorium.

Many Roman Catholics in Ireland also listened to the broadcast and some wrote addressing their letters, "Dear Father Fuller . . ." A Christian worker in Ireland gave a pretty accurate idea of the popularity of the broadcast there with the following letter:

Thousands of Irish Catholics are listening to messages over the air from Radio Luxembourg. A week or two ago four young Christians were holding an open-air meeting in Dublin's city center. When the listeners numbered about two hundred, a girl playing a piano-accordion said to the crowd, "We are now going to sing 'Heavenly Sunshine,' and I want you all to join in." And they did! Imagine one of the main thoroughfares of a city like Dublin resounding with a song from Roman Catholic lips, "Heavenly sunshine! Heavenly sunshine!

Hallelujah, Jesus is mine," and that toward the end of the Marian Year, when every attempt has been made to focus the people's attention on "Mary the Mother of God" as mediatrix between God and man and co-redeemer with Christ for the world. Obviously the words had already become familiar through the radio.

A Roman Catholic servant in an Irish country mansion recently asked the daughter of the household if she liked to listen to the radio. "I do," she replied. "Well, I hope ye'll turn it on of a Thursday night at 11 o'clock," he rejoined, "and ye'll hear, miss, what I call real Christianity."

Another letter tells more of what was happening among Roman Catholics in Ireland:

Dear Mr. Fuller,

We had an evangelist at our church last Wednesday, who has recently been to Southern Ireland. They have a few workers there at present, but he says your broadcast seems to be the only steady Gospel message they get in a 95 percent Roman Catholic population. He told of meeting a monk who had listened to you for seven years before finally accepting Christ as his Savior. I thought you would like to hear this, Dr. Fuller.

Of the many who wrote from England reporting their conversions, the following written in April, 1953, serves as an example:

Dear Mr. Fuller,

I am a British soldier here in Germany. I would like you to know that I listen to your Revival hour every Thursday.

A little while ago I was one of the biggest drunks in the camp. Even when I went on leave I used to go in pubs (beer houses in England), but one night I turned on the radio and heard your religious service and I was deeply moved. I tuned in again the following week and heard you again. My life has been changed. I have given up drink, and don't smoke now. My life is changed completely. I am now on God's side, and I wouldn't change it for the world.

I was a prisoner of war in this country during the war, and I hated the people here. But since I have gone on the Lord's side, all hatred has gone and now I am trying to teach the German people. I am telling them that God is the only one to turn to.

I would also like you to know that I am going to be married in a couple of months and that I am marrying a Christian girl, a girl who is working for good. Queenie (that's her name) sings hymns all over the country, and helps to bring more to God's kingdom.

Please give my regards to your wife, and I believe you have a son. If this is correct, give him my regards too.

I think "Heavenly Sunshine" is wonderful. I have just been listening to it sung in Spanish during your Revival Hour.

In 1959 my father and mother visited me in Basel, Switzerland, where I had gone with my family to work on a degree in theology. One Thursday evening at 11 o'clock I tuned in Radio Luxembourg so my father could hear his program. It was the first time he had ever been to Europe, and he was so glad to hear the broadcast over that station which had been mightily used of God to the winning of souls in the British Isles.

Long Beach became well known in England through Radio Luxembourg. In July, 1956, a traveler to London wrote,

Dear Charles Fuller,

Yesterday while we were seeing Windsor Castle here in London, I was talking with the bobby at the main entrance, and he asked me where I came from. I said, "California," and he said, "Could you possibly live near Long Beach, California? I hear the most wonderful religious service from there on Radio Luxembourg." I asked him to write to you, but he said he wasn't very much on writing, so I said I would do it. He said, "Be sure to say that I like it *very* much."

Other foreign radio outlets and shortwave stations made the broadcast heard virtually world-wide. A seaman wrote,

Dear Brother Fuller,

I am a sailor on a British ship, and during my years of traveling around this old world, in almost every port I have picked up the "Old Fashioned Revival Hour." The first time was back home in Scotland. Back in the old country many tune in to the Luxembourg station, and I personally know that many from Petershead, in the north of Scotland, right down to the very south of England, never miss hearing you. Over in Europe, too, I've picked up your broadcast in many ports, radiating out from the powerful transmitter of Luxembourg as far south as the Mediterranean Sea, as we headed for Egypt and the Suez Canal. Then once we get clear of Aden and the Red Sea, going down the Indian Ocean, I've picked you up coming from Ceylon. This station is also very powerful and can be heard from South Africa right over to the Australian coast. In the Pacific, Manila is so powerful that I have found you all around China, Japan, and the islands of the Pacific, very clearly. Then on the way from Japan to San Francisco I listen to Manila most of the way, but as we near America I find Quito, Ecuador, comes in better.

Recently on two occasions I have been in Long Beach. The first time was for a weekend and I located the Municipal Auditorium right away on Saturday, looking forward with great expectancy to your service the next day. But how disappointed I was when the ship sailed early Sunday morning. I couldn't see you, but I listened that afternoon as we headed south for the Panama Canal. The last time, we expected to be in Long Beach over the New Year, but were ahead of schedule and left on the last day of the old year. . . . I leave America in a few weeks, returning to Britain, and I anticipate leaving the sea. But Brother Fuller, if I do not see you on this earth, I shall meet you in heaven.

The ministry of the broadcast extended not only to most of the globe but also brought a saving knowledge of Christ to people in all sorts of situations. Miss Rose Baessler, Charles Fuller's secretary from 1940 to 1963, estimated that during the 1950s, an average of four hundred conversions a week were reported by letter. And of course many other converts never bothered to write.

An incident which also hints at the many who found Christ through this ministry occurred when a master of ceremonies was about to introduce Charles Fuller to speak before four thousand ministers of the Southern Baptist Convention. He put him on the spot by asking how many of the pastors there had had any converts added to their churches as a result of the "Old Fashioned Revival Hour." Sometimes ministers regarded the broadcast as a competition which drew support away from their churches, and as the master of ceremonies posed this question, there flashed across Charles Fuller's mind the thought of how hard it would be to speak to such a group if few or no hands were raised. But to his great relief fully two-thirds of those ministers raised their hands, and this was all the more remarkable because it happened only three years after he had gone coast-to-coast so he could be heard in the South. Thus he was greatly encouraged to proceed with his sermon on 2 Timothy 4:5, where Paul exhorted a pastor to be diligent in carrying out the work of an evangelist.

A letter written in 1949 by a young pastor from Illinois provides an example of how the radio ministry helped pastors:

For ten years I have enjoyed the "Old Fashioned Revival Hour," but have often wondered, "Is it really doing the job—is it reaching the unsaved? It is fine that the Christian is being strengthened, but do the lost tune in on the program?" I confess I didn't think so. But in my pastoral calling to the unsaved in this, my first charge, I am amazed to find that almost everybody knows the "Heavenly Sunshine" man. Best of all, they listen, not only to the music, but just as eagerly to the messages. It's the best music on the radio, I am told, and Reverend Fuller preaches the Bible so plainly and understandingly that we just can't miss it. That's what they, these unchurched, unsaved people say to me.

Yes, the Holy Spirit through your broadcast has planted the good seed and now I, as a young pastor, am privileged to come along and reap the harvest.

Let me give you an example of this. Last month I was able to lead to the Lord a coal miner who had been hospitalized after being severely crushed under a rock slide. Every rib as well as his back was broken. While under the rock he had cried out, "God, help me, for if I die now, I die in my sins." Now this man had been a real prodigal, but in his extremity he knew he was a sinner, and he knew he needed salvation. Where had he learned this? After he was gloriously converted, I learned that even in his unsaved state he had been listening to the "Old Fashioned Revival Hour," and there he had learned the way of salvation.

Charles Fuller also helped pastors by providing them with encouragement in difficult circumstances. In 1954 a pastor from the state of Washington wrote:

Dear Brother Fuller,

I am pastoring a small community church while carrying on my studies at college. A few months ago I came home from the church so discouraged that I thought maybe I had better give up and turn the preaching assignment over to someone else. Feeling the need of help, I tuned into your program in time to hear you say, "You pastors, laboring in the country areas, take heart." And then you quoted "Be ye steadfast, unmoveable," "In due season you shall reap if you faint not." I needed just such encouragement, and I have stayed with it and seen God working in people's hearts since then.

A similar letter came from the wife of a seminary student in Boston in 1957:

Dear Dr. and Mrs. Fuller,

Once again you are hearing from those who have enjoyed the "Old Fashioned Revival Hour" for many years and are finally saying thank you. Many times I have been tempted to write but until now I have been a miserable procrastinator. I can recall sitting with my family Sunday evenings after church in our living room, and the joy when we listened together—that was back before World War II. Then I can remember college days when the music of the program, wafting down dormitory corridors, would bring many a girl into my room to hear Dr. Fuller and the wonderful words of life.

But the time that your ministry has meant the most was three years ago when my husband, a student in seminary, accepted a call to a little church in the vicinity here in New England. It was a church which down through the years had slipped away from the Old Book, and its light had all but gone out. No evening service, about three or four members at prayer meeting, about twenty-five in the morning service. Having come from a wide-awake evangelical church, we almost "froze to death" spiritually in the cold atmosphere. But my husband made a covenant with the Lord that he would preach the Word, and we prayed and worked with the people. We began an evening service; sometimes we had as few as twelve in attendance. It was discouraging, and even heartbreaking, as only a preacher's life can be at times.

There were two things, however, that kept us going; the knowledge that God had put us there for a purpose and was using us; and the privilege of listening to the "Old Fashioned Revival Hour." On Sunday mornings the old parsonage was filled with the blessed strains of "Heavenly Sunshine," and our hearts were thrilled and lifted by the message in song and word. Especially would we be blessed when Dr. Fuller would pray for those "laboring in the out-of-the-way places" because we knew he meant us! When the program was over my husband would say, "Well, I'm all fired up now!" And little John, aged two, would clap his chubby hands at the first chords of "Jesus Saves" and say, "Oh, It's Walk-a-Church Day!"

As a result, revival came to that church! God honored His Word as He had promised He would, and souls were saved. One Sunday morning when John gave the invitation, seven came forward—something that hadn't happened in that church for a long time. From that time on, souls were saved frequently, and attendance quadrupled, actually! It's now a God-blessed church, with a full-time pastor, and when

God called us to a new work we left many new and wonderful Christian friends to carry on the work there. So you see, you have had part in another revival without realizing it!

Charles Fuller's ministry was also felt overseas on the mission fields, both by encouraging those who were missionaries and by being the means God used to call others to become missionaries. A missionary from Indonesia wrote:

For over eight years we supported the "Old Fashioned Revival Hour" by our prayer and offerings. Now as new missionaries, we are working among the mountain people near Molino, Celebes, Indonesia. For some time we have been hungry to enjoy an hour of fellowship and music around the Word again. I never dreamed I could get your program, which we have loved so long, but last night while I dialed the shortwave radio, I heard the one word, "Brother . . ." in a voice so familiar that I was startled, for it was unmistakably your voice, Mr. Fuller. Imagine our joy to be able to turn the dial back and be able once again to get your program, with all that it means to us.

In 1946 Charles Fuller preached to his largest visible audience, about 68,000 who came to the Chicagoland Youth for Christ program held on Memorial Day evening. The following story, taken from the February 7, 1954, issue of the Sunday school magazine *Power,* tells of the effect the message preached that evening had in the life of Kenny Joseph, one member of that audience. As a high schooler, Kenny had had something of an inferiority complex and so jumped at the chance to join a gang called the "Cobras." Occasionally he got into street fights with this gang, and he began to develop a police record and spend some nights in jail. He also began to add to his wardrobe by shoplifting.

But one day as he boarded a streetcar he saw a sign that read: "Chicagoland Youth for Christ Rally, Soldiers' Field. Charles E. Fuller, speaker; Gil Dodds in exhibition mile run. All seats free." Since it didn't sound too much like a church meeting, Kenny decided to go. He had been an athlete and wanted to see Gil Dodds run. But he felt uneasy in the unmistakably religious atmosphere of the 68,000 who were there. He wished he could leave and was glad when it started to rain. People were beginning to leave, and he was about to go himself.

174

But then Charles Fuller stood up and led the whole audience in prayer, asking God to stop the rain. Kenny sat dumbfounded as the rain stopped. (Torrey Johnson has said that the rain stopped as though Someone turned it off like a faucet.) Kenny realized he had seen a miracle. All resistance to God was broken down, and when the invitation was given at the close of the meeting, he joined eight hundred others who went out and knelt on the field accepting Christ and His forgiveness. Desiring Bible knowledge, he enrolled in a Christian college. Kenny also went to the police with the clothes he had stolen and said he wanted to make his wrongs right. As, he neared the end of college, he told the Lord he would be a preacher if He would give him that desire. God worked and led him to become a missionary in Japan.

It is also interesting that the medical missionary, Dr. Dean F. Kroh, who is well known as "jungle doctor" in the books bearing that title, was converted through listening to the "Old Fashioned Revival Hour" one evening in 1941.

On October 1, 1951, a woman in South Carolina was listening on her radio as a missionary was being interviewed by a local radio announcer. The missionary told how one night as he was listening to Charles Fuller, his heart melted and he fell on his knees and with tears gave himself to the Lord. The announcer asked, "Did you write and tell Dr. Fuller about it?" The missionary replied, "No, I didn't. I suspect if everyone who has been saved by Mr. Fuller's preaching would write, he would be reading letters for the next thousand years."

At a banquet honoring Charles Fuller and Harold Ockenga, the founders of Fuller Theological Seminary, Billy Graham said, "I've met people all over the world that say they were converted to Christ under the ministry of Charles Fuller—people he'll never know anything about until he gets to heaven."

In 1949 the door opened again for the broadcast to be aired over the stations of a national network, this time that of the American Broadcasting Company. Early in 1944, when Charles Fuller had learned that he was soon to be off Mutual, there was the possibility for a few weeks that the "Old Fashioned Revival Hour" could go onto the ABC network. It had recently been formed as a result of an antitrust action against the National Broadcasting Company, and for a few years this network was called the "blue" network.

But the ABC network quickly adopted the policy of NBC and CBS, which allowed no paid-for religious programs. Later on, however, as the 1940s drew to a close, television began taking over the popularity that radio had been enjoying. With advertisers buying more television time, the ABC network officials responsible for Sunday daytime programming became interested in the high popularity the "Old Fashioned Revival Hour" had been maintaining year after year.

The makeshift network of independent stations that had carried the broadcast since 1944 had never been as satisfactory as being on a national network, and so Charles Fuller quickly decided to go on ABC, even though it meant broadcasting by electrical transcription from 8 to 9 A.M. Sundays in each time zone. He dropped some of his independent station time spots in exchange for the two hundred eighty ABC stations that would now carry his broadcast, and again a portion of his audience were unable to locate the program. As a result, while the number of letters had been gradually dropping each year since 1944, the biggest drop occurred in 1949 when he shifted to the ABC network. Charles Fuller had known how risky it would be to subject his audience to the change involved in getting back on a network, but he was convinced that such a decision would help him reach more people in the long run. Then, too, he had hopes that once he was on ABC, he would be able to negotiate an arrangement for broadcasting "live" across the nation.

In June, 1950, one year later, ABC granted him this desire. Now he could broadcast from the Long Beach Auditorium to the Pacific Coast from 1 to 2 P.M. Sundays and on across the nation so that he was heard from 4 to 5 P.M. in the East. This plan meant shifting the time of the Long Beach meeting to 1 o'clock on Sunday afternoons. But just as the broadcast had improved when it originated before a large visible audience, so now it improved even more as everyone realized that what was happening in Long Beach was being heard "live" over more than two hundred eighty stations across the United States and Canada. The next seven years, during which this arrangement continued, were indeed the golden years of the "Old Fashioned Revival Hour."

The year 1950 saw an increase in the number of letters coming in, and this indicated how much better a "live" afternoon broadcast was than the transcribed, 8-to-9 A.M. spot. But even though 1950 saw more letters coming in than 1949, the increase did not equal the volume of letters that had come in during 1948. The reason was that television was continuing to replace radio's popularity. Thus Charles Fuller seriously faced the question of whether he should not start a television counterpart to his radio broadcast.

Accordingly, in the fall of 1950 he contracted with ABC to carry a half-hour program on Sundays called "The Old Fashioned Meeting" on twenty-five of its TV stations across the country. This meant assembling the choir, quartet, Rudy Atwood, and George Broadbent on a sound stage in Hollywood on Tuesday evenings where a "kinescope" would be made. A kinescope was television images transferred to motion picture film, which could then be copied and sent to the various television stations for release two or three weeks later. (Instantaneous transmission of television coast-to-coast was not achieved until the summer of 1951.)

Charles Fuller knew how enervating it was to produce a telecast. Back in 1943 he had assembled his choir and quartet in the television studio atop Mount Lee in the Hollywood Hills one evening to make a telecast that was seen locally on the several thousand sets that were then in the Los Angeles area. He remembered the hot lights, the time spent getting "made-up," and the necessity both to look and sound well. The whole experience had been, as he described it, a "nightmare." But he was willing to endure all this again in 1950, because if television was going to make radio ineffectual, he wanted to be ready to shift to this new communication medium.

There was indeed a considerable response to this telecast, but after about three months Charles Fuller could see that it was not going to pay its own way, and so "The Old Fashioned Meeting" was dropped after a run of six months. Whatever effect television would finally have on radio, he was convinced that God did not want him to be a television preacher.

Year by year television did increase in popularity, and each year the response to the "Old Fashioned Revival Hour" decreased a little. Nevertheless the Nielsen ratings showed that it was the third most popular broadcast during daylight hours on Sunday (the other two were secular programs) and that it was certainly at least as popular as Billy Graham's "Hour of Decision" program, which had commenced in 1950 on ABC. Thus though the response in the 1950s

Above: *The Fullers in costume and make-up for short-lived telecast series, the "Old Fashioned Meeting," early 1952.* **Below:** *Mrs. Fuller makes suggestion during public broadcast; charter seminary board member, Arnold Grunigen, listens in.*

An ABC radio official presents Charles Fuller with a gold microphone during anniversary broadcast in January, 1950.

With Miss Rose Baessler, his secretary from 1939 to 1963.

was down a third from the peak year of 1944, Charles Fuller still preached to an audience that numbered in the millions as he stepped before the microphone at Long Beach.

As the year 1955 approached, the extent of Charles Fuller's ministry became remarkable not only because of its great outreach but also because it had now been going on for so long. He had counted the broadcast made in August, 1925, as the beginning of his radio career, and the broadcast in January, 1955, became the time to celebrate thirty years of radio broadcasting.[8] The ABC network, the city of Long Beach, and many evangelical leaders joined in helping to celebrate this momentous occasion. The ABC network produced a special half-hour program which reviewed the main features of Charles Fuller's life. Roy McKeown, leader of the Los Angeles Youth for Christ, put on a "This Is Your Life" program for my father. Then during the anniversary broadcast itself, a high executive of the network appeared on the program and gave Charles Fuller a gold microphone to commemorate thirty years of radio broadcasting. Evangelist Merv Rosell led the ceremonies that took place right after that broadcast in the Long Beach Auditorium. Letters and telegrams of congratulations were read from dozens of evangelical leaders around the world. The mayor of Long Beach read a proclamation making that day "Charles Fuller Day." Transcontinental World Airlines flew, free of charge, a Mr. Joseph Pixley from his home in Cimarron, Kansas, to be at Long Beach for that thirtieth anniversary broadcast. He had written the preceding November and said, "Next to going to heaven, I would like most to attend a broadcast of 'The Old Fashioned Revival Hour' in Long Beach." When his telephone rang on Christmas Day and he was told that he would be flown to Long Beach for the broadcast, he was overjoyed. His presence there symbolized the great numbers of the unseen audience who had never gotten to Long Beach but wanted to join in the thirtieth anniversary celebration.

Charles Fuller took off a few Sundays after that anniversary broadcast and had evangelists like Merv Rosell speak for him. He felt that after preaching fifty-two Sundays a year for so long, he was entitled to take a little rest. It wasn't long, however, until he was back again, preaching as regularly as ever. But in the summer

[8] I am not sure why the second Sunday in January rather than the third Sunday in August was reckoned, from 1947 on, as the anniversary Sunday.

of 1957, the ABC network informed him that soon its new policy would be to limit all programs to half an hour. Charles Fuller then decided that his thirty-third anniversary broadcast on January 12, 1958, would be the last public broadcast of the "Old Fashioned Revival Hour" from the Long Beach Municipal Auditorium. That preceding April he had just turned seventy, and he had been noticing how tired he became each Sunday after mounting the energy necessary to conduct the hour-long broadcast and make the large audience at Long Beach feel welcome. Thus when ABC's policy announcement came through, he felt that he should now reduce the broadcast to a half hour and originate it from the ABC studios in Hollywood without a visible audience. Something of what this meant and how Charles Fuller was thinking at the time can be sensed from the following letter which he sent out to his mailing list on December 10, 1957:

After January 12, 1958, the "Old Fashioned Revival Hour" will cease to be an hour long as it has been in the past, and we will no longer broadcast from the Municipal Auditorium at Long Beach. Rather, it will become a one-half-hour studio program. How we shall miss meeting our radio friends each week! It has meant so much to us to shake hands with you and look into your faces. This change will, of course, mean that we will not be able to have as much music, so since the choir could give greater variety, we reluctantly decided to give up our wonderful quartet which has been such a blessing to us all. Rudy Atwood and George Broadbent [on the organ] will still be with us. What an upheaval this is for us all. . . .

Although it has become necessary to go to a half-hour program, yet by the grace of God these ether waves are still open to us for the preaching of the Gospel, and we must be obedient to our calling to preach the Word and to beseech men and women to be reconciled to Christ.

The way radio listeners responded to this announcement is typified by the following letter, which was written December 16, 1957:

Dear Dr. Fuller,

Praise be to God the Hour will not disappear altogether! What a dark world this would be without the weekly light of your dear program. While I know you are discouraged I thank you for continuing your work. I know you are tired and long to be Home with Jesus, but we do need you, Dr. Fuller. . . . I know I should not be afraid to face the future without your teaching and guidance, for I'll always have my Bible, but your Hour is the only church I have, and I just don't know what I'd do without it. I am so sorry that the Hour must be condensed—how I will miss the quartet!—but I am so thankful that *you* will still reach us.

The auditorium at Long Beach was filled almost to capacity for that last broadcast from the place where an hour-long broadcast had been going out each Sunday for almost twenty years. For the last time on the broadcast, the quartet sang "This World Is Not My Home," "I'm on the Battlefield for My Lord," and then finally, "Peace, Peace, Wonderful Peace, Coming Down from the Father Above . . ." The three grandchildren, Janice (6), Cathy (4), and Steven (2), joined with their grandfather to sing "Trust and Obey," with Steven sometimes way off key. For the last time the audience stood up to sing "Heavenly Sunshine" and turn around to shake hands with everybody. They also joined in singing "Meet Me There" and "What a Friend We Have in Jesus."

All this had much sentiment-producing potential, and Mrs. Fuller was afraid her husband might break down completely. A few tears could be heard in his voice during the early part of the broadcast, but he rallied to preach very powerfully on "Seven Marvels of Mercy" from Isaiah 1:18, "Come now and let us reason together, saith the Lord, though your sins be as scarlet, they shall be as white as snow; though they be red like crimson, they shall be as wool." The seven marvels of mercy were (1) that God forgives at all; (2) that God forgives *all;* (3) that God reasons with *sinners;* (4) that God reasons with sinners even after all He has done for us; (5) that God not only forgives but also transforms the sinner; (6) that God makes the sinner a *new creation;* and (7) that the longsuffering God pleads with people and says "Come *now."* Many raised their hands to accept Christ, and after the broadcast about twenty of these came forward to make a public confession of Christ during that last after-service.

At the close of the after-service Charles Fuller had everyone sing "God Be with You Till We Meet Again," and then for the last time he and his wife stood at the foot of the platform to shake hands with hundreds of friends. Mrs. Fuller wrote in her diary, "Leaving, we looked back at the old auditorium and said, 'Good-by.' The Gospel went out from there year after year to a world-wide audience, and we have had blessed fellowship with radio friends from all over the world in that place. We shall henceforth miss meeting our radio friends. Yes, we turned, waved, and said 'Good-by' to the old Long Beach auditorium."

This was the last day that the faithful ushers and personal workers assembled to make their vital contribution to the production of that public broadcast. For several months two or three of them kept going to the auditorium each Sunday at 12:30 P.M. to welcome people who still came to attend the broadcast and to tell them that the public meeting had been discontinued. Some people were coming there hoping to attend the broadcast even three years later.

THE HALF-HOUR BROADCAST

The shift to the half-hour broadcast did not require much reshuffling of station time. The program continued to be heard on the two hundred eighty ABC stations coast-to-coast on Sunday afternoons, and the remaining time spots on the four hundred independent stations were simply pared down to thirty minutes. The biggest change came in having to work out a new program format. So in the January, 1958, *Heart to Heart Talk* Charles Fuller asked people to pray that "as I preach and as the musicians sing, the Holy Spirit may empower and work through *every second* of the thirty minutes—opening the hearts of listeners everywhere to spiritual truths and to their great need of Christ." Three months later he felt that the new format was a success. "Now that we can look back on several weeks of the new release of the broadcast," he said,

. . . I believe most of our radio friends are confident the change was of God's leading, and that the new set-up will enable us to get the Gospel out more effectively than ever. We are taking a few more local stations in areas of dense population which will give us fine coverage. . . . It was hard for us to make the change, but while many of our radio family were greatly disappointed over losing some features of the Long Beach meeting, yet they are surprised how much can be put into the half hour without any feeling of hurry or pressure.

One great advantage to the new set-up was that Charles Fuller could preach the sermons for two weeks during one Sunday afternoon, when Leland Green, the choir, Rudy Atwood, and George Broadbent gathered for a recording session. While he still had to prepare fifty-two sermons a year, yet the sermons were now only about half as long, and he needed to be ready to preach on only twenty-six Sundays a year. For forty years he had preached virtually every Sunday, but now he could take off two or three weeks in the winter and still have the whole summer free.

Now he had time to take trips to the "out-of-the-way places" he used to visit and to which he visualized his broadcast reaching. In the April, 1958, *Heart to Heart Talk* he reported how he had been planning for some months to take a trip:

I felt I needed the rest—driving and looking at the grand open spaces, for I love the desert and the grandeur of God's handiwork there.[9]

But about ten days before the time to start I began to feel an urge to take a few meetings with some of the pastors and friends out there. So I had a friend do some telephoning to arrange for three meetings. When he called one pastor to say we would like to come to his church, he said, "You must be kidding. Charles Fuller wouldn't want to come to my church. It only holds fifty people and we could not give him an offering." My friend said, "He is not coming for an offering. He wants to have fellowship with your people." "Oh, that would be fine," said the pastor. There wasn't much chance to advertise, but he rented a small hall for $4 and the word got around. It was a very cold, snowy night but when Mrs. Fuller and I reached the appointed place, the hall was nearly filled and it was warm and cozy. We sang "Heavenly Sunshine" like Long Beach, and after the message we had a wonderful time of fellowship. An offering was taken and given to the pastor for his encouragement. There seemed to be very little interest in the things of God in that busy growing town, and the pastor is having a hard time.

Charles Fuller went on to describe meetings in two other towns in Arizona, but the excerpt just cited shows how much he now missed broadcasting with a visible audience. The choir, however, was always on hand when he taped these half-hour broadcasts, and

---

[9] Mrs. Fuller lovingly accompanied him on these trips, but having been raised in Oregon, she would have preferred to go to some damp, rainy, foggy place!

having them there helped convince him that he really was speaking to someone by means of that impersonal microphone. His first experience in radio broadcasting had been from the KTBI studio at Biola in Los Angeles, and he recalled how he thought he might be wasting his time and breath because no one was listening. But when his own broadcasts became a success, he soon learned how vast were the numbers that the microphone helped him reach. Even so, he did better when he could actually see some of the people to whom he was speaking.

However, while Charles Fuller was now preaching again from a studio, with what was, at best, only an artificial audience, his great ability to project himself to people on radio was still abundantly manifest. Once when asked how he was able to do this, he replied that though he knew that an unimaginably large audience was listening, yet he would completely forget about the numbers and picture some lonely miner in a little cabin or someone else who was alone and facing an insurmountable problem. From this, one might conclude that Charles Fuller was good at counseling individuals, but the fact is that while a large audience of people brought out his very best, talking with a single person with a problem sapped his energies so quickly and completely that he usually found some way to avoid such situations. (This, incidentally, was perhaps one of the reasons why he was not the most successful pastor at Placentia.)

Because of this God-given ability to reach out to people by radio, the "Old Fashioned Revival Hour" continued to be very popular, even though it was now a half-hour broadcast with no visible audience. On April 17, 1960, a lady from Denver wrote to tell how she had been converted listening to him preach. Then she added,

Each time I hear your voice, there still comes a tear to my eyes, for who knows what would have happened to me if I had not heard your voice the first time. May God bless you and thank you again for *caring* and *pleading* for the lost. They can be saved. I was.

Other reports of conversions continued to come in as well:

Thank you for saving me from suicide. We moved to Newark, thinking that my husband could get work in a big city. For ten days he roamed the streets looking for some kind of work, and two days ago he said he would not come home until he got a job. In the meantime my little girl took ill with a high fever, and I was desperate because I had no money and did not know where to go to get help. I just thought I would end it all by turning on the gas, when I remembered the radio. I thought perhaps I could hear a little jazz or something funny, and the first thing I heard was, "The Lord's our Rock, in Him we hide, a shelter in the time of storm." I had forgotten all about God, and I dropped to my knees, asking Him to help me. Things turned from that time on, and my husband came in saying that he had found work. Thank you again for saving me from such dreadful cowardice.

January, 1960, was celebrated as the 35th anniversary on the radio, and the National Religious Broadcasters gave the "Old Fashioned Revival Hour" an Award of Merit in which the president of the NRB said,

To the Rev. Dr. Charles E. Fuller for distinguished leadership in the field of religious radio, for significant contribution to the principles, policies, and practices for which the organization stands: for outstanding faith, vision, and courage in the fullest possible use of mass communications media for the proclamation of Christ's Gospel.

Your fellow-broadcasters through the land join in felicitating you, Dr. Fuller, upon your thirty-fifth anniversary in the broadcasting of the Gospel of our Lord and Savior, Jesus Christ. We implore upon you and your radio ministry our heavenly Father's richest benedictions.

On this anniversary the Los Angeles County Supervisors gave Charles Fuller a scroll commemorating his years of radio broadcasting. Mr. Kenneth Hahn, one of the supervisors, while officiating at the ceremony, recalled,

I just grew up on the "Old Fashioned Revival Hour" and cannot remember the time when I did not hear it! My mother was left a widow with seven sons, a staunch Christian woman and a wonderful mother, and I can remember many a Sunday when, after church, we all drove to Long Beach to the auditorium to see and hear Brother Fuller. We loved every part of the program, and it had a tremendous influence on us boys. Then when I was out in the Pacific during the war I nearly always could find the Hour, and it meant so much to a serviceman far from home. I have loved you and your work, Brother Fuller, and I wanted to honor you on this wonderful anniversary.

Many were the plaudits received during these autumn years of Charles Fuller's ministry, but there were still severe battles to be fought. Late in 1959 Radio Luxembourg changed its policy regarding religious broadcasts and refused to sell any more time to the "Old Fashioned Revival Hour," so Charles Fuller fell back on the transmitters of Trans World Radio in Monaco and North Africa. Then in 1963 the ABC network chose to drop the "Old Fashioned Revival Hour" along with most of its religious programs. In the August, 1963, *Heart to Heart Talk* Charles Fuller said,

After the last Sunday of August the Hour will not be heard on a great many of the powerful ABC stations. The reason is not that the Hour has a poor listening audience, for it has an excellent one, but the ABC network has changed its policy for releasing paid religious programs over stations which it owns.

However, we have been working hard to get stations in different areas which will be affected by these changes, and we have been quite successful. In a few days you will receive a printed sheet which will tell you the stations and hours when you can get the program.

Many changes have come through the years, but by prayer and God's help we have survived and grown and the Gospel has continued to go out clearly over a very large area of the world. But *this change* is hard to take, so we are asking our friends to stand faithfully by, as in the past.

Thus even in his seventy-seventh year Charles Fuller had to keep fighting to go on preaching the Gospel by radio. As in 1944, so now he and his radio agency, the R. H. Alber Company, had to negotiate with independent stations to make up for the loss of the first-rate network stations.

But Charles Fuller's weariness increased, and he would sometimes share something of this with his hearers. One of them, however, replied with a poem and a word of encouragement:

> An open door, it is God's way
>   to reach the sinner in this day.
> An Iron Curtain it can probe,

The message goes around the Globe.
A precious gift—His Church should know
This open door is radio.

The writer continued, "Don't you dare talk of quitting or dropping stations, Brother Fuller. Shame on you! I'll bet you think maybe you are getting old, but you better think of Caleb. Next Sunday give 'em both barrels. The world needs to know." Charles Fuller obeyed this man's advice and went right on preaching on the radio for two more years, even though Mrs. Fuller was by now an invalid and was soon to pass away. The only thing that caused him to stop preaching was a heart attack, but his broadcast has continued on since then without a break. Indeed, Charles Fuller had been firing, as it were, through a second barrel for twenty years. We have talked mostly of his work on the radio, but he had also greatly multiplied his ministry through a seminary which he founded in 1947. When asked what the great ambition of his life was, he often replied, "My ambition is to see the world evangelized in this generation. I believe two things must be done before my responsibility has been fulfilled. First, to seek to be as effective as possible in preaching by radio; and second, to train others to preach."

8. Training Others to Preach

RADIO WORK WAS unquestionably the great work to which God called Charles Fuller. But we have also noted his recurrent interest in training people for Christian service. Thus he took on the heavy responsibility of being president of Biola's board of trustees from 1928–32, and even devoted some time to teaching at the Los Angeles Baptist Seminary in the late 1920s. Then for seven years after he left Calvary Church his energies went exclusively into building his radio ministry. But one night in November, 1939, God woke him out of a deep sleep and began to lay on his heart a burden (to quote from his statement made at the convocation for the founding of Fuller Seminary in 1947) "for a Christ-centered, Spirit-directed training school, where Christian men and women could be trained in the things of God, to become steeped in the Word, so as to go out bearing the blessed news to lost men and women." This burden which came upon him then was more than just a passing fancy, for I well remember how, one evening that fall, he drove my mother and me out to the La Puente hills in the eastern end of the San Gabriel Valley and walked around what was then still a rural area, wondering whether God might not have him build a school there sometime.

We have also noted how rapidly the radio ministry grew, especially after America entered World War II and people became more conscious of spiritual things. After hearing Charles Fuller pleading for souls Sunday after Sunday, there were some who felt led to entrust monies to him to use either to get the Gospel out by radio or in some other manner. They felt that he was in a better position to know how to use it for the spread of the Gospel. For example, a bachelor who had been a regular listener to the "Old Fashioned Revival Hour" was drafted into the service, and as he came through Los Angeles to go out to the Pacific to fight, he called and asked Charles Fuller for an appointment. "I may not return," the GI said, "and if I don't, please invest this money in missions in my name." Such requests raised the question of whether the Gospel Broad-

189

casting Association should receive monies designated for ministries that might not specifically involve radio broadcasting. While its by-laws stated that it was primarily concerned with broadcasting the Gospel by radio, they also allowed it to acquire and expend funds for "the general purpose of carrying on religious, missionary, charitable, benevolent, and educational work." Thus the trustees of the GBA were legally justified to accept and channel monies designated for nonradio broadcasting projects. Nevertheless, they felt that in order to do this, it would be better to establish a new religious, nonprofit corporation. So in October, 1942, the GBA voted to establish the Fuller Evangelistic Association especially "for the purpose of training, or assisting in the training, of men and women for the Christian ministry and for evangelistic work."[1] While the two associations were to be entirely separate, yet the majority of the board members of the FEA was to be made up of board members of the GBA.

This new corporation also gave Charles Fuller a more efficient means for disbursing the income of the Immanuel Missionary Fund, which his father, Henry Fuller, had set up in 1918. At this point it is interesting to recall the vision that led Henry Fuller to set aside a fund of some $100,000 for helping foreign missionaries. For twenty days during September, 1918, Henry Fuller, still active at the age of seventy-two, had been busy sorting the one thousand dollars worth of oranges from his grove that came by on a conveyor belt each day. But as his eyes busily directed his fingers, his thoughts were far away. He was thinking of what to do with his fifty thousand dollars of Liberty Bonds, and the thought flashed across his mind, "Why not use them all to invest in missionary work?" Believing this to be from God, he said, "Yes, Lord, I will use them all for thee." He reported how a bit of God's glory then came down from heaven and filled his heart with love, joy, and peace.

As he continued sorting oranges during the days that followed, he recalled how much money he had loaned out in the preceding years—some of which was never repaid—since he had planted his orange grove. He remembered how he had spent more for travel

---

[1] Up until 1968 this corporation's name was the Fuller Evangelistic Foundation. At that time the board voted to substitute the word "association" for "foundation." To avoid confusion, this later name will be used throughout the book in speaking of this corporation.

and in investment in various business enterprises than he had for the Lord's work. So he decided to put all the Liberty Bonds into a trust and to add another fifty thousand dollars besides, and to make a close friend, Mrs. Grace D. Woodson, a co-trustee with him. Not only the interest from this money but also some of its capital from time to time was to be used to help support missionaries around the globe. Mrs. Woodson suggested that the trust be called the Immanuel Missionary Fund, and by the time of Henry Fuller's death in 1926, fifty-four missionaries in various parts of the world were being supported.

After his father's death, Charles Fuller was appointed co-trustee of this fund with Mrs. Woodson and together they continued to carry out the purposes for this trust that had been outlined by Henry Fuller. When the FEA was established in 1943 with virtually the same goals as the Immanuel Missionary Fund, Mrs. Woodson, a sponsor of the new association, agreed with Charles Fuller to put the Fund under the administration of the FEA.

There were two tasks upon which the newly constituted FEA embarked, the establishment of a Fuller Seminary of Missions and Evangelism, and a Department of Field Evangelists. Before proceeding with the way the seminary developed, it is well to describe the evangelistic outreach of the FEA, since the zeal that Charles Fuller gave to this department, while at the same time he was struggling to found a seminary and to keep an international radio broadcast going, indicates how serious was his commitment to the task of world evangelization.

To fulfill his dream of getting the Gospel out into the neglected areas, Charles Fuller set up a Department of Evangelism which guaranteed the expenses of an evangelist so he could hold a campaign in an impoverished area whose churches could never hope, otherwise, to have the renewal and encouragement that an outside speaker could bring. The FEA offered to make up the difference between what such churches could pay and the cost of supporting an evangelist. In 1948, sixteen evangelistic teams held one hundred eighty campaigns in such areas in the United States and Canada. Some of these evangelists and their wives traveled with house trailers so they could work more easily in the out-of-the-way places.

Thus Mr. Harry Sprague, who worked with the FEA for twenty-five years, gave a typical instance of how during an open week between scheduled campaigns, he and his wife drove into the railroad town of Imlay, Nevada, where the Sunday school had closed three months before. Despite a lack of enthusiasm on the part of the former Sunday school officials, he persuaded them to let him advertise a Daily Vacation Bible School to be held in the local school building each day of that week. By the third day fifty young people from that unchurched area were coming for a whole morning of instruction in the Bible. They followed the "Heavenly Sunshine" D.V.B.S. material which Miss Irene Hunter, also of the FEA, had written up and which was being used in two thousand churches across America. Having reached the young people, the Spragues found that they had a point of contact with the adults also, and were able to hold an evening service in which several adults made a public profession of Christ along with twenty-seven younger people who had been attending the Daily Vacation Bible School.

Two other evangelists had jeeps which enabled them to get into the mountainous areas of Kentucky and West Virginia, where they would give similar reports of people won to Christ. Such reports were a great encouragement to Charles Fuller. We recall how he himself had done this sort of work in the summers shortly after his conversion, and even now as he stood before the microphone Sunday after Sunday, he visualized himself speaking to someone living in some such inaccessible spot. His radio broadcast kept him tied down Sunday after Sunday to the Southern California area, but how he did praise God for making it possible through the newly formed FEA to have these consecrated evangelists standing in for him in many places across the land.

The evangelists also found their linkage with the FEA and Charles Fuller to be helpful, for the broadcast was well known to people in these areas, and a good majority of the audiences already knew "Heavenly Sunshine." As one evangelist working in the southeastern part of the country put it,

To be associated with Dr. Fuller in any capacity gives one a solid acceptance with the Christian public. I find that I am received in the utmost confidence, and don't have to go through that period of breaking down people's reserve and of getting acquainted with them.

But during the very time that Charles Fuller was marshaling evangelists to go out into the neglected areas, he was also working hard to carry out that vision God had given him in 1939 of establishing a school to train others to preach.

THE FOUNDING OF FULLER THEOLOGICAL SEMINARY

In the summer of 1944, a year and a half after the establishment of the FEA, a first step was taken toward launching the Fuller Seminary of Missions and Evangelism. The FEA bought a piece of property to the north of the California Institute of Technology in Pasadena. During the war, Cal Tech had been using this property for military research, and it was hoped this could be zoned for a school. It was soon apparent, however, that after the war the neighborhood would not approve a zone variance.

Selling this property, the FEA was then able to procure a five-acre plot of ground very close to the civic center and only one block away from the main library. A high school had once stood there, and this plot was now the largest piece of unused property in the center of Pasadena.

Charles Fuller announced that when steel and materials became available after the war, he would erect on the property six concrete buildings that would be designed by a top architect and be a credit to the city of Pasadena. In the meantime, however, he had a temporary location where the school could hold its classes when it planned to open in the fall of 1945. The Lake Avenue Congregational Church had voted in a recent meeting to permit the new school to hold classes in its three-story educational building until it could construct its own buildings.[2] No longer planning to start a seminary, Charles Fuller decided the school would be a college of missions and evangelism. It would offer a five-year course of study for high-school graduates and would lead to a Bachelor of Theology degree. A shorter course, also stressing missions and evangelism, would be available for college graduates. Charles Fuller believed that as many as 500 students would apply for the entering class, but from these only the best qualified 125 would be accepted.

But as the war dragged on for another ten months, it became ap-

---

[2] Charles Fuller and his family had been members of this church since they moved to the Pasadena area in 1933. Dr. James Henry Hutchins, who had been pastor of the church since 1921, had been a very close friend of the family from the beginning. He had served on the board of trustees of the GBA since 1937 and was a charter board member of the FEA.

parent that this school could not be started in the fall of '45, so the fall of '46 became the next target date. It was a good thing Charles Fuller had this extra time, for many steps had to be taken before a school could actually be training and graduating students. The first step was to find a man to head up the school who would be an experienced educator and also zealous for evangelism and missions. Such a man was Dr. William Evans. When Charles Fuller was a student at Biola, he had regarded him as one of his most valued teachers. After leaving Biola, William Evans had become director of the educational department at the Moody Bible Institute of Chicago. Steeped in the knowledge of Scripture and a powerful speaker, William Evans was now constantly in demand to preach at Bible conferences. In the fall of 1945, he accepted Charles Fuller's offer to come and set up a new school. As dean he plunged into the task of recruiting faculty, mapping out the curriculum, and planning how to carry on the school during the period before the buildings could be erected on the Walnut Street property.

By September, 1945, Dr. Samuel Zwemer, the great missionary to the Moslem world for forty years and recently a teacher at Princeton Seminary, had moved to Pasadena in preparation for the school's opening a year later. The Rev. Armin Gesswein, who had taught evangelism at Gordon College in Boston, also moved to Pasadena with a view to teaching evangelism in the new school.

During January, 1946, the FEA received permission from the state to conduct a college or seminary and to grant degrees. By that time Dean William Evans had published a brochure giving a general outline of the Fuller College of Missions and Evangelism that was to start that next September. Now the plan was to admit only students who had completed two years of college, so that with an additional two years of training provided by this new school, they would receive a Bachelor of Arts degree. Along with the usual biblical and theological studies that would occupy most of those two years, they were to have a sequence of courses stressing missions and evangelism. This brochure listed several others who would make up the charter faculty, among them Robert H. Glover, the well-known writer on missionary subjects. An architect had now begun to draw plans for the new school, and the FEA Board had authorized borrowing several hundred thousand dollars from the bank to erect the buildings on the Walnut Street property.

But by the spring of 1946, plans for opening that next September were going awry. William Evans was not in good health, and it did not appear that Dr. Samuel Zwemer, now seventy-nine years old, would be able to carry much of a teaching load. Then, too, Charles Fuller was appalled at the figures which the architect gave as an estimate of the cost of the buildings. In the postwar inflation the cost was "three times" more than he had estimated. He also found that it would be some time before the nation, until recently tooled only for war, would be able to satisfy the tremendous demand that had built up for peacetime goods. He couldn't even produce kitchen equipment in order to remodel homes next to the Walnut Street property for married students.

But even more important than these problems was the task of obtaining the right person to head up the school. William Evans had now stepped out of the picture, and Charles Fuller cast about for a younger man who, as an educator and sharing his vision, would make the school a reality. In April, 1946, he wrote to Dr. Harold J. Ockenga, for ten years pastor of the historic Park Street Congregational Church in Boston. For some time Charles Fuller had had Harold Ockenga in the back of his mind as one who would be eminently qualified to head up such a school. As pastor at Park Street Church, Harold Ockenga held an annual missionary conference during which many thousands of dollars in pledges for the support of foreign missions were received as fifty or more missionaries would take their turn speaking in day-long meetings that lasted for a week. That very spring of 1946 the missionary conference had raised $75,000 for missions. Harold Ockenga was also qualified as an evangelist in that he had a backlog of about two hundred requests to hold evangelistic campaigns around the country, but because of his pastoral duties he accepted only three or four a year. He was a scholar as well, for he was not only a seminary graduate (Westminster Seminary, 1930) but had also earned a Ph.D. from the University of Pittsburgh in 1939. By 1946 he had authored six books, among which were *Our Protestant Heritage* (1938), *Everyone That Believeth* (1942), and *Our Evangelical Faith* (1946). He had achieved such prominence as a leader of evangelicals in America that he was elected as the first president of the National Association of Evangelicals when it was organized in 1942.

Charles Fuller and Harold Ockenga had been friends for some

years. Harold Ockenga had fully supported Charles Fuller's evangelistic meetings in Boston in May, 1939, and October, 1941. When Harold Ockenga came to Southern California on a preaching mission sometime around 1941, Charles Fuller had shared with him the burden he had for founding a school, and in the course of suggesting that he would be the one to head up such a school had driven him around the Pasadena area, showing him where he might well reside. But nothing came of this at that time.

However, as everything now hinged on getting someone to head up the school, Charles Fuller's thoughts again turned to Harold Ockenga, and he wrote him a letter in April, 1946, in which, after describing the advances that had been made in securing property and outlining the curriculum, he said,

I feel that with Dr. Evans and myself both getting on in years we should have a younger man trained to carry on in case of illness in either of us. Therefore I am looking for a man between thirty and forty-five or fifty years of age, preferably a seminary graduate who is spiritual and scholarly, and who has had experience in some line of Christian work since leaving seminary.

If you are able, Dr. Ockenga, to put me in touch with such a man, I shall greatly appreciate it. . . . Frankly, Dr. Ockenga, I have entertained the wish that you might be free some day to head this college. This suggestion may sound absurd to you, but I am sure you will pray with me about it, won't you? You know the Word of God tells us, "Ye have not because ye ask not."

Harold Ockenga replied that "you very graciously raise a question which is flattering and which I would be willing to seriously consider. God has been leading me in this realm of missions and evangelism in a very interesting way." Harold Ockenga went on to describe what God had been doing through him in missions and evangelism, and then he added, "It is quite possible that within five years from now, if God abundantly blesses your school, that I might be interested. Of course it would have to be a leading from Him." But he could suggest no one who could take over the leadership of the school in the very near future.

No one else who was approached at that time could help Charles Fuller solve the all-important question of the school's leadership. The property originally purchased for $90,500 could now be sold for $150,000, and so Charles Fuller could easily have scrapped the whole idea of founding a school and channeled all his remaining energies into his radio work and to developing the evangelistic department of the FEA. He really wanted to do just that, but try as he would he could not shake off the conviction that God wanted him to found a school. So he contacted a number of other Christian leaders, either asking them to recommend someone or sometimes suggesting that they themselves might be the ones, but nothing came from these inquiries. To one such person he wrote in the fall of 1946 as follows:

Oh, brother, God has laid so heavily on my heart the need of this type of school for training men for the preaching of the Gospel in these terrible days, but I am not qualified to plan such a curriculum. I see this great need, but I am not an educator. I must have the help of men of like vision. I cannot understand why God has laid this so heavily on my heart, but I wondered in the same way when he so definitely called me to preach the Word and I felt so inadequate; and later still when He called me to use radio as a means of reaching the lost. I felt so absolutely inadequate that I drew back and argued with God and told Him I wasn't the man for this; I wasn't a polished speaker, etc., but as I yielded He has worked and undertaken in such marvelous ways just because it is His will and His plan. . . . Well, if this is not of Him I want none of it. But I am confident this is God's plan, but it may not be His time.

With no outward indication for many months that God was working to found a school, it was only natural that Charles Fuller should say that "it may not be His time." But he kept complaining to his wife that he could not shake off the conviction that he must somehow found a school. He would find himself waking up at night with this burden and praying about it until he dropped off to sleep again. Finally one morning in exasperation Mrs. Fuller said, "Charles, you'll be sixty years old in April. Either get the school started now, or stop talking about it."

Charles Fuller agreed and decided that the one last step he would take was to invite Harold Ockenga and his wife to spend part of their winter vacation with him and Mrs. Fuller at their Palm Springs home. A few months earlier, Harold Ockenga had agreed to be a consultant for the proposed new school, and so Charles Fuller sug-

197

gested that they spend three days together, away from it all, out on the desert. The Ockengas concurred, and in February, 1947, they arrived in Southern California. After being met at the airport, they were shown the five-acre property in Pasadena and walked over it in the warm sunshine. Then the Fullers drove them one hundred miles east to their desert home where, surrounded by the sage brush and snow-capped peaks, these two leaders of the evangelical cause and their wives began to talk about the kind of school that was most needed.

Both men agreed that such a school should provide scholastically sound training in scriptural exegesis, theology, and church history and at the same time imbue students with a vision for missions and evangelism. Harold Ockenga felt that the needs of the evangelical cause would be served best by a school providing postgraduate theological training on a seminary level, as Charles Fuller had originally planned. But Mrs. Fuller asked, "Do enough evangelical scholars exist to start a seminary?" Much to the encouragement of the Fullers, Harold Ockenga quickly listed off a dozen men who would qualify. The more the four talked, the more excited they became, and Charles Fuller became convinced that now God was indeed opening the door for him to go ahead with the school.

The result of that Palm Springs conference was the decision to form a board of trustees for a school to be called Fuller Theological Seminary, and Harold Ockenga very willingly consented to be a member of that board. They were thinking then of opening the seminary eighteen months hence, in the fall of 1948. "Who knows," said Harold Ockenga, "but what I will be led to come on at that time as president?"

Right after the next Sunday's broadcast, Charles Fuller flew across the country to talk personally to other men whom he wanted as board members, and by the time he returned home, three men, Mr. Herbert Taylor of Chicago, Dr. Rudolf Logefeil of Minneapolis, and Mr. Arnold Grunigen of San Francisco had agreed to come on the board. Herbert Taylor was the president of the Club Aluminum Company and was also president of the Christian Workers' Foundation. He had played a vital role in the development of the Inter-Varsity Christian Fellowship and in the massive Youth for Christ rallies in Chicago. Rudolf Logefeil was a prominent physician in Minneapolis. Arnold Grunigen, a stockbroker in San Francisco, had been very active in the International Christian Business Men's Fellowship.

In conjunction with frequent communications with Harold Ockenga in Boston, approaches were made to several men to come on the faculty of the seminary. Dr. Wilbur M. Smith, professor of English Bible at Moody Bible Institute and editor of the annually published Peloubet's *Select Notes on the International Sunday School Lessons,* indicated that he was open to coming. Charles Fuller also began serious conferences with his architect over plans for erecting the seminary buildings but was very troubled because the architect still advised against planning to build until materials were more readily available. Charles Fuller feared that if he stopped moving forward in getting buildings for the seminary the men now willing to be on the charter faculty might lose interest.

But then he learned of the sale of the five-acre Cravens estate with its thirty-two room mansion on South Orange Grove Boulevard in Pasadena. Here was a piece of land just as large as that on which he had been planning to build, but with a building already on it which could easily provide offices for half a dozen faculty. Its enormous living room could be both a chapel and classroom, and its large bedrooms could be used as classrooms, dormitories, and library stacks to house the 14,000 books that Wilbur Smith had in his own personal library and the 4,000 volumes the FEA had been collecting for a school library. The surrounding five acres would provide ample land for building additional structures. Its value was assessed at $145,000, and Charles Fuller got authorization from the FEA to bid that amount on April 2, 1947. Any other interested parties could also place their bids by May 2, at which time it would go to the highest bidder. Charles Fuller, however, was quite confident that he could get it. Even if he had to go a few thousand dollars higher in his bid, the price would still be a marvelous bargain.

In the meantime Wilbur Smith had written and said he wished that somehow the new seminary might start in the fall of 1947 instead of 1948. Charles Fuller had asked Harold Ockenga what he thought of the idea, and he had replied, "Yes, that can be done, but it will take work." They did not want to risk losing Wilbur Smith's interest and so agreed that as Harold Ockenga returned from the National Association of Evangelicals meeting in Omaha, Nebraska, he would stop over in Chicago on Thursday, April 17, and confer with Wilbur Smith and Charles Fuller, who would fly in from Los Angeles.

This historic meeting was held in a private room at the Union League Club in Chicago. Wilbur Smith wanted to know what position Harold Ockenga would occupy in the seminary. He would be president *in absentia* for the time being, Harold Ockenga replied. He would work to recruit the charter faculty and map out the curriculum. Then they agreed that if three faculty members, besides Wilbur Smith, would be willing to start teaching by that next September, they would then go on ahead with this earlier date. They also agreed to meet again a month hence in Chicago in the offices of Herbert J. Taylor's Christian Workers' Foundation in the Civic Opera Building. Harold Ockenga would contact several prospective faculty members, and if any of these would be willing to move to Pasadena, they would be invited to participate in this forthcoming meeting.

Dr. Carl F. H. Henry, then professor of theology and philosophy at Northern Baptist Seminary, had been one of the names Harold Ockenga had put on the list of evangelical scholars at the Palm Springs conference with the Fullers in February. Dr. Henry had indicated that he would be interested in casting his lot with the seminary for that next fall, but was doubtful that a seminary could start on such short notice. In his earlier days he had been a newspaperman and had had some experience in handling publicity. He felt that more time would be needed to advertise the new seminary to the Christian public, and before the May meeting he had conferred with Wilbur Smith and together they sent the following telegram to Charles Fuller:

We cannot announce plan without good advertising literature and catalog. This could not be available until July. Moreover we need assurance of one more professor and registrar before advertising can be written. Ten months of preparation and wide publicity in press not a wasted year. We all believe this is our life-work. Great things are before us.

But by now Charles Fuller was not at all willing to postpone starting the seminary until September, 1948. God had remarkably worked in enabling him to buy the Cravens property for no more than the $145,000 he had put down. Before the final chance to bid, it was known that two other parties were interested in the property. One party had wanted to make a swank social club out of the estate. But for some reason neither of these parties showed up for the final bidding session, and the judge ruled that the property should be deeded over to the FEA. Later, neither of the two men could quite understand why he had not come to place his bid. "Why did we let that man Fuller beat us to it?" one of them complained. "Well," reasoned the other, "maybe he prayed."

To finance buying the Cravens property, Charles Fuller sold two-thirds of the Walnut Street property and leased the other third. Now that he owned this highly improved Cravens property, Charles Fuller did not want to waste money maintaining it for eighteen months before it would be used. Also, by announcing the seminary's opening over the radio, he could give it a boost and visibility far beyond what the printed word could do. And how could he be sure he would still have this vastly effective medium of communication a year hence? Then, too, Charles Fuller, with his characteristic urge to get the Gospel out to as many people as quickly as possible, did not want to delay sending out the first graduates for a whole year. If they could start with fifty men in the fall of 1947, that would mean fifty men ready to preach the Gospel in the spring of 1950, and why lose a whole year getting such men out? So he wired back to Drs. Henry and Smith as follows: "God has worked so marvelously we should do our very best. Do not favor seventeen months' delay unless He absolutely closes doors."

But as this second crucial meeting convened in Chicago on Wednesday-Thursday, May 13–14, 1947, none but Charles Fuller really believed the school would begin that next September. In Drs. Smith and Henry, only two of the four faculty that would be needed were on hand. Indeed, Dr. Everett F. Harrison, professor of New Testament at Dallas Seminary, whom Harold Ockenga had contacted, had indicated a willingness to consider moving to Pasadena by September and would be joining the meeting the next day, but who would that fourth man be?

The meeting began with a prolonged season of prayer. Then Harold Ockenga began the discussion, following a carefully prepared agenda. Wilbur Smith has written how in that time together "there seemed to be an unusual consciousness of the presence of God, giving wisdom, liberty in discussion, prompting suggestions, keeping us from disastrous mistakes, and, hour by hour, knitting us together in a fellowship which we knew was rare upon earth, even in Christian educational institutions."[3] As the meeting progressed that day with Charles Fuller recounting the wonderful way God had procured the Cravens property, the possibility of opening the seminary's doors four months hence seemed to grow. But they needed a fourth man. Carl Henry suggested that Dr. Harold Lindsell, a colleague who was professor of missions and associate professor of church history at Northern Baptist Seminary, would certainly be a suitable man. After earning a doctorate at New York University, he had been a professor of church history and missions at Columbia Bible College in South Carolina for two years. When contacted he said he was interested and would be on hand that second day when Everett Harrison would also be present.

At noon that second day deliberations on starting the school began in earnest. After two hours of quiet, calm discussion and prayer, everyone agreed that the announcement to open the school *that coming fall* should be made. Along with their teaching duties, Carl Henry would be the dean for at least a year, and Harold Lindsell would be the registrar. Carl Henry would prepare a very attractive advertising layout which would be sent to several religious magazines as one way to announce the opening of this new seminary. Charles Fuller agreed to announce the opening of the school over the radio on June 22, to coincide with the announcement coming out in the July magazines.

As Charles Fuller flew home from Chicago after that fateful meeting, his heart was filled with joy and thanksgiving to God for working so wonderfully to bring about agreement to launch the school beginning that next September 29th. But he also trembled to think of how much work would have to be done by then. Fortunately, I had just arrived home from having spent one year at Princeton Theological Seminary, and I did a lot of leg work. I purchased the pulpit and folding chairs to put in the new chapel, as well as desk chairs and blackboards for the classrooms. I wrote to each of the professors to get lists of books they wanted for classes

---

[3] Wilbur M. Smith, *A Voice for God* (Boston: W. A. Wilde, 1950), p. 188.

that fall, and proceeded to open up accounts with various publishers under the name of the Fuller Seminary Book Store.

Mr. Ernest Buegler, an ex-army chef who had used his culinary skills to feed students at Prairie Bible Institute in Canada and later at Moody, was busily at work setting up the kitchen and dining room facilities. Half of Wilbur Smith's 14,000 books arrived at the Cravens mansion early in June, and workers busily built shelves in one of the large bedrooms where his library would be stored.

Miss Mary Ashley (now Mrs. Daniel Lansing), who had been a secretary with the FEA, set up a registrar's office and began to process the applications which were already coming in. At that time she was functioning as the registrar's secretary, since Harold Lindsell, the registrar, was committed to spend the summer in New Hampshire and could not come west until September. But on his way to New Hampshire early in July, he and Carl Henry spent an afternoon with Harold Ockenga at Park Street Church, mapping out the curriculum for the first year and sketching out the catalog that had to be published immediately and sent to prospective students.

The "Old Fashioned Revival Hour" was not on any network at that time, and so some broadcasts were recordings of services conducted at Long Beach as much as a month earlier. For all stations to have announced the new seminary by June 22, Charles Fuller had to make the announcement at the Long Beach service on May 31. Some stations on the west coast were carrying the broadcast "live," or later that same day, and so inquiries about the new school had been coming in ever since the end of May. I recall one man who was to be a member of the seminary's first class telling how he was sitting in his car with his girl in front of her Oakland home, listening to the broadcast that Sunday and heard Charles Fuller tell of the new seminary that would soon open. For some time he had received much spiritual help through the "Old Fashioned Revival Hour." Now he was about to graduate from the University of California (Berkeley), and when he heard that Charles Fuller was starting a seminary, it came to him in a flash that God wanted him to begin training there that next fall. (According to surveys of entering classes made during the early years, more than half the students who enrolled, until about 1960, said the chief reason they came was the blessing they had received from the "Old Fashioned Revival Hour.")

From the applications that were coming in it was clear that a large percentage of the students would be married. Many of these were veterans who had been in service for several years after graduating from college. But where could adequate housing be found for these married students? The FEA owned a few old houses across from the Walnut Street property, which had been remodeled so they could house several couples, but many more apartments would be needed. My father was staying at the Mount Hermon Conference Grounds that summer, and I remember how burdened he became as the weeks drew nearer to the time when married students would be arriving. He had real estate agents looking for an apartment complex that could be purchased, and what a great relief and answer to prayer it was when a phone call came from Miss Rose Baessler, his secretary in Pasadena, telling of a complex of sixteen apartments that was available.

But a much more serious crisis was developing. The Cravens property was part of a mile-long row of estates on South Orange Grove Boulevard that had been built two or three decades earlier by immensely wealthy people. The "golden age" of that street had now passed, and Pasadena's zoning commission was being petitioned to allow a hotel and multiple dwelling units to be built there. Everyone felt quite certain that the street's zoning category was going to be changed, and so Charles Fuller had indeed acted responsibly to purchase a property for a school even while it was still zoned only for residential use. The man who wanted to build the hotel was bringing his petition before the commission in June. Many felt that his petition would be granted, and so it seemed that the FEA could then ask for a use variance to permit the Cravens property to be used for a school. (For many years there had been a fashionable girls' school directly across from the Cravens estate.)

Unexpected opposition to the building of a hotel developed, however, and this same opposition also vented itself against granting a zone variance for a school. Now Charles Fuller went through one of the hardest times of testing in his life. At the rate the registrar was receiving applications, it was clear that there would be about forty students arriving in just a few weeks. Four professors had now burned their bridges behind them and had either arrived or soon would be coming. They were making down payments on homes in Pasadena. The thirty-two room mansion had been fitted out as a school with desks in the classrooms, books in the library rooms, faculty offices set up, and eating facilities established; but the property was still zoned for residential use only.

Satan hurled fiery darts at Charles Fuller during those rapidly passing days of the summer of 1947. Would he not be the laughing stock of the world to have announced on an international broadcast the founding of a school on a piece of property that the law said could not be used for a school? I remember my father remarking to a friend what an awful thrust of anguish he felt one day that summer as he drove past the Walnut Street property and wished he had hung onto it instead of buying the Cravens estate. But then he said, "God has remarkably lifted the burden since then and has given me a peace that passes all understanding." At another time he and my mother were tempted to say, "Just think how much trouble we could have avoided if we hadn't started a seminary. We could have simply gone on with the radio ministry and the FEA and enjoyed the fruits of our labors during our remaining years." But he also remembered how he had tried, without success, to shake off the conviction that he ought to start a seminary. Then, too, God had miraculously worked to help him out of many impossible situations before, and surely this present crisis would be no exception.

The solution to the problem did not come, as hoped, through getting a zone variance before school started. Rather, it lay along the rather humiliating pathway of having classes meet in the assembly rooms of the educational building of the Lake Avenue Congregational Church. Three years earlier the church had voted to let the Fuller College of Missions and Evangelism hold classes there until it could construct its own buildings, and as Charles Fuller consulted with his good friend, the pastor, Dr. James Henry Hutchins, he said he believed that the decision made then would apply for the seminary now.

But the decision to follow this option was delayed as long as possible. Another meeting of the zoning commission was coming up soon after classes were to commence, and there was hope that the city authorities would let the school carry on at the Cravens estate until the final decision was reached. Admittedly, there was some wishful thinking in this because it was hard to concede that the Cravens estate, whose procurement had been the chief encouragement to start the school in 1947 instead of 1948, could not be used now for a school after all.

Above: *Harold Ockenga, Charles Fuller, Everett Harrison, Harold Lindsell, Wilbur Smith, Arnold Grunigen, and Carl F. H. Henry stand in front of building on Cravens estate, original location of the seminary (1947).* **Below:** *The first entering class of Fuller Seminary, following opening convocation at Pasadena Civic Auditorium, October, 1947.*

Fuller Seminary's first president, Harold Ockenga, looks on as Dr. and Mrs. Fuller break ground for erection of permanent building; at right, board member Dean Stephan and James Henry Hutchins, the Fullers' pastor.

Sharing experiences with seminary class in evangelism.

On Monday morning students did begin to register for classes at the Cravens property, and the next day a qualifying examination in Greek was given and some classes were even held there. But on that day the city fire marshal had to inform the school that while students could be housed and fed and professors could have their offices there, no actual class instruction could be carried on. On Wednesday evening of that very next day the seminary's opening convocation was scheduled to be held in the Pasadena Civic Auditorium, and President Harold Ockenga was going to bring the inaugural address. The "Old Fashioned Revival Hour" chorus and quartet would sing, but that Wednesday morning the duty fell to me to stand at the driveway entrance to the Cravens property and tell each student as he drove up to turn around and go two miles away to the Lake Avenue Church, where classes would be meeting instead.

There was some confusion, but the thirty-nine men who had come to this new seminary for training were able to carry on with their scheduled classes in Greek exegesis, introduction to the New Testament (Dr. Harrison), apologetics (Dr. Smith), revelation and inspiration (Dr. Henry), and church history (Dr. Lindsell). The assembly rooms in the church's educational building were large enough, but we members of that first class will never quite forget the incongruity of hearing Carl Henry's insights into the theory of religious knowledge while sitting on kindergarten chairs taking notes. But within a day or so the classroom desks that were at the Cravens property were set up in these rooms.

The final zoning decision for South Orange Grove Boulevard was to permit garden apartments but no hotels or schools. So the seminary classes continued to meet in the Lake Avenue Church for the next six years, until property was procured back near the center of Pasadena, on Oakland Avenue, and the permanent buildings the seminary now occupies were completed for the classes beginning in the fall of 1953. Indeed, it was inconvenient for faculty offices, the library, and single student housing to be located at the Cravens property, two miles from where the professors actually taught, where the daily chapel service was held, and where the study hall with its reserve and reference books was located. But a school's worth depends far more upon its faculty than upon its physical features. Dr. David Hubbard, who has been president of the seminary since 1963, was a member of the third entering class, and one day he remarked to me, his dean, "You know, even though we were sitting in kindergarten rooms in those days, we still had a great school because we had a first-rate faculty," and I heartily concurred with him. This policy of having a first-rate faculty has continued over the years as the number of the faculty for the seminary has grown from four to seventeen men.

Twenty-five hundred people attended the convocation for the new seminary at the Pasadena Civic Auditorium. Charles Fuller shared his vision for founding a seminary and then introduced Harold Ockenga, the president of the seminary, who spoke eloquently of just why it was so important for men who were already college graduates to spend three more years in preparation for the preaching of the Gospel, and why the general Christian public should not only support those carrying on ministries that are presently reaping fruits but also a seminary which would train to-morrow's Christian leaders. "We fling out the challenge of the Christian Gospel," Harold Ockenga said.

Now there is a task to be done. And that task is not going to be done by the ordinary Christian alone. It's going to be done by those who are prepared to do it. It must be done by the rethinking and re-stating of the fundamental thesis and principle of Western culture. There must be today men who have the time and energy and the in-clination and the ability and the support to be able to redefine Chris-tian thinking and to fling it forth into the faces of unbelievers every-where.

In other words, we need to rebuild the foundations and to restore the breaches. Where the foundations are destroyed what will the righteous do? We need men who can once again in an intellectually respectable way present an apology for God, and for His creation of the world, and for the soul, and for eternal life, and these things must be brought out so that our young men, and those who are going to take the places of leadership, will once again believe in the eternal law of an eternal God.

Now I have said something about our intellectual purpose and goal. Let me say something about the spiritual program. The Lord Jesus laid down His program, and the trouble with so many of us is that we don't follow His program. Here it is in all of its simplicity. He placed missions first. And I'll tell you that though we stress the academic preparation of these young men to preach and stand out before the world, yet their first and primary task is to be missionaries to the world. We must have hearts full of passion and zeal, that are on fire for Jesus Christ to win souls.

Harold Ockenga went on to tell of the need for graduates from such a seminary. He pointed out that every day one Protestant church in America was closing its doors, and that most of the major denominations were not training enough men to fill the pulpits of the remaining churches.

Now you say, Is it time to be building a theological seminary when the world's on fire? Such a question is legitimate. Well, if you don't build a theological seminary and train the men, and you don't send them out, who is going to do it? Are you going to do it? Is an untrained man going out? Who is going to occupy till Jesus comes? Listen to me, my friends, the quickest way to evangelize the world is to have divinely called, supernaturally born, spiritually equipped men of unction and power to go forth. We will *not* default. God helping us, we will occupy till Jesus comes.

He concluded his address as follows:

Pray for the school, for these men [the thirty-nine students who had enrolled were sitting near the front], pray for the faculty, pray for Dr. Fuller, pray that the needed funds will come in because though we have launched an expenditure of hundreds of thousands of dollars and have a fine start in every way, yet, my friends, it is only the beginning of what must be done. I say again, I envisage a school that can become the center of missions and evangelism on the basis of a Gospel of which we need not be ashamed because we can give a reason for the hope that is within us.

Thus Fuller Theological Seminary was launched, and the vision and burden which had weighed so heavily on Charles Fuller for the past eight years had finally become a reality. Yet, as Harold Ockenga had said, "It is only the beginning of what must be done." The seminary has made great advances in the years since the "small beginnings" of 1947, and the purpose of the remainder of this chapter is to show the crucial ways in which the seminary affected the last twenty years of Charles Fuller's life.

For many years the primary burden for the financial support of the seminary was on Charles Fuller's shoulders. Indeed, the school had enough money through the FEA to make "a fine start in every way," as Harold Ockenga put it in his inaugural address. But soon the faculty would have to be quadrupled so that students would be trained in all phases of a seminary curriculum. Then, too, large sums would be needed to erect the buildings the school would need. Since the Cravens property could not be used, money would also be needed to buy new land for the buildings. As Harold Ockenga closed his inaugural address by soliciting prayer that "the needed funds will come in," Charles Fuller knew how much the financial responsibility of the seminary rested on his shoulders.

Some may wonder why he would start a seminary without being quite sure where all the necessary money would come from. But as Harold Ockenga remarked at Charles Fuller's funeral in 1968, "Here was a man of faith who took great risks for God." When the FEA was founded, God had made it clear that it was to be used to found a school. Obeying God, then, meant using what the FEA had, to get the school started and trusting God for the rest. Charles Fuller was obedient to the heavenly vision, and God has marvelously blessed the seminary as it has grown these past twenty-five years.

Others may wonder why he did not look to his large radio audience for support for the expansion of the new school. This, however, was impossible, for the audience had to keep sending in twenty thousand dollars a week at that time just to keep the broadcast heard on its six to seven hundred outlets each Sunday. Charles Fuller had had enough experience in radio broadcasting by then to know that if he gave appeals to raise money for something besides the radio work, support for the radio work itself was very likely to decrease. Then, too, he knew that not everyone in the radio audience shared his vision for training men in a theological seminary. At the beginning his vision had not been to found a college but a seminary, and I well recall how often he talked of the need of establishing what he liked to call "a Cal Tech of the evangelical world." He wanted a school which would be as effective in getting out the Gospel as the California Institute of Technology had been in advancing science. By and large, however, the evangelical world and the people supporting the "Old Fashioned Revival Hour" were more interested in supporting a broadcast which was winning souls now than a seminary which would train men for effective work several years hence. Charles Fuller also sensed that the ordinary evangelical was a little distrustful of theological seminaries with all their emphasis on study. So he knew it would be impossible to depend on the radio audience for the development and support of the seminary.

A way that seemed open to him for raising the necessary funds was to visit wealthy evangelical leaders and try to enthuse them with his vision of the need for a theological seminary. In the spring of 1948 Charles Fuller went on several fund-raising trips in between Sunday broadcasts. But he was never a very good money raiser. He loathed asking individuals for money, and the strain of traveling all week and returning to preach on Sunday drained off all his energy. As he flew into Los Angeles late one Saturday evening in April, 1948, he was exhausted and downcast. Mrs. Fuller drove him home and put him to sleep in the guest room so he might be ready for his heavy responsibility the following day of preaching on the broadcast. But the next morning, while tiptoeing around so as not to awaken him, she was alarmed to hear sobs coming from the guest room. Going in she heard him say, "Oh, Lord, I'm so glad you're going to take me home. I'm so glad to go. I've done the very best I knew how to get the Gospel out. It's been a long battle, but you've been wonderful, Lord. But we're so far behind in getting the needed funds for the seminary, that I'll be so glad to go home now and be at rest with You."

Mrs. Fuller could see that her husband was suffering a very severe emotional breakdown, and she hurried to call the family doctor. Obviously, Charles Fuller would not be able to broadcast that Sunday, and when the doctor arrived, he predicted that from his experience with emotional breakdowns as severe as this apparently was, it would be months before Charles Fuller could broadcast again. Mrs. Fuller then called Wilbur Smith and asked him to preach that Sunday. But what would happen for the Sundays ahead? How could the broadcasts and the seminary carry on if Charles Fuller would be laid aside for months?

During that next week, however, he began to rally much more swiftly than the doctor had thought possible. As the coming Sunday drew near he had faith, against the doctor's advice, to attempt to preach. We all were very apprehensive as the time for the sermon approached. As he began, his voice was shaky and his hands trembled, but as the sermon progressed he began to preach with increased power. By its conclusion all the shakiness had gone and he was speaking with complete liberty and boldness. Over one hundred people came forward to accept Christ when the invitation was given. But as if that were not enough, Charles Fuller then gave an invitation for people to dedicate their lives to full-time vocational Christian service and to the amazement of everyone many more people responded. Not many after-services at Long Beach were like this one, but God was working that day to show that indeed His strength is made perfect in weakness. God also answered the prayers of many thousands who had heard that Charles Fuller was ill. In the May, 1948, *Heart to Heart Talk* he said,

I wish to thank each one of you for your prayers on my behalf, and for the many encouraging letters you sent during the past weeks. You will never know how they helped me during the time of utter exhaustion and weakness.

I have always been so well and strong . . . but this past year has been one of greatly increased responsibilities and intensified attacks on the part of the enemy as we have enlarged our borders under God's blessing.

Speaking to his radio audience through these monthly letters or over the radio, Charles Fuller could not say that the "greatly increased responsibilities" of the past year stemmed from the task of getting a theological seminary started.

The problem of providing the seminary with the financial undergirding it needed was a primary concern for him for the first sixteen years of its existence. God worked many miracles during that time to balance the budget and to enable the school to grow. But in 1963, when Charles Fuller was seventy-six years old, Dr. David A. Hubbard became the seminary's third president, and under his able leadership and that of other dedicated seminary board members, the financial responsibility for the seminary was basically shifted to other shoulders.

Another great difficulty which Charles Fuller constantly encountered as the result of having launched the seminary was the many criticisms that were directed against the school. The root cause for these is that a seminary or school will, by its very nature, be different from an evangelistic radio broadcast. In seeking to reach the millions who listened to his radio sermons, Charles Fuller naturally limited his remarks to those matters of greatest importance to the majority of such an audience. But stressing such matters meant not talking about other important matters. No evangelical found grounds for criticizing Charles Fuller as he continued to preach from Sunday to Sunday the simple truths of salvation by faith in Christ who died and rose, the need to live a life consistent with faith in Christ, the Second Coming of Christ, the Resurrection, and the future judgment.

But when the seminary was founded, American evangelicals were facing the very difficult problem of separation from apostasy—that is, the question of whether a local church belonging to a denomination many of whose leaders had become Liberal, should not separate from that denomination. A number of evangelicals had followed the answer to this question given by the American Council of Churches and its chief spokesman at that time, the Rev. Carl McIntire, editor of *The Christian Beacon*. For a church to belong to the American Council, it had to remove itself from all association with a denomination that was represented in the predominantly liberal Federal Council of Churches.

A larger group of evangelicals, however, followed the answer given to this question by the National Association of Evangelicals and particularly by Dr. Harold Ockenga, its president for the first two years. While remaining with a denomination represented on the Federal Council of Churches, a church could nevertheless join the NAE and thus join hands with many other evangelicals to accomplish tasks requiring a united effort.

Charles Fuller's own church, the Lake Avenue Congregational Church of Pasadena, joined the NAE, and his own sympathies were with it rather than with the alternate answer to this problem. But when he stepped before the microphone to use the twenty minutes allotted him each week to speak to millions, he was obviously not going to say anything about the issue of "separatism" and "come-outism." But when Harold Ockenga, as the president of the newly founded Fuller Theological Seminary, gave the inaugural address for this school, he had to say something about how the seminary would relate to the burning question of separatism. While a radio

214

broadcast seeking to win the lost would never touch upon such an issue, a school for training the ministers of tomorrow's churches could not avoid it.

Thus in his inauguration address Harold Ockenga said,

We do not intend to be ecclesiastically bound. We will be free. But we are ecclesiastically positive. In our church relationships, though we are interdenominational, we do not believe and we repudiate the "come-outism" movement. We want our men to be so trained that when they come from a denomination, whatever that denomination is, they will go back into their denomination adequately prepared to preach the Gospel and to defend the faith and to positively go forward in the work of God. We will not be negative.

No sooner had these words reverberated through the evangelical world than Charles Fuller began to receive irate letters from long-time supporters who, holding to the American Council position, felt that he had betrayed them and therefore wanted their names taken off his mailing list. But as the founder of a school, he stood behind the answers his seminary had to give to this and other crucial questions that would never be brought up on an evangelistic radio broadcast.[4]

Charles Fuller also lost radio supporters because of the stress of Harold Ockenga and the seminary on the need for evangelicals to relate the biblical teachings on love to the injustices of society. In their battle against Liberalism, Fundamentalists had, correctly,

---

[4] A careful reading of Harold Ockenga's famous statement quoted above will show that while he committed the new seminary definitely to the NAE position, he certainly did not make students coming from separatist churches unwelcome, for he said, "When students come from a denomination, *whatever that denomination is* [italics added], they will go back into their denomination adequately prepared to preach the Gospel . . . and to positively go forward in the work of God." Thus he was not repudiating all churches who at sometime in their history had been formed from a separation from a church deemed apostate, for had he meant that, he would have repudiated the Reformation itself. What he was repudiating was the *spirit* of separatism, which, with its implicit negativism, no sooner accomplished one split than a new one would develop within its midst. Many Fuller Seminary students have come from and gone back into denominations recently formed by a separation. But we are not aware of any Fuller graduate who has split a church, because the school's emphasis has been "to positively go forward in the work of God."

criticized the Liberals for teaching man's need to reform without stressing his need first to be regenerated. But Fundamentalists, in emphasizing regeneration, had sometimes sounded as if, in their concern for saving the individual, they had no concern to remedy socio-economic injustices.

As a leader of what might be called "the second generation of Fundamentalism," Harold Ockenga wanted to reawaken the social conscience of evangelicals. He had been particularly interested in Carl Henry's book, *The Uneasy Conscience of Modern Fundamentalism* (1946), which had taken evangelicals to task for neglecting social ethics for several decades, and this book's appearance was unquestionably one of the reasons why Carl Henry's name stood high on the list of those qualified for the faculty of the new seminary. But many evangelicals regarded this emphasis on social ethics as diluting the Gospel. As a result, more letters came into Charles Fuller's office from long-time supporters who now wanted their names expunged from his mailing list.

The same sort of problem continued through to the end of his life and beyond. He lost more radio supporters through the seminary's refusal to condemn the *Revised Standard Version* of the Bible. While it refused to condemn this version, as many Fundamentalists were doing, it also refused to give it a blanket endorsement. Instead, the seminary chose to maintain toward that translation (and others that have also appeared) a critical stance of testing it against the original Hebrew or Greek. The seminary has maintained a similarly critical stance toward the World Council of Churches. While refusing to endorse this council, the seminary has also refused to condemn it. The school has not wanted to close doors to any opportunity to represent the evangelical point of view before the leaders of that group. But through the years many hundreds of supporters have withdrawn their names from the broadcast's mailing list because the seminary which Charles Fuller founded and of which he was, for many years, the board chairman, maintained dialogue with the World Council of Churches.

A particularly heavy wave of criticism came with the publication in 1959 of Dr. Edward Carnell's book *The Case for Orthodoxy*. Edward Carnell was the president of the seminary from 1954 to 1959 and had been a professor there since 1948. In that book Edward Carnell had the courage to point up certain inconsistencies and foibles in the evangelical world, and with a prophetic note he had reminded Christians everywhere of the sobering implications of the command, "Love thy neighbor as thyself." In so speaking he violated some sacred cows, but he did this because he was convinced that a Christian school renounces its God-given commission when it seeks only to please the constituency from whom it derives its financial support and fails to remind the churches of some emphases of Scripture that they may not want to hear.

Over the years Charles Fuller lost many thousands of supporters of his broadcast because they did not like certain things the seminary said. Receiving letters from disillusioned supporters always caused him extreme anguish of soul, and in his weaker moments he would wonder whether the seminary faculty realized how much it was costing him for them to have the freedom to speak out on the burning issues affecting the evangelical cause. But then would come his better moments when he would remember that a seminary can adequately train those who will lead the churches only when it frankly airs the basic issues that confront the churches. The price of having a "Cal Tech of the evangelical world" was high, but then really small in comparison with the benefits which have been channeled throughout the world by the now more than twelve hundred graduates of the seminary.

Another source of anguish which the seminary brought to Charles Fuller was the inability of three of the Presbyterian members of the faculty to be admitted to the Los Angeles Presbytery after they had moved to Southern California. In November, 1953, Drs. Gleason Archer, Everett Harrison, and William LaSor were refused admission to the Presbytery because "to hold positions on the faculty of the . . . Fuller Theological Seminary, which, judged by past attitudes, records, and statements of some of its present officers and faculty members, will aid the [seminary] in such a way as to hamper the approved program of the Presbytery of Los Angeles." In talking about "past attitudes, records, and statements of some of its present officers," the Presbytery was thinking, in part, about what Charles Fuller did in previous years in relation to Placentia Presbyterian Church and to Dr. John MacInnis, a Presbyterian minister who resigned as dean of Biola just before Charles Fuller became president of the board there. As one member put it during the discussion on the floor of Presbytery,

A great deal of the attitude of this Presbytery is centered around . . . Rev. Charles E. Fuller. While he was a member of the board of trustees of the Los Angeles Bible Institute in 1928, according to the judgment of the Presbytery of Los Angeles . . . he did . . . "great wrong to a member of the Presbytery, the late John Murdock Mac-Innis, in private and in the public press, making it appear that Dr. MacInnis was of unsound faith and lacking in respect for Jesus Christ and the Holy Scriptures, in spite of repeated avowals on his part of loyalty to the historic standards of the Presbyterian Church . . ."

Another person remarked that

Mr. Fuller joined the Presbyterian Church in the little town of Placentia, and was in due course ordained as an elder. . . . Mr. Fuller had not been an elder long before it was discovered he was circulating literature among the young people without the approval of the session. This literature caused marked division and feeling. The session appealed for unity of action and spirit of cooperation. The appeal was apparently of no avail, for the session's record indicates the futility of all effort to have [Fuller's] teaching and actions in harmony with the feeling of the session. Ultimately, an independent church, the Calvary Church, was organized with Mr. Fuller as the pastor-founder . . . and in due course the sanctuary was built in Placentia some two blocks from our Presbyterian Church. . . . We all make mistakes, to be sure, but so far as I know, this former elder and founder of that church and the founder of the seminary in question has never repented of this act, but rather, if records that come to me are true, it seems to reveal a pattern that continues to be characteristic.

It hurt Charles Fuller to realize that three of the seminary faculty now had to move their ordination to other denominations, partly because of his actions in the 1920s. But both he and the faculty rejoiced as the graduates of each class from 1950 onwards began to serve Christ across the nation and around the world. Any thought of wishing the seminary had never been started were overcome by considering that of the two hundred fifty men who had graduated by 1955, thirty-seven were already serving on the foreign field and fifteen more had been accepted by mission boards and would soon be overseas. Of those already on the mission fields, six were in the Moslem world, eleven were in Latin America, four in Africa, eight in Asia, four in Oceania, and four in Europe. A glance at the bulletin published late in 1955 shows some of the places in America where the most recent graduates had gone to pastor churches: Trenton, Michigan; North Freedom, Wisconsin; Montrose, California; Santa Ana, California; Culver City, California; Battle Ground, Michigan; Chattanooga, Tennessee; Denver, Colorado.

Often letters came in from radio listeners blessed by graduates from the seminary. For example, a lady from Iowa wrote,

Dear Mr. Fuller,

I realize you are a very busy man, but I'm sure not too busy to hear about one of your students, a graduate of the class of 1952. He is our *Pastor*. You would be very proud of him if you would hear him preach. He is a spirit-filled man; not only does he preach the Word, in all its entirety, but he lives it as well. No one could possibly have a greater burden for the lost than he does, and for the backslidden members on the church roll. He devotes his entire time to God's work in calling, witnessing, teaching, and preaching. He has only been with us for six months, but many souls have been added to our church and many who were not coming are coming again. How it must thrill your heart to see these men go out, in service for the Master, to teach and preach like you.

A lady from Oregon wrote,

Dear Dr. and Mrs. Fuller,

Last summer I was in another town, and went to a church of the same denomination where I usually attend, but was so disappointed. The minister held a Bible in his hand and talked, but didn't make a grain of sense. The next Sunday I attended another church. But it also seemed cold and lacking in the presence of Christ. Well, the following Sunday as I went out the front door I prayed, "Please, God, take me to the right church." I walked around the corner to a very small frame building which looked as if it had been a residence converted into a church. The moment I stepped inside, I was so overcome by the feeling that Christ was there that it was difficult to keep back the tears. I said, "Thank you, God." Then the minister appeared and really preached the Word of God as I hadn't heard it preached in a long time. He was one of your graduates, I learned later.

When I came back home I asked God to direct me to a good church there. He did, and I found a church where God's Word was really preached, and the minister, I find, is a graduate of Fuller Theological Seminary.

Some of the seminary's graduates were doing just the things that were closest to Charles Fuller's heart. One man was working in the hill country of Kentucky, in the "out-of-the-way places," and wrote, "I can never thank you enough for the fine training received at the seminary. We want the Lord to use us here in this portion of the world's harvest field. You, Dr. Fuller, have many friends here." Mr. Akira Hatori graduated from Fuller Seminary and returned to Japan, where he preaches daily on a nation-wide broadcast. Shortly after leaving the seminary he wrote my father:

We praise His name for His great power manifested in your radio ministry. It has been a wonderful encouragement and testimony to me as I undertake the same ministry in Japan. Being a graduate from your seminary and being given the same radio ministry, your name and testimony never leave my mind.

Thus Charles Fuller's vision not only to get the Gospel out by radio but also by training men to be effective witnesses themselves has surely been realized over the years. Furthermore, the effort to have a school which would send men back into their denominations to do a positive work for God there was proving very successful. At the time of Charles Fuller's death, the more than nine hundred graduates of the school were serving in forty denominations. One hundred three were serving in the United Presbyterian Church, U.S.A.; seventy-seven were in the American Baptist Convention; sixty-eight in the Conservative Baptist Association; twenty-nine in the Baptist General Conference; eighteen in the Congregational Church; sixteen in the United Church of Christ; fifteen in the Methodist Church; and fourteen in the Christian and Missionary Alliance. A considerable number of graduates were also working with nondenominational groups: twenty-two with Wycliffe Bible Translators; twenty with Young Life; eighteen were Inter-Varsity staff members; five were with Campus Crusade for Christ; and three were working with the Navigators.

One particularly encouraging bit of news that Charles Fuller heard in 1965, two years before his final illness, was that the two faculty members (the third had gone to another school) who had had to relinquish their Presbyterian ordination in order to continue to teach at Fuller had now been readmitted to the local Presbytery.

The Presidency of the Seminary

Charles Fuller always realized that he lacked the gifts and training necessary to organize a seminary and run it himself. So much depended on having the seminary led by an educator who also shared his zeal for evangelism. Harold Ockenga was the leader who, especially during those crucial first years of the seminary's history, set the tone for the school by the faculty he recruited, by the kind of curriculum he set up, and in many other ways as well.

During those early years Harold Ockenga was open to the possibility that God would lead him to become the resident president of the seminary. When the three-story classroom and administration building was completed at 135 North Oakland Avenue and at last all the school's facilities were assembled at one location, Harold Ockenga knew that the time had come for him finally to decide whether or not to move to Pasadena. In the months leading up to the board meetings and his visit to Pasadena in the spring of 1954, he went through much soul-searching over this question: should he leave Park Street Church with its ever-growing missionary outreach and key ministry for the evangelical cause in the difficult New England area? God had given him a great gift for expository preaching, and his two sermons on Sunday were aired over a powerful Boston radio station. He had been a pastor for almost twenty-five years; should he now leave all this behind to become primarily a seminary president? To make the transition from Park Street to Pasadena would be very difficult, but there was the seminary now fully established and needing the day-to-day supervision of a resident president if it were to grow properly from this point on. What should he do? He decided to put out a "fleece" as a means for knowing whether or not God wanted him to make this move.

The board was naturally very eager to learn what Harold Ockenga's decision would be. Charles Fuller had great hopes that he would decide to come, but he also appreciated how difficult it would

Charles Fuller congratulates his son, Daniel, on his inauguration as dean of faculty in 1962, after completing studies in Europe.

Above left: *With seminary students (left to right) Chris Smith, Paul Birch, Ed Gregory, Michael Cassidy, Dick Peace, and Don Ehat (seated) who formed original Africa Enterprise team. Dr. Fuller encouraged founding of organization in 1963.* **Above right:** *Robert Gerry, member of first graduating class, tells Dr. Fuller of his work with Christian Literature Crusade in Japan.* **Below:** *Part of student body and faculty in fall of 1959.*

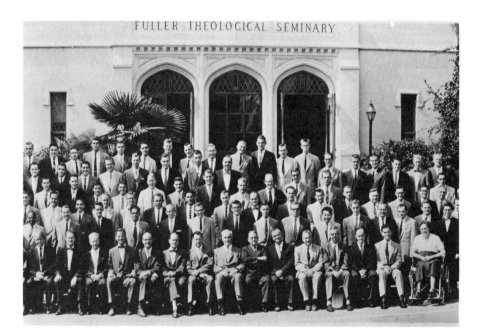

be for him to leave behind all the work that was being so blessed in Boston. In particular he wondered how Harold Ockenga could be happy in Pasadena without a regular preaching schedule.

That spring Charles Fuller turned sixty-seven, and he realized that he would not be able to carry on the broadcast indefinitely. He was feeling more weary after his Long Beach broadcasts than in previous years. The thought occurred to him, might not the time now be right to turn the broadcast over to a younger man, and if so, why not turn it over to Harold Ockenga? Then as president of the seminary he could still have a regular preaching schedule and be heard by many millions. But then what would he, Charles Fuller, do for the remaining years of his life? He would no doubt greatly enjoy taking a vacation for awhile, but would not the time soon come when he would be restless to be preaching over a microphone again?

One night during Harold Ockenga's visit Charles Fuller became so exercised over the matter that he had difficulty sleeping. Harold Ockenga was staying in the downstairs guest room, and early the next morning Charles Fuller decided to have a talk with him. He went down to his door and said, "Harold, are you up? I must talk with you."

Harold Ockenga answered, "Come in, Charles, come in," as he pulled on a robe and offered his friend a chair.

"Harold, I could hardly sleep last night thinking about an important matter. I've come to a decision. I want you to take over the 'Old Fashioned Revival Hour.' "

Harold Ockenga covered his face with his hands and gasped, "Oh, Charles, that's the fleece! I told the Lord that if the door would be opened for me to carry on my preaching ministry by being on the 'Old Fashioned Revival Hour,' I would take this as an indication that I should move to California and become the president of Fuller Seminary."

The board and faculty were elated when they learned that Harold Ockenga had decided to move to Pasadena, and plans were made for him to be there as resident president that next September. But after a few days Harold Ockenga began to have second thoughts. He went through great agony of soul as he returned to Boston and announced to his congregation that he would be leaving them soon. The Park Street congregation was also deeply distressed. Some of them organized a caravan of cars to drive up to New Hampshire where he was vacationing to show him just how much they wanted him to stay. He was deeply touched by their love, but the courage to reverse his decision came only after much prayer during that vacation time.

It was by no means easy for him to counter the announcement he had made publicly at his church and which had gone out as a news release on the national wire services. Many another man, fearing the reproach that such a change of mind would bring, would have doggedly gone through with the original decision. But when Harold Ockenga, through much prayer, realized that God did not want him to take the "fleece" as a final indication of His will, he wired the seminary to cancel all forthcoming publications that were about to announce his coming.

Subsequent events seem to have confirmed the wisdom of this decision. As Harold Ockenga continued on as pastor of Park Street Church for another fifteen years, its missionary outreach and ministry continued to grow. As for Charles Fuller, whereas he had moments when he felt tired and thought it would be a relief to stop, yet it was God's plan for him to go right on preaching Sunday after Sunday on the "Old Fashioned Revival Hour" for yet *another thirteen years!* When Harold Ockenga visited me in 1961 while I was studying theology in Switzerland, he remarked how thankful he was that he had reversed his decision in 1954. "Wouldn't it have been awful," he said, "if I would have gone ahead and become speaker on the broadcast back in 1954! How could your father have stood it to be on the sidelines all these subsequent years?"

When it was clear that Harold Ockenga would not move to California, it was then necessary to find another president, and the board of trustees offered the post to Edward Carnell, the professor of apologetics and systematic theology since 1948. A man with great scholarly and teaching abilities, Edward Carnell accepted the presidency with the understanding that he would function more as an academic headmaster than as an aggressive fund raiser, a task for which he regarded himself as definitely unqualified. Harold Ockenga then became president of the board of trustees, while Charles Fuller became executive vice-president of the board.

Under Edward Carnell's leadership the seminary made some

225

notable advances. The most significant of these was achieving full accreditation in 1957 from the American Association of Theological Seminaries, the nationally recognized accrediting agency for theological seminaries. One problem that had stood in the way of accreditation was that the seminary, though it had become a separate corporation in 1951, was financially dependent to a large extent on the FEA. But in 1956 the FEA deeded to the seminary the land on which its building now stood, and also the assets that were posted as collateral for the loan which had made it possible to build.

Evangelist Billy Graham also came onto the board of trustees during Edward Carnell's presidency. During the spring of 1956, Billy Graham was holding a crusade in the Cow Palace in San Francisco, and as Charles Fuller visited that crusade one evening and the two men were sitting together, Charles Fuller invited Billy Graham to come on the board, pointing out how that would demonstrate their oneness in the cause of evangelism. Billy Graham agreed and later said, "I personally feel a sense of mission about the work being accomplished by Fuller graduates, and I like to think of it as 'scholarship on fire.' " For himself, Charles Fuller said, "God has used Billy Graham to point thousands to Christ, and I am confident that by his part in helping to direct this young seminary, he will greatly multiply his own ministry." After five very fruitful years as president, Edward Carnell resigned and returned to his teaching and writing. He had passed out the five-hundredth diploma that commencement evening in 1959 when he announced his resignation. Now the board of trustees was again faced with the question of who would be the president of this flourishing seminary which now had three hundred students from one hundred colleges and universities and from forty denominations.

For the next three years Harold Ockenga was acting president again. He continued to make several journeys a year to California. (In 1967 he estimated that in the past twenty years he had traveled to Pasadena one hundred thirty times and had been a guest in the Fuller's home seventy-five times.) A most notable achievement during these three years was the construction of the McAlister Library Building, where the school's fifty thousand books could be adequately housed and where more than two hundred thousand could eventually be accommodated.

In 1962 Mr. C. Davis Weyerhaeuser became the chairman of the board of trustees, and a committee was formed to find a resident president. Its efforts were rewarded when Dr. David A. Hubbard became the seminary's third president in 1963. Graduating from the seminary in 1952, David Hubbard had then earned a doctor's degree in the field of Old Testament from St. Andrew's University in Scotland. Committed to evangelism as well as scholarship, he had held month-long preaching missions while studying for his doctorate in Scotland. He had then taught at Westmont College and been chairman of the biblical department there. He had sung in the "Old Fashioned Revival Hour" choir for several years both before and after his study period in Scotland. Charles Fuller had had him preach on the program in January, 1962.

Dr. Hubbard was thirty-five when he became president. Admittedly, he was a young man for such a responsible post, yet the board was convinced that he was remarkably well suited for the task. Almost twenty years before, Charles Fuller had talked of his need to find a younger man to carry on the school. More than anyone, Harold Ockenga had been that man for sixteen years. But now in David Hubbard, Charles Fuller had that younger man who could fully shoulder the responsibility of the seminary, and who would, in time, become the featured speaker on the broadcast.

9. Last Days

PLANS FOR NEW developments in the seminary were under way soon after David Hubbard occupied the president's office. I was inaugurated as dean of the faculty several months prior to his becoming president. Now he appointed me to head up a committee to make recommendations for revising the curriculum for the three-year seminary course. Harold Lindsell, who was still with the seminary as vice-president, was appointed to head up a committee to design the requirements for a fourth year of study that would lead to the Doctor of Ministry degree. A number of other seminaries were moving in this direction, and the faculty of Fuller Seminary saw such a program as an opportunity to upgrade training for the ministry.

Primarily through the initiative of board member C. Davis Weyerhaeuser, the seminary further broadened its horizon by launching a satellite School of Psychology. Men enrolled in this school would take much of the theology and biblical studies of the divinity program and then would continue for another four years to earn a Doctor of Philosophy degree and be qualified as clinical psychologists. During David Hubbard's first year as president many conferences and consultations were held to make plans for such a school, and when Dr. Lee Travis agreed a year or so later to be the dean of this new school, final steps were then taken to commence its operation in the fall of 1965. The School of Psychology has been in operation ever since, and as of fall, 1971, has conferred degrees on seventeen graduates who are serving the churches in various ways as Christian psychologists. Not only do these men uphold a Christian approach to psychology in the various clinics in which they now serve; many also work in conjunction with churches as counselors to whom pastors can refer problem cases that require special help.

It wasn't long after the seminary began to think about having a satellite school alongside its main program that wheels began to turn inside the mind of Charles Fuller, who as a member of its board of trustees was still very involved in the ongoing life of the school.

Though seventy-seven years old now, he dreamed of promoting still another venture that would help finish the task of evangelizing the world. Why not have alongside the main seminary program also a satellite school of missions? His seminary now had a full-time president with the energy, time, and ability to launch and administer several new programs, so why not let him use all this to start a school of missions? Charles Fuller and the board of trustees soon thereafter directed David Hubbard to launch plans for such a school.

Actually the thought of having such a school in conjunction with the seminary had been in the back of Charles Fuller's mind for the past seven years. In going through my father's sermons and records of the broadcast shortly after his death, I was amazed to find the following statement made during the course of a sermon preached on the "Old Fashioned Revival Hour" in 1957, when the program still originated from Long Beach:

Pray for laborers! God speaking tells us that the laborers are few, that the multitudes are scattered as sheep having no shepherd. I am informed along this line that in the Protestant branch of Christianity, there are some 30,000 home and foreign missionaries. The world's population I believe exceeds two billion people. And I have been told that if the Protestant branch alone would really catch the vision and give as God leads, and have a compassionate heart and pour out as God has prospered, 350,000 missionaries would be sent as flaming evangels across the nations. And who knows but that if we could send 350,000 true missionaries, the world would be evangelized in one generation and Jesus would come—we would hasten His coming. The crime of it is that a lot of the present 30,000 missionaries are living on some things hardly able to keep body and soul together. Pray! And if we pray in real honest faith believing, God will answer by asking some that pray to go, and others to give of their substance, enabling others who feel the call, to go. Did it ever occur to you that actually every born-again believer is a foreign missionary? Let me explain. Colossians 1:13 tells us that at conversion you and I who have received Christ are delivered from the power of darkness and translated into the kingdom of God's dear Son. Couple that with Philippians 3:20. It informs us that our citizenship is in heaven. You and I are strangers and pilgrims here. This world is not our home. And in the true sense of the word every believer is a foreign missionary, a witness here on this earth unto Jesus. Let's all begin at home, in your neighborhood, your business, and your circle of friends—begin at Jerusalem

229

Judea, Samaria, and then to the uttermost parts of the earth. Begin first and say, Lord, lay some souls upon my heart and help me to win those souls to thee. That's what the Church of Jesus Christ needs.

And may I be just a little personal. May I just take you into my confidence. Ten years ago God raised up Fuller Theological Seminary in Pasadena. This Seminary stands true to the inspired Word of God, true to the faith once delivered. At the end of ten years, God has given us four hundred graduates, highly trained but above all spiritually minded and enlightened. Ninety of these four hundred graduates are either on the mission field or are learning the language, ready to take their place to witness for Jesus Christ. Twenty-two and a half percent of our graduates are on the mission fields. But I'll tell you something that is on my heart—and in the night hours I have been awakened time after time to pray—and that is that God would somehow lay it upon the hearts of the people world-wide to stand by in prayer and help us to make the Missions and Evangelistic departments of the Fuller Theological Seminary the best, highest, truest training departments in all the world for missions and evangelism. That is my burden, and I will be so glad if the Lord permits me to see that before He comes or He takes me home. We have a fine Missions department and a fine Evangelism department under Dr. Booth, formerly of Providence, Rhode Island, and God is blessing. The boys are soul-winners, the teachers are soul-winners; but I want to see a training school that will outshine anything, for God's glory. Will you pray with me? Oh, the need is so great. I can hardly sleep. And I want to say to you—what joy, what heart satisfaction, to see God's choice young men and women, not only to be trained as missionaries and teachers, but to be His sent-forth ones into the fields where millions have not yet heard the precious name of Jesus. Old Fashioned Revival Hour friends, under God I believe that is what he would have all of us do on this Hour—to emphasize missions and evangelism in these closing days.

Thus in the fall of 1964, David Hubbard appointed a school of missions committee, with Dr. William S. LaSor, professor of Old Testament at the seminary since 1948, as its chairman. He was a master of a dozen or more languages and a specialist in Semitics, but he had always been very concerned about foreign missions, and he threw his whole heart into directing the committee to dream and plan about such a new school. That committee was greatly helped by Dr. J. Christy Wilson, Sr., who was teaching a missions course at Fuller Seminary at that time. For many years he had been a missionary to the Arab world and was cast somewhat in the mold of

Dr. Samuel Zwemer. Dr. J. Kenneth Strachan, general director of the Latin America Mission, had also been teaching Missions with his particular emphasis on "Evangelism in Depth" at the seminary since the preceding spring. These two men met with the committee each Monday afternoon and helped direct its thinking on whether the world missionary enterprise would be helped most by a school whose curriculum was built around linguistics, comparative religions, anthropology, theology, or the history of missions. Would the teaching of a school of missions sufficiently differ from that of a seminary to justify setting up a separate school? David Hubbard, William LaSor, and I picked the brains of many a missionary leader as he came through Pasadena that year in order to get some lead on how such a school might be set up.

Early in 1965 our attention focused upon Dr. Donald McGavran, who several years before had founded an Institute of Church Growth in connection with the Northwest Christian College in Eugene, Oregon. Donald McGavran had been a missionary in India for thirty years. A characteristic trait of his work there was his conviction that the task of a missionary was not fulfilled simply by proclaiming the Gospel whether or not any conversions resulted. He was impressed that Paul had not stayed long where there was little or no response to the Gospel but had used his time and energy among people who were responsive. Therefore in 1937 Donald McGavran had asked the leaders of his mission to send him to an area in India whose people gave evidence of being more receptive to the Gospel.

Donald McGavran also knew that the people in Africa, Asia, and Latin America are bound together in more tightly structured societies than in North America and Europe. In a country like India, people act more in concert with their family and social group than they do as individuals. Thus as he and his wife evangelized the villages of this part of India, they worked more to see groups of families turn to Christ than to single out individuals with whom they would then work. As a result, a church would be established in a village as a group of families turned to Christ. When the McGavrans left that area in 1954, there were on-going churches of about ten families in each of fifteen villages.

Encouraged by this experience, Donald McGavran made a study of missionary enterprises in other lands, in order to understand why churches in one area had shown growth over the years, while other

231

missionary efforts sometimes had only a handful of converts to show for it all. He began to discover certain principles which explained, in part, why some churches grew while others languished, and he spelled these out chiefly in two books, *The Bridges of God* (1955) and *How Churches Grow* (1959), which were widely read in the missionary world.

As a result, missionaries increasingly consulted him about the peculiar situations in their own fields. To satisfy this demand, in 1961 Donald McGavran began the Institute of Church Growth at Eugene, Oregon. This school of missions was set up to help missionaries who had already been on the foreign field; it was not for college or seminary graduates who were yet to go abroad. Each year about fifteen missionaries home on furlough and from many different mission boards came to study with Donald McGavran. During this time he would help them formulate the questions that should be asked about their fields in order that the crucial factors influencing or hindering the growth of churches would come to light. As these missionaries would propose changes in the strategy to increase the rate by which converts would become active church members, McGavran would cross-examine them to help them think out their strategy with greater clarity.

Mr. Alan Tippett was one of the first missionaries to come to Eugene. An Australian, he had been a missionary in the Fiji Islands for twenty years. He studied with Donald McGavran the first year, and then as he worked toward his Ph.D. in anthropology at the University of Oregon only a block away, he began to teach part time in the Institute of Church Growth. He received his doctorate in 1964, so that both he and Dr. McGavran, who had received his Ph.D. from Yale some years before, constituted a small but qualified faculty for a school of missions which already had a clientele of career missionaries.

As the committee at Fuller Seminary carried on conversations with missionary leaders, the name of Donald McGavran and the term "church growth" kept coming up. Why shouldn't a school of missions primarily emphasize the question of why churches grow? With such an emphasis in the forefront, a school would be less prone to veer away from the task of evangelism than might be the case if its primary emphasis were, say, linguistics, or anthropology. Then, too, Donald McGavran already had a functioning school of missions that missionary leaders the world over regarded as contributing vitally to their task. So we began conversations with Donald McGavran to explore the possibility of his moving his school to Pasadena. How much better it would be to commence with a school of missions that was already functioning and serving the missionary cause! In the spring of 1965, an invitation was extended to him and Alan Tippett to move their Institute of Church Growth to Pasadena, where their school would become another satellite school to the Fuller Theological Seminary. They accepted the invitation, and the School of World Mission and Institute of Church Growth opened on the Fuller Seminary campus in the fall of 1965 with Dr. McGavran as dean under President Hubbard and Dr. Alan Tippett as the second faculty member. Sixteen career missionaries from twelve lands came to study that first year in Pasadena.

Thus at a time in life when Charles Fuller would have been perfectly justified to settle back and carry on his radio broadcast until the Lord took him home, 'he once again ventured forth for God, like Caleb, and brought substance to the vision God had given him since 1957. But in enabling this school to begin, God did exceedingly abundantly above all we could ask and think. A school of missions had been regarded as a place where young people fresh out of college or seminary would get further training in missions before going overseas. But when we talked in such terms with mission executives, we noted that they were dubious that this type of school would be of much help. They were not sure that what they needed most were missionary candidates who had had an extra dose of classroom courses in missions. They feared that graduates from such a school with a degree in missions might be somewhat less teachable and might find it harder to learn the lessons that only mission field experience provides. But now God had worked to raise up a school which *veteran missionaries* attended while on furlough. Because such people were already experienced missionaries, they could far more readily appreciate and profit from the teaching of such veteran missionaries as Donald McGavran and Alan Tippett. And missions executives have certainly shown no small interest in such a school, for each year more have seen to it that their key missionaries take a course of study at Fuller's School of World Mission and Institute of Church Growth.

At the present time (fall, 1971), this school has a faculty of six and a student body of more than eighty missionaries and nationals, from forty-one separate countries. Some two hundred fifty missionaries have attended there in the past seven years, and sixty-four of them have received degrees. Many a missionary will testify how much this school has helped him. It has become so popular among missionaries that it is regarded as *the* place to go if one can possibly work it out during his furlough.

Today Donald McGavran remains actively engaged in teaching, but has transferred the deanship of the school to Dr. Arthur Glasser, once a missionary to China and then home director for North America of the Overseas Missionary Fellowship (formerly the China Inland Mission). The most recent addition to this school's faculty is the Rev. C. Peter Wagner, who graduated from Fuller Seminary in 1955 and then spent sixteen years as a missionary in Bolivia. The board of the Fuller Evangelistic Association recently brought him on to serve also as its executive director.

In the spring of 1965, while plans were moving swiftly to open the doors of the new School of World Mission in a few months, Charles Fuller also called upon David Hubbard to preach for him occasionally on the "Old Fashioned Revival Hour." In introducing him to his radio audience, he said,

Beloved friends, we're so thankful to our Lord for directing Dr. David Hubbard to us to become president of the Fuller Theological Seminary in Pasadena, California. Dr. Hubbard is doing an excellent job, and I've asked him to come and give a message today on the "Old Fashioned Revival Hour," that you, too, may come to know him and learn something of his vision for the work.

We're so thankful God is opening so many doors to Dr. David Hubbard, using this dedicated and gifted young man to speak in colleges and universities over the United States and Canada. If you have the opportunity to hear him, you should do so. A warm welcome to you, David. The microphone will be yours in a few minutes, and may God's blessing be upon you.

Miss Mae Douglas was another person who had come on the scene in these days to provide support for Charles Fuller. In December, 1963, his faithful secretary for twenty-five years, Miss Rose Baessler, had passed away, but the Lord led in bringing Mae Doug-

234

Fuller Seminary School of World Mission, 1971.

Charles Fuller is greeted by David Hubbard and Carl F. H. Henry on arrival at Congress on Evangelism in Berlin, fall, 1966.

Sermon preparation in his study at home.

las to become the executive secretary for the GBA and FEA. In the months and years ahead, as Charles Fuller's strength declined, and ever since his death in 1968, her gifts of wisdom, intelligence, and initiative have been essential for enabling us to carry on the work of the radio and the FEA.

Shadows were lengthening for Charles Fuller as the School of World Mission opened its doors in September, 1965. Mrs. Fuller's health had begun to deteriorate that preceding June, and by now she was bedridden a good part of the time. The physicians could not diagnose her ailment even after they had made an exploratory abdominal operation in December. During the winter and spring months of 1966 Mrs. Fuller spent most of her time propped up on the couch in the living room, while her husband constantly hovered and worried over her. In May she became so weak that she was taken to the hospital.

She was conscious for ten more days, and Charles Fuller spent most of his waking hours with her at the hospital. Even when she lapsed into a coma, he remained near at hand and spent his time preparing the next sermons to be preached on the "Old Fashioned Revival Hour." Though now cut off from her, he nevertheless felt close to her as he wrote sermons, for he said, "This is what she would want me to be doing—working as hard as I can to keep getting the Gospel out." Then early in the afternoon of June 11, 1966, when Charles Fuller had returned home for a few minutes, the phone rang and the doctor sadly informed him that Mrs. Fuller had passed away. He penned a note that day which was later discovered among his papers:

"June 11, 1966. 2:30 P.M. Grace at home with the Lord. 54 years—nine months of wonderful life together. Good night, 'honey.' We will see each other in the coming eternal morning. Charles."

A great sense of loneliness came upon Charles Fuller after the well-attended funeral at Lake Avenue Congregational Church and the committal service at Forest Lawn Memorial Park. The broadcasts for that summer had all been made up to the next October, and so he did not have, during those difficult months, the camaraderie of the choir which he enjoyed so much on Sunday afternoons as they all met together to make recordings. But he spent his days working on sermons for the forthcoming broadcasts that would be recorded in the fall. He announced that he would be commencing another series on "The Tabernacle in the Wilderness." It was of great help that I and my family lived only four blocks away, for he often had meals with us and loved to hear about the latest things the grandchildren were doing. On Sundays we would all attend church together. We also planned a trip that summer of 1966 to Wawona in Yosemite National Park, arranging things so that my father could live at the hotel while the rest of us camped nearby.

Charles Fuller was also helped in getting through that summer by accepting an invitation from the Young Life Campaign to spend two weeks at their Malibu resort on the shore of British Columbia. He greatly enjoyed watching how the Young Life staff presented the Gospel to these mostly non-Christian young people and how they were successful in winning many of them to Christ. He found companionship in the other guests who were there, and reports came back of the great blessing that he was to all.

Knowing how lonesome my father was, I urged him to accept an invitation to be one of the delegates to the Congress on Evangelism to be held in Berlin in November, 1966. Evangelical leaders the world over would be at that congress, and he would meet many who had followed his ministry by radio over the years. He finally decided to go, and it seems that there in Berlin God gave him a little glimpse of the great effect of his ministry. Christian leaders from all over the world, people who were total strangers, kept seeking him out to tell him that it was through his ministry that they had either been converted or led to dedicate their lives to the preaching of the Gospel. So many kept coming to him that some days he found it hard to get back to his hotel for a full night's rest.

While in Berlin, evangelist Merv Rosell recorded an interview he had with Charles Fuller so that he could later play it on his (Rosell's) broadcast. The following excerpts from this interview give an insight into my father's thoughts after preaching the Gospel for fifty years:

Fuller: "Well, Merv, I'll tell you, I think that evangelism is the very heart of the whole thing, and let me just say this: in 2 Timothy 4 it speaks of preaching the Word, but also it says there, do the work of an evangelist. . . . And I mean work, traveling under all kinds of conditions and all kinds of problems that come up and pressures and you know the misunderstandings.

It's a terrific job, and you've got to be as wise as a serpent and as harmless as a dove, and yet not in any way trim your message or give up any principles, and just stand there and preach the Word in no uncertain terms.

Rosell: Dr. Fuller, what would you advise the young people to do?

Fuller: I would advise them first of all to let the Word of God dwell in them richly; that is, master it. . . . Then it is so important to know the will of God, and that which you feel at home in and love to do. God will open the door. You must remember we are ordained from before the foundation of the world to bring forth good works and fruit, and before you and I came into the world, God had a plan on the boards of the architectural plans in heaven about exactly what we are going to do. And when I found out that according to Ephesians 2:10 "we are His workmanship, created in Christ Jesus unto good works which God had before ordained that we should walk in them," I simply said, "Well, Lord, show me your plan for me." I don't know what His plan is for others.

Rosell: Right. We must get it from God.

Fuller: We must get it from God. And he that doeth the will of the Father shall abide forever. The moment that you are in that will, then all things work together for good—I don't care what it is.

Rosell: Now let me personally and publicly thank you for all the encouragement you have given to me in my campaigns and to Billy Graham and to all of the men who are working so hard for Jesus Christ and the evangelists here—many of them owe tribute of thanksgiving not to you but to God for what you have done in faithfulness. And I recall the happy days when on the platforms [at Philadelphia and Des Moines and Waterloo, Iowa] you encouraged me to go on and win souls for Jesus Christ. . . . Have you any idea, Dr. Fuller, of the people you have preached to since you went on the radio?

Fuller: Well, Merv, I don't know about the figure, whether it's right or not, but the radio officials tell me that my audience runs twenty million a Sunday . . . [But] the Lord will tell me when I get to glory.

238

Rosell: You're going into the room and check the statistics?

Fuller: I sure am.

Rosell: Get the Nielsen Rating in glory.

Fuller: Merv, you know that we talk about our converts, and you know, I've learned this—some Sunday school teacher or some godly mother has planted the seed, and we water. Sometimes we also plant the seed and someone else waters it, and if I ever have a part in somebody's salvation or conversion, well, praise the Lord! I don't care who did what as long as people are brought across the line.

Rosell: We are workers together with Jesus Christ. And now let me say to the radio audience, I am sitting with Dr. Fuller in Congress Hall, Berlin, where the benediction of his presence is a blessing to all the evangelists who have gathered from around the world, and we want to express again, Dr. Fuller, gratitude from the hearts of all the radio people for your ministry to Jesus Christ, and will you pray for me.

Fuller: I will, Merv.

Charles Fuller's spirits were greatly lifted after his return from Berlin. He found it possible to go on living in the apartment, even though its atmosphere in every corner reminded him of his beloved helpmeet. He found surcease from loneliness through spending whole days in Bible study and preparing messages for the broadcasts. Evenings he would spend either with close friends, many of whom were board members of the GBA and FEA, or with Ruth and me and the grandchildren. He also took walks through the California Institute of Technology, whose campus was just a block away from his apartment. During Easter vacation he took us to Grand Canyon National Park, which we all enjoyed thoroughly.

On April 7, 1967, the Fuller Theological Seminary celebrated its twentieth anniversary and honored its founders Charles Fuller and Harold Ockenga, who just twenty years before had met in Palm Springs and Chicago to launch the seminary. This was an unusually happy meeting. Accolades came to both men from many of the almost one thousand graduates of the seminary as well as from

Christian leaders everywhere. Over five hundred guests jammed the Viennese Room of the Huntington-Sheraton Hotel in Pasadena. Billy Graham was the featured speaker, and he spoke warmly of his indebtedness to Charles Fuller and Harold Ockenga:

Now my sermons may not have helped very many people, but the sermons and the life of Charles Fuller and Harold Ockenga have blessed and inspired and enriched my own life. Both of these men in their own unique way have encouraged me in my ministry. I've gone to both of them for advice and counsel for many years. They've never been too busy to give me their time and to help a struggling young preacher many years ago in many ways that they'll never know. There are no two men more deserving in the Christian world today of the honors that have been bestowed on them tonight. It's difficult for us to remember in 1933. The churches were empty. The church treasuries were emptier. There was no Gospel on the radio, very much, hardly any. Religion was hardly ever in the newspapers, except on rare occasions. And we were in the midst of an even greater spiritual depression. And Sunday after Sunday there was the voice of Charles Fuller, crying in the wilderness. Spreading an umbrella of the Gospel across the world. And I used to listen. And I thought, if I could ever meet that man and shake his hand. I finally met two men that had met him, and that was a tremendous privilege.

Dr. Fuller came into the lives and into the homes of millions and millions of people as a friend. We all thought we knew him personally, and I think we do, and did. And then to get to know him and see that his life backed up everything he said on the radio. And to get to know Mrs. Fuller in even a small way, as I said today, one of the great women of our generation. And I'm sure if I understand the Scriptures correctly, that she is a witness to what is happening here tonight and rejoicing with us and standing waiting until we get there. And we're going to have a banquet in the sky when our Lord Jesus Christ will hand out the rewards and every man will have his praise of God.

Charles Fuller also made some remarks, and the following excerpt was really his last public statement about the deep intentions that had shaped his ministry:

And I pray God that we may reach the last possible soul, and get the good news of God's love before them and give them a good chance to accept the Savior and Redeemer. And I hope and pray that God will give me the chance to do it someday, even now. I'd love to go out and stay in the wilds, and meet the corner groceryman or meet the gas station attendant, or to go to a homestead and just sit down and talk about the things of the Lord. And I'll say this one thing. That I'm not thinking about the number listening in on the program. When I'm preaching over the air, I'm preaching to grandma who's sitting in the rocking chair. I'm talking to some poor lonely soul that needs Jesus Christ. One time from Long Beach I stopped in the middle of the broadcast. And I said, "Someone, somewhere, is about ready to take his or her life." And the following Wednesday came a special delivery letter from Indianapolis from a young woman from an Iowa farm who went the downward path, and she was starting for the bathroom to take some poison when that voice came out from over the radio, "Please stop. Jesus loves you. Kneel by your bed and give your heart to Christ." And in the letter she said that she had been obedient, and thanked me for it.

So I thank you for all of these commendations and resolutions. I don't know what else to say except to say from the bottom of my heart, thank you.

Seven weeks after this banquet, our phone rang about 5:30 one morning and my father said, "Dan, I've got a bad pain in my heart —have had it for some time during the night. Please call the doctor and come over and see me." After examining him, the doctor recommended that he be taken to the hospital for further observation, and there it was learned that he was suffering from congestive heart failure. But he improved sufficiently to return to his apartment and be cared for there by a private nurse. A month later, however, his condition worsened and this time he spent almost two months in the hospital. Several times the doctor thought he was on the verge of passing away. But his very strong constitution was not yet quite ready to give up, and he rallied sufficiently to be moved to a convalescent home in northern Pasadena.

He stayed there for six months until he passed away on March 18, 1968. Until after New Year's Day he was well enough to receive visitors and even have me take him out for automobile rides. David Hubbard[1] and I visited him almost daily. Scores of people came

---

[1] In December, 1968, the board of trustees of the Gospel Broadcasting Association voted to bring Dr. David A. Hubbard on as executive director and featured speaker on the "Old Fashioned Revival Hour," and he has been the speaker on the broadcast, now called "The Joyful Sound," ever since March 2, 1969.

to see him there and to tell him how much his ministry had meant to them over the years. His spirits improved enough that fall for him even to feel that he might be able to resume preaching on the broadcast, though he was now past eighty. He worked on outlines for some sermons on the psalms.

His spirits were also buoyed as he looked forward to New Year's Day and the three football games he could watch on his television set. He did watch the games that day, but evidently he got so involved in them that he used up too much strength watching the sport he had played so well in college and had loved ever since. Thereafter he seemed to lose enthusiasm for everything except to urge us to keep the broadcast going.

One of the last things he said to me was, "As I look back on my life, how glad I am that I have spent it preaching the Gospel. I'm so glad I gave my life over to the Lord to become a preacher that day I knelt in the packing house in Placentia." I have often reflected on how great a blessing it is to be able to say, as death is approaching, that one has spent his life doing God's will. One's life is wasted unless he can say this.

The Lake Avenue Church was crowded for Charles Fuller's funeral. Harold Ockenga recounted the various ways he and Charles Fuller had worked together during the past thirty years. "We were closer as friends than I have been to any other living man in connection with any other work which we have undertaken." Their work together had been chiefly in the founding of the seminary, and Harold Ockenga recalled that he had spent seventy-five weeks as a guest in Charles Fuller's home during the years he had come west on seminary matters. "I saw him there in the home," he related,

. . . and consulted with him and enjoyed his counsel. Almost every morning when we were together he would come down to the area where I was staying, just after breakfast, and we would first talk about the matters of the seminary, and about the whole evangelical picture in the world, and about his vision and the vision which God had given me. And then we would pray about these things and commit them unto the Lord and believe that the Lord would answer prayer. We had a very close fellowship in prayer.

On my thirtieth anniversary in Boston [in November, 1966], he came, as he did also on the twenty-fifth anniversary. I remember we went up into the hotel room and talked these things all over, and then we knelt down. And Charles put his hands on me, and he prayed for me at that time in a wonderful way.

And I remember then, just last fall, when I said good-by to him in the convalescent home not far from here, and said to him a few things of personal note, then I put my hands on him, and prayed in like manner for him. And God has blessed us in these ways in a remarkable vision with a friend. And when I remember him, I remember him in this way.

David Hubbard also spoke and recalled,

How many times he has said to us at the seminary, and to me personally, day after day, time after time, "Preach the Word." . . . He was a great one to quote Scripture to me if I'd be riled up about something. I'd bring a problem—"A soft answer," he would tell me, "turns away wrath." "Live peaceably with all men." "Seek peace and pursue it." I can hear his words now. Time and again, even in these last months, I would leave his bedside and he would say, "Dave, God will give you wisdom. God will give you wisdom." And he believed this, and I believed it, and there was something of the strength of his faith that buoyed my own even in the midst of his weakness.

After the funeral a procession of nearly one hundred cars followed the hearse to Forest Lawn. Perhaps Rudy Atwood's statement of how he felt and what he did when he returned home from that funeral can express the feelings of many of us: "I remember, after Dr. Fuller's funeral, I came home, sat down at the piano, and played, 'He the Pearly Gates Will Open.' As I thought of the loss of that great Christian warrior, and his abundant entrance into Our Lord's presence, I felt the need of the comfort and inspiration of that old hymn."[2]

---

[2] Rudy Atwood, *The Rudy Atwood Story* (Old Tappan, N.J.: Fleming H. Revell, 1970), pp. 68 f.

INDEX

244

INDEX